# Blacktown

# Blacktown

## Shane Weaver

*Books Alive is an Australian Government initiative developed through the Australia Council.*

Pseudonyms have been used and other details altered where necessary to protect the identity of people and organisations mentioned in this book.

BLACKTOWN
A BANTAM BOOK

First published in Australia and New Zealand in 2003 by Bantam
This edition published in Australia and New Zealand in 2004
by Bantam

Copyright © Shane Weaver, 2003

All rights reserved. No part of this publication may be reproduced, stored in a retrieval system, transmitted in any form or by any means, electronic, mechanical, photocopying, recording or otherwise, without the prior written permission of the publisher.

National Library of Australia
Cataloguing-in-Publication Entry

Weaver, Shane.
Blacktown.

2nd ed.
ISBN 1 86325 461 7.

1. Weaver, Shane. 2. Weaver, Shane – Childhood and youth.
3. Adult child abuse victims – Australia – Biography.
4. Abused children – Australia – Biography. 5. Boxers (Sports)
– Australia – Biography. I. Title.

362.76092

Transworld Publishers,
a division of Random House Australia Pty Ltd
20 Alfred Street, Milsons Point, NSW 2061
http://www.randomhouse.com.au

Random House New Zealand Limited
18 Poland Road, Glenfield, Auckland

Transworld Publishers,
a division of The Random House Group Ltd
61–63 Uxbridge Road, London W5 5SA

Random House Inc
1745 Broadway, New York, New York 10036

Cover design by Darian Causby/Highway 51 Design Works
Cover photograph courtesy Getty Images
Typeset by Midland Typesetters,
Maryborough, Victoria
Printed and bound by McPherson's Printing Group,
Maryborough, Victoria

10 9 8 7 6 5 4 3 2 1

*For Mum, who saved me*

# PROLOGUE

### It's okay to look back at the past, but don't stare

NOW, WHEN MEMORIES ARE GHOSTED like leaves fluttering fitfully across the graveyard brain, I recognise the people buried there.

I see his drunken silhouette lurching across the paddock. He lost his balance in the Korean War when flying shrapnel smashed his spine, ripping the feeling from the left side of his body. 'Arm's useless as a tit on a bull. Stupid leg won't do what it's told.' The combination of booze and bullets leads his limbs in a deadwood dance. Floppety, bobbety, jerk and jig. Daddy's coming home and God only knows who's pulling the strings.

You're lucky to see him coming. There's no warning on the worst nights. Suddenly, the house is plunged into darkness. He's turned the power off at the box outside. The lights go out and the wireless dies and we scurry like blind, panic-stricken rats to cower in cupboards or under beds.

Fear is selfish. I don't think about Mum or my two younger brothers. Not for a second. I'm a foetus, balled up on the floor under my bed, eyes clenched tight as angry fists and the whoosh of the blood thumping through my heart, roaring like the ocean in my ears. Terrified that he'll find me again.

Daddy can smell my fear. Daddy can see in the dark. Daddy can hear my voiceless screaming. And now, as the door opens wider, it's time to slip away. Let me introduce you to my family . . .

We are the Reynards. We live in a grey, three-bedroom fibro house in Edward Street, Blacktown, on the dirty edge of Sydney's western suburbs. There's a song they play on the wireless that sums up our cookie-cutter neighbourhood. Referring to the houses, the chorus goes, 'And they're all made out of ticky-tacky and they all look just the same.' Our neighbourhood is made up of war service and Housing Commission estates. Courtesy of Daddy's damaged back, we live in one of the former.

Ours is the sixth house before a creek that interrupts the street about three-quarters of the way along. There's a huge paddock on one side. The Roberts family lives next door on the other side. The McKinnons' house is over our back fence. The railway line is a ten-minute amble away at the top of Edward Street. When a train thunders past, it muffles the sound of the wireless in our kitchen. Our family comprises five people and two cats. There's Mummy, Daddy, me, my brothers Kelly and Tony, and Cha Cha and Hot Cha Cha.

Actually, my brothers and I aren't really Reynards. We're Weavers. And my name's not really Shane. It's Patrick. That's because Daddy is not really Daddy. Legend has it that our 'real' father went to the shop to get milk and bread when I was about four. He kept going.

To cut to the chase, Mum first met Saul Reynard as an army mate of my real father, Ryan. After Ryan had disappeared, the chivalrous and crippled Saul offered to take his place in bed. Mum was heavily pregnant and said yes, but we kids had to come along for the ride. The ride lasted nearly 20 years and we picked up another brother and two sisters on the way.

Each of us reacted differently to the journey. My youngest sister, Sarah, killed herself in 1999. Beth, my other sister, is a born-again Christian. She has surrendered her nightmares of Daddy's beer breath and dirty hands to a God who can forgive anything. Kelly is living under an assumed name in Queensland, alienated from the rest of us. If he's true to form, he's scamming suckers for a quid. Tony is a psychiatric outpatient sitting in his lounge room with the blinds drawn, his paranoia, his dope and Tom Waits and John Lennon for company. My youngest brother, Richard, is 41, single, desperately lonely and still apologising to the world for being Saul's blood son.

And what about Mum? Well, the best answer is to tell you who Mum is today. You see, she's been so many different people over the last 40-odd years. You'll meet them all, but for now, it's enough to know that Mum appears to be the archetypal, white-haired pensioner, living with her little dog, Sherna, in a government flat in Kelmscott, Western Australia. She's as happy as you can be with one daughter dead and the rest of your children in varying stages of decay. I don't mean to imply that she is bitter. She's not. Survivors know better than anyone that because life is seasonal, hope is eternal.

My name is Shane. I'm 48 and I'm an alcoholic. I've been the victim and the tormentor. I've been a human boxing bag and an Australian professional champion. I've seen behind the locked doors of lunatic asylums, both as a resident and as a nurse. I've been the raging storm and the supplicant sheltering in the peace that surpasses all understanding. I've eaten from rubbish bins and dined at some of the finest restaurants in the world. Seven years ago, my doctor said I was dying. Today, I'm here to tell you that there is life after death.

But first, I must take you back to the beginning. I must, because this is the only way for me to make any kind of sense of it all. I can't promise it will make sense to you. I can only promise you that what I say will be the truth, as I remember it.

# ROUND 1

THE SCREEN DOOR OPENS AND bangs shut. The silence that follows is like the collective intake of breath between the split second a guillotine falls and when it thuds home. A silence that's painful because of the awful inevitability it imposes.

He must be standing stock-still by the fridge, just inside the kitchen door. Blinking into the blackness, adjusting his vision before the hunt. Maybe he's cleaning his glasses on his hankie. And then he starts. An almighty crash as the electric frying pan with its hot fat and fried sausages smashes to the floor.

'You call this dog's shit dinner?!'

He's screaming, and even though I can't see him, I know the veins in his neck are knotted like ropes, and his nostrils are flared like a wild beast's, and he's dribbling with rage, and he has the electric cord. And he's coming.

It's too late to wish. Too late to hope. Too late to pray.

The next part of the ritual is the strangest. Daddy moves as quietly as he can down the hall towards our bedrooms, almost as though he doesn't want to disturb anyone. The only sounds are the creaking of the bare floorboards, the dragging of the dead-leg shuffle, and the whispered war cry that always precedes the pandemonium. 'Cha Cha, Hot Cha Cha, Cha Cha, Hot Cha Cha.' The soft sibilants and singsong absurdity give an incongruous nursery-rhyme tone to Daddy's approach.

When I was six, I'd brought two starving kittens home from the paddock. I'd stuffed them down the front of my T-shirt so they couldn't get away; they'd returned the favour by peeing on me and scratching my chest. Mum had said I could keep them if I hid them from Daddy. One was male, the other female. She knew he'd hit the roof if he saw them. Considering how he treated us, there was no telling what he'd do to the kittens. But you could bet he'd make a show of it. Grimly she said they would be named Cha Cha and Hot Cha Cha. It was Mum's way of turning the horror into a pantomime, and I still remember when we grew brave enough to laugh about it. But first, another eight years would pass.

No one's laughing now. The Cha Cha chant is in the bedroom. I hear Tony whimper and I know he's hiding under his bed. Four years my junior, Tony is five. For a second I wish he'd be foolish enough to run, drawing Daddy's fire. My guts are a loose gravy of terror and self-loathing. Part of me wants to comfort my little brother, but somewhere else, more desperate, more pressing, I know it's every kid for himself and I'd watch my little brother being beaten senseless to save my own skin. But Tony isn't going anywhere. He's paralysed by fear and, besides, I'm the favourite whipping boy. I'm the 'Mummy's boy' and the 'biggest Weaver bastard'.

I scream as the first lick of the electric cord stings my back. Unable to get a clear shot, he rips the bed away from the wall. I feel like a soft-shelled crab when the rock it's scrunched under has been flung aside. And I beg for mercy as 'Cha Cha, Hot Cha Cha' explodes into an obscene torrent of spit and fire.

I don't know where Mum has been hiding. But I hear the shrill siren of her scream as she leaps onto Daddy's back, sinking her teeth and nails into him, tearing at his face and knocking his glasses to the floor. 'You fucking bitch!' Turning from me he staggers backwards, crashing into the wall, and Mum, winded, slumps to the floor.

Mum is five feet tall and weighs less than seven-and-a-half stone. Picking her up and tossing her over his shoulder, he hisses, 'You so much as poke your fucking head out and so help me God, I'll gut her like a fish.' He closes the door gently on the way out.

How long do I lie there until I get up and put Tony into his bed? Where has Kelly been hiding? Maybe he managed to get outside. Maybe he was outside when it all started. He's eight and smart enough to smell catastrophe before it comes crashing down on us. After what seems like ages, Mum's screaming stops and only her sobs and the squeaking, grunting big double bed punctuate the still of the night.

I wake, ashamed that I have surrendered to sleep. I know I should've stayed awake for Mum's sake. Even though I'm powerless to protect her, she deserves to have someone who loves her enough to witness her pain. Instead, I'd parachuted into dreams while she suffered on her own.

Sunlight floods the room. But it isn't a glorious announcement of a new day. It's too bright, too sharp, too focused and in your face. A cruel light, demanding scrutiny of things I have no wish to see. Tony is still sleeping, his face puffy and flushed from crying and his brow furrowed in the old-man-worried way that some boy babies have. Kelly is in his bed, the covers pulled up over his head. He's still wearing his shoes and I know by the labour of his breathing that he's awake.

The first thing that strikes me after the brilliance of the new day is the profound depth of the silence. Not peaceful. Different too from the hair-trigger silence of last night. It's leaden and heavy with consequence. A silence set to burst. As I make my way to the lounge room, I know that something is waiting.

The door to the big double bed is shut. But I know Daddy has gone to work. He's a 'permanent temp' working in a government department. His war service pension guarantees his job for life, as long as he plays the game and clocks on daily. No matter what happens, if the next day is a workday, he's gone before sunrise.

At first glance, the lounge room is the same as after any other fight night. Broken glass, spilled ashtrays, and the vomit reek of stale Reschs beer. It takes a few moments to see the rest. Clumps of fuzzy brown stuff on the wooden floor. Some wet with blood. Hair. Taking a brown paper bag from the kitchen, I set about picking it up. I half-fill the bag and put it in my pocket. What am I thinking? Maybe that we can somehow put it back on her head. Maybe that we can use it as evidence. Or maybe it just seems somehow wrong to throw it in the bin, something so intimate, so much a part of her.

She must have heard me. The door to the big double bed opens. She moves in tortured slow motion, like every muscle is racked with pain, every socket screaming. She moves like she's just awoken from the ice age and is still numb from the freezing cold, waiting for the blood to rush to her limbs and restore her. But it's her face that shocks me. It's a swollen mask. Her eyes are blue-black slits. Her lips are split and bloated and caked with dry blood. She looks like she's been partially scalped. And as she hugs me, sobbing so it tears my heart, I understand the words blubbering from her ruined mouth. 'I'm so sorry, Shane. I'm so sorry.'

Her breath stinks like a dead bird and I bury my face in her shoulder, ashamed that the sensitivity of my nose somehow betrays a callous disregard for her pain.

I go and clean up the grease and sausages from the floor. No one ate dinner last night so I make toast under the grill and cake it with dripping from the fat we keep after frying food. It's cheaper than margarine, and I reckon it tastes even better, especially if you sprinkle it with salt and pepper, because it has the flavour of mince. After our toast, I help Tony get dressed for school and we leave the house. I know that when we get home Mum will have cleaned up the mess and, except for her ruined face, the world will be back to normal. Until next time.

# ROUND 2

GROWING UP IN BLACKTOWN IN THE 1950s was like falling out of an arse. It stank, and had the awful finality of gravity. Plop and there you were. Stiff shit, kid. Fuck-all you could do about it.

One thing Blacktown was big on, though, was equality. Every man and his dog was dirt poor. Having the arse out of your pants was the common denominator. Everyone knew when their neighbours' pension or dole cheques lobbed, and we rostered our borrowing and paybacks accordingly. No one ever lent money, and no one ever asked. As the eldest, it was my job to 'loan' half a cup of sugar or a few slices of bread or a slab of 'marge' or 'a smidgen' of milk ('even powdered would be good').

Because of Daddy's fondness for a beer or 50, my demands on the neighbours' generosity were more frequent than welcome. Sometimes, one particular set of neighbours, who Mum said were 'snooty', refused to open the door. But I knew when they were home because they had one of the first black and white TVs in town and I could hear the volume go down as soon as I knocked on their door.

When we'd run out of options and the fridge was empty as our bellies, Mum would send me to the butcher's shop near our primary school. The 'Butcher Lady' was a kind old woman with knowing grey eyes, a pinkly powdered face and tightly permed, blue-grey curls. She always wore bright red lipstick that stamped her daytime expression with a permanent pucker of happy surprise. I waited until there were no customers before sauntering in. I said I wondered if they had any spare dog bones today. I always did my best to sound like my dog and I couldn't really give a toss one way or the other. She smiled sagely at the butcher man, who I think was her son, and said, 'Sure thing, sonny, can't have your dog go hungry, eh.' And then she took out a big straw broom and swept up the bones from the sawdust on the floor and wrapped them in big sheets of clean white butcher's paper. Sometimes she gave me sixpence to buy a one-scoop ice-cream cone from the milk bar next door.

I felt like a hero after my trips to the Butcher Lady. Mum fussed, saying how proud she was of her 'little man'. She oohed and aahed as she unwrapped the parcel tenderly, saying, 'Look how much meat there is on this one,' and, 'Why, this isn't a bone, it's a blinking chop!' and, 'Won't this make a lovely thick soup now.' And later she made a huge pot of steaming soup with the bones and sometimes celery and carrots – and always tomatoes.

Almost everyone in Blacktown had a garden of sorts. Whatever you could grow you didn't have to buy. The garlic-munchers and wogs kept terrific gardens with fat tomatoes, strawberries and mulberry trees. We used to sweat on mulberry season. Big, fat, purple clusters. We set out on mulberry-gorging expeditions that were fraught with danger because, if they caught you, the landowners kicked your arse all the way home. Every time you stuck your hand over the fence there was the exquisite terror of not knowing if some mad 'eye-tie' would grab it and wrench you over into his yard. I remember when it happened to Chuckie Williams, a kid who lived in our street. One minute he was on our side of the fence, and the next, he was gone. Snatched away by some hairy wog who really gave him what for. We ran home, looking like vampires with the blood of forbidden fruit staining our mouths and splashed over our bare chests and bellies.

Daddy was devoted to his tomato garden. Some weekends he spent hours digging, weeding and feeding the soil for his beloved tomatoes. And it paid off. They were magnificent plants bearing bountiful and tasty fruit ('only a drongo calls a tomata a veggie; it's a fuckin' fruit!'). So we ate lots of tomatoes. Often. Spag with tomato sauce. Tomato stew, with or without meat, depending on how close it was to pay day. Tomato soup and tomato salad. Tomato and Kraft cheddar on toast. We had tomatoes to snack on. We took soggy tomato sandwiches with dripping instead of margarine to school for lunch. For a change we took slabs of bread and whole tomatoes and a big pinch of salt wrapped up in newspaper. To this day Mum still says, 'If you've got tomatoes, you'll never go hungry in this world.' And to this day, not a single kid in our family can so much as stomach the thought of eating a fucking tomato.

Ironically, the tomato garden was responsible for the only bonding that ever occurred between Daddy and me. Not that he let me into his beloved tomato patch. I was the 'Weaver bastard' and couldn't be trusted near anything as precious as a tomato plant. But I had a role. When he hobbled in from the garden, Mum and I did shifts, taking turns to massage Daddy's back and neck and his knobby arm and wasted left leg.

The scar ran in a thick, ragged, barbed wire welt from the base of the hairline on the back of his neck, all the way down his spine. It followed the bumpy march of the vertebrae. And our family was stitched into the wound as surely as if we were catgut. Mum and I would rub and knead for hours till our hands ached and the Dencorub burned and our efforts became so feeble that we were reduced to 'useless bastards' and told to 'Fuck off!'

That was easier said than done. There weren't too many places to fuck off to in Blacktown. No youth groups or parks or Police Boys' Clubs. The paddock was it. I'd lie on my back in the long grass for hours on end, looking up and drifting with the clouds, unweighted by thought and liberated by mindlessness. I'd go wading in the creek, searching for turtles and eels. Or I'd wage war on the funnel-web spiders that were legion. I'd poke a long piece of grass or a skinny stick into the holes in the ground they lived in. Not hard enough to kill them in their homes. Just enough to make them very cranky. My heart jumped to see their fat, hairy bodies bloat the entrance before they came leaping out, rearing their legs in the air like shrunken, mutated, bucking broncos. (You had to be careful because sometimes they'd emerge from a back entrance and sneak up behind you.) And then I mashed them with a rock.

But the house was a monstrous magnet, and forces over which I had no control compelled me to return to it. It was where I slept and ate and read my books and dreamed of faraway lands where genies lived and boys risked walking the plank for the sake of a chest filled with glittering treasure. I knew every nook and cranny and every stain on the wall and crack in the ceiling like I knew the contours of my own face. But the main reason I was always drawn back was because this was the house where Mum lived.

I hated that house. Sometimes I lost it completely and ran around the outside, howling and smashing the walls with my fists, punching holes in the fibro. I smeared the blood from my torn knuckles around the jagged edges. The house looked like it was wounded, but it was the people inside who were haemorrhaging hope.

We never had visitors. Only bill collectors, strangers who'd mistaken our address for someone else's, and the police ever knocked on the front door of 63 Edward Street. We always went around the back. Three concrete steps took you to a tiny verandah and a laundry that looked and stank like a sweatbox. A screen door opened into a claustrophobic kitchen where scuffed, blue lino with faded yellow flowers covered the wooden floor. The ends curled up like dog-ears on a book, and if you weren't careful or you were running to get out, you'd trip. An off-white fridge, ancient even by Blacktown standards, leaked when the weather was really hot. In summer, it sat in a puddle like it had had an accident.

Beyond that, a Lilliputian lounge room was furnished with three second-hand chairs and a fawn, vinyl lounge. The wooden floor was bare and the estapol finish that may once have been shiny was now dull and it looked dirty, no matter how hard Mum scrubbed it. Dad had built a mantelpiece against one wall, and it was stuffed with back issues of the *Reader's Digest* and a few of Dad's beloved ships in bottles sat on top. Blacktown-ubiquitous, sky-blue venetian blinds covered two big windows that looked out onto the dusty street.

Most of the time I spent in the lounge room was with my nose stuck in the corner. As punishment for the slightest misdemeanour, which could be as nebulous as 'What's that stupid face for?', Dad would order us to stand in the corner for hours on end. We never knew if he was in the room with us, watching us and waiting for us to make the fatal mistake of trying to steal a quick look. Eventually, I felt my knees buckle and my body swaying. This was dangerous: if you so much as fidgeted or tried to shift your weight, he'd smack you in the head from behind so hard your face would collide with the wall.

I was lucky. Being the tallest, my nose was too high for the mantelpiece, and often I was fast enough to beat Kelly to the corner by the front door. Sticking my nose right on the crack, I closed my eyes and sucked in the fresh air, pretending I was outside.

I'd imagine I was Superman. Squinting my left eye and telescoping my right to take in the sweeping vista of the outside world, I saw myself soaring high above the trees across the road, a triumphant speck in the pale blue sky, my mum safe and smiling in my mighty arms, streaking away to 'Truth, justice and the American way'.

The McKinnons had a black and white TV and, unlike our 'snooty' neighbours, they'd welcome a gang of kids into their house to watch George Reeves starring as the caped crusader from Krypton. Four o'clock in the afternoon was a treasured time. Together, we sat glued to the box, reciting the intro with the announcer, word for word. 'Look, up in the sky. It's a bird, it's a plane, no, it's Superman.' He was faster than a speeding bullet, more powerful than a locomotive and able to leap tall buildings in a single bound.

One ripped shirt away from the bumbling, tongue-tied reporter for the *Daily Planet* newspaper, the man of steel was coiled and waiting to explode in a lightning bolt of electric blue, yellow and red. Even though he was black and white on TV, he appeared in full colour on the covers of my comic books, and my imagination always painted him in vibrant, vivid tones. I was enthralled by the idea of looking like a wuss on the outside but being invincible underneath. I painted a big red S on a white T-shirt and, running along as fast as I could, I bounced on the ground before taking off and flying around the yard with my arms outstretched, making a whooshing wind sound.

Pointing to my T-shirt one day, Mum said, 'S for Superman, eh?'

'No,' I said, puffing out my chest, 'S for SuperShane.'

I was SuperShane. I was invulnerable. Sure, Dad might be able to hurt Shane the skinny little boy, but nothing he did could ever penetrate the armour or crush the spirit of SuperShane.

And I found another place he couldn't reach me. I waited for twilight. Daddy was never home from the pub and Kelly and Tony were off doing God knows what. I longed for the lull between dusk and dark. I sat on the fence separating our place from the Roberts family next door. Often Cha Cha joined me. In our backyard, next to the tomato garden, we sat quietly, a boy and his cat, and calmly, patiently, we waited. I never had to hurry or worry. It always came to me. A peace so overwhelming and all-enveloping that I fell endlessly into it and kept on falling and falling for what seemed like forever. The staccato chirrup-chirrup-chirruping of the crickets flooded my mind. Finally, the falling gave way to a feeling like the deep acquiescence before drowning, where the panic is spent, surrendering to the faraway frontiers of liquid sleep. And then, the miracle. I would buoy up from my body in a flash and float away, adrift in the darkening sky. I was a thinking balloon, a distant thought bubble, high in the heavens, surveying the roof tops of the neighbours' houses, the familiar world laid out like a 3D map way below.

Looking down, I saw the young boy's body sitting on the fence, trapped in the misery of circumstances beyond his control. My eyes misted. Then my own feelings of freedom soared, leaving empathy far behind, and suddenly I was lost again in the wonder and the rapture of leaving. It was short-lived; I could never go too far nor far enough, tethered always by an invisible umbilical cord to the house at 63 Edward Street.

# ROUND 3

AN UNLIT, NARROW HALLWAY LED from the lounge, down past the bathroom and on to three bedrooms. Dad and Mum had the room with the big double bed, and we kids slept and wept in the two poky bedrooms at the paddock end of the house.

My bedroom was a trap. When Dad filled the doorway there was no way out. Hiding under the bed was useless; it was the first place he looked. So I hid in books. I became Huckleberry Reynard, and my best friend Tom Sawyer and I smoked cigarettes and had excellent adventures in a world where adults barely existed. One day, after we'd been gone for ages, everyone assumed we were dead. They searched the creek for our corpses but found nothing and went ahead and organised a funeral. We were very much alive, though, and we watched the solemn proceedings from our hiding places in the trees. Mum looked really pretty in her black dress. The tears were spilling down her face and I wanted to call out, Hey, Mum, it's okay I'm alive, but her sorrow made her achingly beautiful and I didn't want to break the spell.

I was never allowed into the room with the big double bed when Dad was home, and he would have killed me had he known I was in there while he was away. But sometimes, when Mum was putting away clothes or making their bed, I'd follow her in and we'd talk while she worked. That's when I found out about the gloves.

Mum kept a pair of long, white gloves in her drawer. The sort that I'd only ever seen in movies and that went right up to the elbows. She never went out socially, she never dressed up, and she never wore them. They'd belonged to her mother and had the subtle, sickly perfume of sweat and talcum powder and wrinkled old ladies. I was terrified of them. Just knowing they were in the house loosed a Pandora's box in my head. I thought about the gloves all the time. I imagined them, disembodied and crawling like a tarantula across the floor and into my bed at night. I imagined them caressing my face and tickling their way down my body and grabbing my white worm. I told Mum about the awful power these gloves had over me. I told her because she already knew something was wrong.

'What's up, love? I know something's troubling you. I can tell. What is it, love?'

I could say anything to Mum. She never made me feel stupid.

'It's the long, white gloves, Mum. Your mother's gloves. They're after me. They want to get me. They want to hurt me.'

I watched the anger flood her face. Suddenly, she seemed much bigger and bolder than I'd ever seen her before. And when she spoke it was with a power and clarity that charged the air and sent my fears scurrying like rats racing from the light of an opened door.

'Then I will break the spell, Shane. Tonight I will set you free from these evil gloves once and for all.'

What I loved most about my mum was that whenever I was afraid, she never invoked the power of logic. She knew that fear was irrational and resistant to reason. Mum understood that if blind terror cannot see, nor can it hear. Instead, she overwhelmed it with the tempest of her own hysteria.

That night she took them from her drawer and we marched, a nine-year-old boy and the world's bravest mum, out into the backyard. She laid the gloves out on the lawn with great ceremony, extending and spreading the fingers. Then, sprinkling them with kerosene she'd milked from the heater, she stepped back and threw a lighted match on them, commanding loudly, 'Demons, in the name of Jesus, be gone!' We watched the gloves catch and burn in the night, shadows leaping and dancing on the ground, the fingers curling and writhing like the hands of a witch at the stake. And then they lay in a pile of grey-white ashes, stirred by the cold night air. And I was free.

While Dad seemed hell-bent on destroying us, Mum had embarked on a lifelong campaign to save us. But it was never going to be easy. She was 16 when I was born. These were the days before women's hostels. Contraception was pulling out early. Incest was a dirty word, too dreadful to discuss in civilised company. The police had better things to do than get involved in 'domestics'. Wife-beating wasn't merely overlooked – a bloke was a dead-set poofter if he didn't give the little missus a decent backhander when she got out of line. In the 1950s and early 1960s in Australia 'a man's home was his castle' and what happened to the serfs was his bloody business and no one else's.

The king despised little boys who dirtied his castle. I'd wet the bed for as long as I could remember. Between the fear of pissing my bed and the insistent expectation of calamity, I was haunted by a recurring nightmare. I dreamt that I came home from school and walked through the back door into the house. None of the other kids was home yet, and the house was hushed and unbearably still. A woman stood with her back to me at the kitchen sink, washing up. The silence was unearthly, no clatter of plates or tinkle of knives and forks. Her back was turned to me. She was dressed like Mummy.

'Mummy,' I said, 'I'm home.'

She didn't turn to face me, continuing her duties at the sink.

'Mummy?'

I sensed that something was horribly wrong. The hairs on the back of my neck prickled. And then she turned slowly and, looking directly at me, smiled sweetly. She was a total stranger, and the overwhelming, other-worldly joy in her smile sent a shiver thrilling through my body. Although she never spoke a word, I knew exactly what she was thinking. The sparkle in her eyes said, 'I am going to cut you up into little pieces, cook you and eat you.' Jolted from sleep I ran screaming from my bed in search of my real mummy. Daddy's most savage abuse was reserved for any kid who dared to step into the room with the big double bed.

But kids never think of the consequences when their actions are fuelled by fear. 'Mum!' My cry shattered the night like glass.

'Shane? Shane!' I heard the panic in her voice, not so much for what had driven me into the room, as for what was about to happen.

'You bastard.' He was up and out of bed, belt in hand, and hunting me like an animal as I scrambled around the house, bumping into tables and chairs in the dark.

After the whipping, he threw me out the back door like a bag of garbage. Worse than the monsters lurking in the night was the sound of Mum's pleas as she begged him to let me back inside. And then the cruel silence when I knew he was smothering her with his naked, twisted body like I'd seen him do when I'd snuck a peek into the room with the big double bed late one night when the light was on.

Years later, I asked Mum what her family was doing while we were being emotionally hung, drawn and quartered. They were otherwise engaged. Her parents had divorced. Her father was a pianist around the clubs with a weakness for young ladies but no time for the young lady who was his daughter. Her mother had designs on a man several years her junior, and no desire to draw attention to her age by introducing a teenage daughter. They happily signed the papers that allowed Mum to marry at 16 years of age.

There was an estranged elder brother, Dickie, who apparently lived somewhere in the Queensland outback, breaking horses and fencing. Mum showed me an article about him in *People* magazine. He had built a yacht slap-bang in the middle of the Aussie desert. There was a picture of a stocky little bloke wearing an Akubra and standing next to a huge boat perched on a sand dune thousands of miles from the sea. He was squinting into the sun and grinning like a madman, but at least he had a dream.

Before the three other kids lobbed and while she still had the time and the spirit, Mum used every second of Daddy's absences to make us laugh like other kids. We had no toys, so feather dusters and rulers became swords. Sometimes, Mum took her mascara and drew pencil-thin moustaches on us, in the style of Errol Flynn. We wrapped tea towels around our hands for protection and engaged in swashbuckling pirate battles that started in the lounge and spilled into the kitchen and out into the backyard. Mum was an excellent swordsman, but we kids always won, and she lay breathless and prone on the ground at our mercy. We always spared her.

Games don't last forever, though, and the real world was just a limp away. The worst times for me were when Mum was in hospital, either recovering from attempted suicides or having babies. Unlike me, it wasn't so easy for Mum to escape into her own head; Dad knew how to break in and get her. And in the real world, it was even more difficult for her to escape. I felt so sad. When I saw my pregnant mum desperately trying to escape from Dad's cruelty, I wished I could've disappeared. Hobbled by her unborn baby, she never got far.

Happiness and babies only went together on American sitcoms or in *Woman's Day* magazines. For Mum, being pregnant was hell, and her pinched face betrayed her fear. I'd watch her hanging out a big load of washing on the line. She'd stop and, clutching her stomach, wince under the weight of the load she was carrying inside her. As her stomach filled with child and her time grew closer, my own fears soared like mercury: I'd be left on my own with him.

But I learned that pregnancy didn't always mean babies. Dad said we couldn't afford another fucking mouth to feed, and he and Mum were screaming at each other in the kitchen. He hit her in the guts so hard her eyes nearly popped out. Her mouth opened wide like someone had just given her a wonderful gift, and she slid to her knees, dry retching and clawing at her belly. My unborn brother drowned in the river of red that swamped the faded yellow flowers on the lino-covered floor.

Mum seemed to be pregnant all the time. I was almost ten the night I broke down in the kitchen and begged her not to go to hospital before Beth was born. She smiled and said she had no choice, but she told me I shouldn't worry as I was never alone. 'Come, Shane,' she said, 'come see.' And she took my hand and led me outside. It was dark. Pointing among the trees and bushes in the paddock across the road, Mum whispered, 'There, can you see her, love?'

'Who?' I asked.

'My mother, my dead mother, she's standing there watching us. Next to that tree. Look, she's waving to us. Can you see her now?' Mum was wringing my hand and whispering too loudly, 'It's your granny. She loves you, Shane, and she'll never let anything happen to you. Not ever.'

I never did see my dead granny, but I knew Mum would be much happier if she thought I believed the spirit of her dead mother was watching over me. Nor was there any doubt in my mind that Mum could actually see her. My mum lived in a world where ghosts hovered just on the edge of reality, and could pass over into the realm of the living as easily as dust and stale air are released from a long-locked cupboard.

'Yes,' I said, 'I can see her, Mum. Now I can see her.'

Then she grabbed me and hugged me so tightly I could hardly breathe and she didn't let go for ages, and I could feel her sobbing inside herself in a private place deep beneath the surface. As we walked back into the house she put her arm around me for support and I put my arm around her and felt the baby blooming there. I knew I had to have a plan if I was going to survive Mum's trip to hospital.

Mum's pregnancy with Beth marked a term of solitary confinement for me. I literally fell between the cracks: I lived under the house. I kept out of the way and became as invisible as a child can be without actually vanishing. I discovered little 'rooms' where the foundations followed the layout of the house. The tiny cell under the bathroom was best because the entry was at such an angle that you couldn't see inside by looking under the house. Also, there was no way Daddy's back would let him crawl under and get me before I could scramble out the other side.

I stocked up on bread from the kitchen, tomatoes from the garden (I knew he counted them, but I also knew I wouldn't be there to face the music), and cans of soft drink stolen from the backyard storage shed of the wog milk bar next to the Butcher Lady's. I took an old blanket, not to keep warm, but to hug and to keep the mozzies off, and some Superman comics. The night Mum went to hospital, I moved in to my new home.

I heard Dad threatening to skin Kelly and Tony alive if they didn't tell him where the fuck I was. But they couldn't. Not if he peeled them like prawns. They didn't have a clue. I didn't dare share my secret hiding place with anyone. Only Cha Cha and Hot Cha Cha knew, and

I loved their purring visits because life under the house was alternately scary, lonely and mind-numbingly boring.

At night, I pretended my little brick box was Superman's Ice Fortress at the North Pole. Even in my dreams I wasn't able to see myself landing a dynamite 'KAPOW!' on Dad's face, but at least he couldn't hurt me. I felt safe. I found a bit of chalky debris left behind by the builders and scrawled Ice Fortress on the brick wall.

Occasionally, I took a gamble and crawled to a spot under the kitchen where I could hear the wireless playing through the floorboards. I was exposed to anyone who looked under the house, but it was worth it. The radio was a comfort. Engelbert Humperdinck sang 'My Ten Guitars', Johnny Cash was falling down, down, down into a burning 'Ring of Fire', and Tom Jones tore my heart out with 'The Green, Green Grass of Home'.

I also found some unlikely friends: spiders. There was an army of them (ironically, we called them 'daddy long-legs') living under the house, nesting in the corners. I had a choice: I could either get on with them, or not. I talked to the spiders. I gave them names. We laughed together. We wept together. We screamed together. We made plans for a better life, and we promised to always be there for each other. But only in whispers.

A rare comic interlude was watching the bottom half of Daddy's legs as he limped around the house calling out for me. His tone changed from a saccharine, 'Shane, come and get some dinner, mate,' to a snarling, 'I'll rip your fucking head off and shit down your neck when I get my hands on you.' It set off the strangest feeling in me; I felt like laughing and crying at the same time, and my lips trembled between the two extremes.

If Daddy were home, I'd stay put. Only when I was certain he was at work or at the pub would I crawl out into the sunlight. Even then, I didn't let my brothers know where I'd been living.

'Where've you been?' Kelly asked.

'Nowhere,' I said, speaking the truth.

Later, Kelly found out about my home under the house, and sometimes, when nowhere was the best place to be, he moved in.

I lived there for ten days, the whole time Mum was in hospital. If I had to go to the toilet (and I was awake), I'd use the furthermost cubicle under the house. If I ran out of food, I'd wait until I could steal scraps from the kitchen or find something worth eating from the rubbish bins in town.

Sometimes, to kill time, I rode the trains to Sydney and back, over and over. I could spot a ticket inspector at 50 paces, and hopped from carriage to carriage to avoid him. Once, a man in a business suit pressed a few shillings into my hand and I went to the old Warrick Picture Theatre in Main Street, Blacktown. I had to plead with the usher to let me in because there was no adult to look after me, and it was eight o'clock at night and I was filthy and had no shoes. I bought a 'choc top' ice-cream and watched a documentary about crocodiles in northern Queensland.

For two hours I lurked in steaming jungles and jumped in my seat when cruel eyes snapped open on floating logs and giant jaws seized unsuspecting prey in a thrashing frenzy of ravenous, razor teeth. To this day, the cinema is a very special place for me. I go as often as I can. For a time I can be a small boy again, when fantasy and escape are more appealing than the real show outside.

I never went to school while Mum was in hospital. I was scared they'd make me go home. For the time being my home was under the house. And then, when Mum came home at last, I discovered the nightmare was just beginning.

I could usually tell when Mum was going to do something bad to herself. She became quiet, like she didn't have the energy to be noticed, and her skin seemed pale and brittle as porcelain and she looked like she'd break if you touched her too roughly. But it was her eyes that were the real giveaway. They looked unbearably, achingly tired, like they were too weary to continue looking at this world any longer. As I watched her, it seemed as though her life was leaking out through her eyes. And as Mum's eyes grew duller and more distant, I knew she just wanted to lie down and never get up again. I tried my best to brighten her up. I told her about the bird that Cha Cha had caught or said how pretty she looked, but Mum was too tired to see me or hear me or care any more.

It was only a few months after Mum had brought the new baby home that she tried to kill herself again. I was in the bedroom when I heard screaming outside. Even though the venetian blinds were closed, I knew it was Mum. I'd heard the sound so many times before. Peering through the blinds, I saw her running along Edward Street in the dust, helter-skelter towards the main thoroughfare leading into Blacktown.

She was naked and seemed hell-bent on throwing herself under a bus. Coming up behind her like a giant lopsided crab was Dad. To run, he had to use the right-hand side of his body to pull the weakened left side into line. He had his dressing gown in his hands and he was trying to catch up with her and stop her and cover her at the same time. He kept swivelling his body as he reached out to grab her.

I'd never seen a naked woman and I was shocked by how white she was, and how her breasts rose and fell as she ran and at the dark triangle between her legs. Everything was in slow motion. Even the animal wail that tore from her throat sounded like a scratched record, slowed and warped under the needle. When he brought her back into the house, she was covered and trembling and he was breathing wildly. He marched her into the room with the big double bed and shut the door behind them. I knew that Mum would have come out when she heard the baby crying, if only she could.

It wasn't long after this incident that she said something that terrified me more than anything Dad had ever done.

'Listen carefully now, love. I have something very important to tell you. The most important thing I've ever said to you. Your real father's coming to pick you up tomorrow. You and Kelly are going to live with your real father.'

Tony would stay because he was too little to travel, and anyway, he had what Mum called Pink's disease, caused by mercury poisoning as a result of the stuff she rubbed into his gums to ease his teething pain. It kept him awake, crying through the night because his body ached right down to his bones. Mum spent hours massaging him and singing to him softly till he dropped off. Some mornings I found her asleep on a chair next to his bed, her hand still stroking him.

Before I could say a word, she put her hand over my mouth. 'Shhh,' she whispered. 'It's for the best, love. I know you love me and you know how much I love you. You're my soulies of the chook. You're my brave little man.' She was sobbing now. 'But all this is no good. It's not fair to you. You deserve so much more, and your real dad can give it to you, love. I can't. I just can't. He's coming for you tomorrow at six o'clock.'

And she left me standing there and went off to cry alone, some place where her pain wouldn't add an unbearable weight to my own.

# ROUND 4

TOMORROW CAME. DADDY KNEW RYAN was coming to fetch us, and he was busy in the tomato garden at six o'clock. He could tolerate this once-only visit if it meant 'getting rid of those useless fucking Weaver bastards forever'. Kelly and I were scrubbed and shining and shitting ourselves on the front verandah at ten to six. Mum had stuffed our clothes into plastic bags. There wasn't much to carry. She had to wait inside because Daddy said there was no way he'd let her 'so much as nod, let alone speak, to that cunt'. But she told us not to worry, she'd be watching through the venetian blinds. I asked Mum what we should call him.

'Call him Dad,' Mum said, 'because that's who he is. And he's the only man I've ever loved.'

I didn't want to go. I wanted to stay with Mum no matter what. Who was going to love her when I was gone? Who was going to look out for the lopsided silhouette lurching across the paddock? Who would warn her to run and hide? Who would bring her bones from the Butcher Lady?

At six o'clock a filthy white ute with Queensland number plates pulled up. There were three blokes in the front. One of them got out and, smiling broadly, put his hands on his hips and said, 'Come on then, boys, what are you waiting for? A telegram?' He spoke in a clear, booming voice, like he had no fear of Daddy hearing him, no fear at all. I turned around and saw Mum's face pressed against the window. She was smiling and sobbing at the same time. She wasn't waving; she was shooing us off.

Kelly and I headed down the footpath, carrying our plastic bags. I looked back. Mum's face was twisted in misery. The strange man with the big voice walked as far as the gate and then stopped and held his arms out.

'Ah, you must be Shane then, eh,' said the stranger, grabbing my free hand and shaking it. 'Which means *you* must be Kelly,' and he tousled Kelly's hair and laughed out loud. 'These are me mates. That's Joe, behind the wheel, and the other handsome coot's Dennis.' Joe and Dennis grinned and said, 'G'day.'

I was wondering where Kelly and I were going to sit when he swooped and picked me up and swung me into the back of the ute. Kelly was next. 'Okie dokie,' our new father said, 'we're off like a bucket of prawns, eh.' He jumped in with his mates and the ute turned around slowly and we drove off. Cha Cha sauntered out onto the road as if to say goodbye, and I wondered if I'd ever see him or Mum or 63 Edward Street again. They tooted the horn a few times. I winced because I knew Mum would get a punch in the face for that.

It was a bloody long drive from Blacktown to Queensland in the back of a ute. The journey was a blur.

Battalions of telegraph poles and trees and more trees flashed by, and days dissolved into nights and flared back into days and then died to darkness again and Kelly and I huddled under the tarpaulin to keep the millions of stars from crashing down on our heads. The man who was our real dad occasionally poked his head out of the cabin and, straining his neck, turned and yelled, 'Hey, are you two blokes doin' okay back there?'

We stopped in a tiny country town and Dad asked, 'Are you blokes hungry or what?' When neither Kelly nor I answered, he said, 'Well, you bloody well *look* hungry. Here ya go. Get a feed then, eh.'

And he gave us five pounds. Each! Geez, we'd never seen so much money, let alone held it in our hands. We went off and bought two huge bags of grapes from a fruit stall and when we offered him the change, he put on a hurt face and said, 'Hey, I gave it to ya, didn't I? Waddaya think I am, an Indian giver?' We ate way too many grapes, way too fast.

Dad said, 'Sorry, boys, but we don't have time to stop. Ave a good chuck and you'll be right as rain.'

We spewed a flying, bitter stream of purple for miles.

It seemed like weeks but three nights later Dad yelled out, 'Hey, are you two sleepy heads awake? This is it. We're home, boys, we're home.'

We stuck our heads out from under the tarp and yawned and stretched and rubbed the sleep and the road grit from our eyes. We were parked between two silver trucks so big you needed a ladder to climb up and get inside. The place looked like a carnival ground with a neon sign flashing 'Open 24 hours' off and on and on and off, and all the lights in a giant shop blazing orange and yellow and blue and red. The unmistakable stench of petrol filled our nostrils. We recognised it because it smelled like Daddy's lawnmower after it'd done a few laps of the yard back at Edward Street. Only 100,000 times stronger.

Our new dad was sort of running on the spot with excitement. 'Come on then, boys, time to meet your new family.'

We followed him into a vast dining room with a wooden floor and tables with blue and white checked plastic tablecloths and salt and pepper shakers and tomato and Worcestershire sauce bottles on every one. Three hippo-arsed truckies in grubby shorts and blue singlets were stuffing their faces with steak sandwiches and guzzling hot coffee. One of them gave us a big animated wink and a toothy grin with a lettuce leaf in it as we passed into the kitchen out the back.

'Well, here they are at last,' Dad announced. 'Shane,' he patted my head, 'and Kelly,' likewise identified by a pat on the head.

He was talking to a short, fat woman who was about three times as big as Mum. A grease-spattered red and white checked apron was stretched tightly over her belly and even though it covered her entire front, it couldn't conceal the pneumatic bosoms that heaved and billowed as she stepped forward to inspect us more closely. She kept blinking to stop the sweat from stinging her eyes and it gave her the appearance of being pissed off at the abrupt intrusion of two scruffy boys into her kitchen and her life.

'Boys, this is my Liza, she'll see ya right, eh. And this is your Uncle Billy, the world's second best chef after my good self, and that there's your Auntie Elsie.'

He went up to Liza and gave her a hug and a peck on the cheek. 'Get 'em a feed, willya, love. They must be starvin'.'

'He looks like he's had a little accident,' Liza said, pointing to the stain on my shorts.

I thought he'd hit me or do his block, and instinctively I started walking backwards.

'Well, it's a bloody long drive,' Dad laughed. 'Enough to piss anyone off, eh. Let's feed 'em first, eh.'

Me and Kelly sat down to T-bones so humungous they spilled over our plates. There was a mountain of chips and a strawberry milkshake each to wash it all down with. I was starving, but I felt guilty with every bite. Mum'd be lucky if she was eating mince on toast.

Home turned out to be a caravan in a place called Waratah, stuck on the map somewhere between Guyra and Armidale near the Queensland and New South Wales border. This was where Dad and Liza ran a 24-hour roadhouse with his sister, Elsie, and her husband, Billy. Long-haul truck drivers and tourists stopped to get fuel, fags and a man-sized fry-up. Dad and Billy were the cooks. Liza and Elsie waited tables and did the washing up.

There were two big caravans, one for Dad and Liza, and one for Billy and Elsie. Because Dad and Liza did the night shift, Kelly and I slept in their bunk. They weren't real rapt about us pissing in their bed, and they took turns to wake us every few hours and lead us into the bush for a leak. It seemed to work pretty well, and there weren't too many dramas. The biggest shock was that when accidents happened, Dad didn't bash the living daylights out of us, or threaten to cut off our dicks.

'Never mind,' he'd say, 'accidents happen. It's our fault for not waking you in time, eh.' He was so damn nice about it that, once or twice, I admit I squeezed out a piss on purpose, just so I could hear him say don't worry, mate, it's okay.

Those nights when it was a bit slow in the restaurant, Auntie Elsie came and sat on the end of my bunk and told us stories. She was heart-attack fat with at least three chins, and arms that sort of stuck out of her body and flapped like a penguin's when she moved. Trouble was, Auntie Elsie thought she was thin and beautiful, and she wore a ribbon in her hair and sort of skipped along like a school kid, humming as she went. Once, I heard Joe say she was about as cute as a tractor. She carried a dirty tea towel with her and always seemed to be mopping sweat from her face.

Auntie Elsie's bedtime stories were at once irresistible and hideous. It was like seeing a squashed wombat by the roadside. You felt sick, but you couldn't stop yourself getting as close as the pong would let you to see the guts pushed up and out through the mouth and spilling from the arse. Her most horrifying tale was about 'a mad bastard' who stole newborn babies and hung them in a graveyard by their noses with the safety pins from their nappies. There was a line of nude babies strung between trees, kicking their little baby legs and howling for their mothers. Her lips tightened and thinned when she got to the worst bits and she watched our eyes like a vulture, feeding off our terror.

Kelly and I had no trouble believing that there was someone out there who relished butchering babies the slow way, so they screamed and squirmed and flapped like blood-drenched washing in the wind until at last death let them go. It seemed to us that cruelty to kids was every big person's right.

Auntie Elsie said it was best if our stories were a secret just between us. She made us promise or the mad bastard might come and get us, she said. I kept my word. Until now.

We went to the local school about 60 miles away. The bus picked us up before the roosters crowed. We were a bit of a novelty at school. We were 'city kids', which was weird really, as (except for my train rides to Central and back) we'd never even been to Parramatta, let alone Sydney. Still, even backwoods Blacktown had shops and a pub and a picture show. All Waratah had was drought-stricken bush and way too many sad, shadow-skinny sheep.

Once, me and Kelly went for a long walk through the brown paddocks surrounding the roadhouse. The grass crunched and turned to dust under our feet. The further we walked, the skinnier and the weaker the sheep seemed to get, until there were just acres of dead sheep. The stink was revolting and you could hear the maggots sluicing through the carcasses. It sounded like the rustle of wind in dry grass, but there was no breeze, not even a whisper, to disturb the awful stillness. The movement of the maggots seemed to invest life into the dead sheep, and their legs lifted and shuddered in the bone-dry air.

I was dying another death. I missed Mum so badly my whole body ached, inside and out. Not knowing what was happening to her always had me imagining the worst. I felt I had betrayed her by leaving her behind without enough to eat and no kindness or caring, while I ate steak and chips and lived with people who didn't whip me or talk to me like I was a dog. I grew more depressed. I couldn't sleep. I couldn't eat. I couldn't play. I just couldn't be bothered. When Dad asked me what was wrong, I told him I had to go home. I had to be with my mum.

'I understand how you feel, sport,' he said, 'but this is your home now. Me and Liza and Uncle Billy and Auntie Elsie, we love ya, mate. You and Kelly mean the world to us. Just give it some time. It'll get better. I swear.'

They gave us carte blanche on the lolly counter. Whenever we wanted, we were allowed to grab. And we did. Often. Chewy cobbers and sticky, multicoloured snakes and gooey bananas and jellybeans galore. After three months, we resembled sausages sizzling on a barbecue – we were bursting out of our skins. We had to get new clothes and our teeth rotted and we'd wake up screaming in the night with our heads on fire with toothache. Dad led us down to the petrol pumps and doused a big gob of cotton wool with petrol.

'Bite on this,' he said, 'it'll kill the pain.'

And by crikey it did. But nothing killed the pain of missing Mum. In the end, Dad gave in and said, 'Okay, okay, I've managed to get word to your mother.' He sighed. 'I think you're making a big mistake, and Liza and I are really sad about this, but you boys are going home on Wednesday.' We'd been away just over six months.

Dad had arranged for us to get a lift with a truckie mate who let us off at Liverpool, about an hour from Blacktown. Mum was waiting when the truck pulled up. She looked so alone and small, standing there in the middle of the vast, vacant parking lot, smiling and crying.

When she saw us climbing down from the cabin, she flung her arms out like she was crucified and we ran like crazy into the warmth of her embrace and I hugged her so hard, so long and so fiercely that we melted into each other.

Our crippled dad never said a word when we got back, but we knew he'd get us for this. We waddled into our rooms and Mum sneaked our dinner in to us. It had been a long time since we'd had tomato sandwiches at night. It wouldn't take long to lose the weight we'd stacked on.

# ROUND 5

I WAS A BOG-UGLY TEENAGER. Kelly and Tony taunted me with cries of 'Nose', on account of the monstrosity stuck in the middle of my face. The mega meatloaf was a Weaver heirloom, but I was the only Weaver boy on this side of the family who ended up wearing it. My skin was a greasy nest for a porridge of pimples. My self-esteem wasn't merely in the gutter, it had run like dirty water through the grille and spilled into the sewer. Laughter was a language I didn't understand. The kids at school reckoned I only smiled if I had wind.

To make matters worse, my bedwetting became more of a problem when I got older, not least of all because a teenager's piss stinks more than that of a young child. I felt like a human cockroach. I felt people were staring at me all the time. I could feel their disgust. I thought they could smell last night's piss on my skin.

The pong problem got pongier after the night Dad caught me in the shower. He came storming in with the electrical cord, rotten drunk and livid because he'd tripped over a cat's bowl on the verandah. My first thought was to cover my nakedness. But when he started whipping, modesty went down the plughole and my only concern was avoiding the lash. Mum heard the ruckus and came to help. He smashed her face with his fist and the next thing, Mum and me were slipping and sliding around on the bathroom tiles in water and blood. The cord was relentless. I didn't know what was worse – the whipping or Mum seeing me naked and flailing around on the floor like a jellyfish with pubic hair. It would be a long time before I took another shower.

All we Weaver boys were nocturnal pissers. The more Dad threatened to cut off our dicks, the more certain it was that we'd wake soaked and stinking. There was a big copper in the laundry, and every day Mum boiled the water and washed and rinsed everything by hand before putting it through the wringer and wrestling it down to the clothesline to hang out to dry. It was hard, heavy work. For Mum's sake as much as mine, I prayed I wouldn't piss the bed.

I'd do whatever I could to stay dry. I'd lie awake as long as possible, worrying my hair, tying knots in it and pulling it out at the roots, but I always fell asleep and in the end it was always the same. In the morning, the floor was covered in hairy little parachutes and I was wetter than a cheerleader's panties. Dad made us shoulder our putrid mattresses outside to air in the sun; I felt like Jesus carrying His cross. I'd imagine all the neighbours jeering, 'Look. It's the King of the Phews!'

Taking a dump was no relief, either. For the first ten years in Edward Street, we had no sewerage. The toilet was a black pan in a wooden box stuck in a fibro shed at the far end of the backyard. The toilet man came once a week, taking the full pan and leaving an empty one in its place. If you forgot to leave out a few cans of beer at Xmas, Easter or on Anzac Day, he'd slop shit all the way down your footpath. When there were three big kids, the pan always spilled over days before 'toilet man day' and Mum would put a bucket next to it.

The shitter ponged to high heaven and the flies were a filthy swarm, even at night. If diarrhoea swept through the family, it was catastrophic.

One such night when the pan was brimming and you could feel the tide lapping on your bum when you sat, I was squatting over the top, taking my weight on my legs and straining to void the fire in my guts. At the same time, every fibre of my being was attuned to the world outside. For a rustle. The breaking of a twig. A cough. Anything. Dad had not come home. Dad was out there. Somewhere.

We kids and Mum never had toilet paper ('a waste of fuckin' money on you arseholes') and my anus was red raw from nonstop shitting and the sandpaper scrape of the *Blacktown Advocate*. Dad took down his own personal supply of three-ply. But the quality of the bog paper was nothing. It didn't matter. I had more urgent priorities. More than anything, I was terrified he'd find me. With my pants down, in pain and trapped. I was frantic. Desperate to finish fast and get out in the open. Out where I could see all around me. Out where I could run.

The black air was hot and thick like molasses and you could cut the humidity with a knife. My ears sieved the darkness for any sound beyond the slow siren of the mozzies, the staccato humming of the crickets and the droning of the blowies. I listened so hard it felt like my ears were bleeding. I kept the toilet door ajar and my eyes probed the night until they itched like ants. And then I saw it.

My heart lurched into my throat and stopped beating. I couldn't believe my eyes. I couldn't swallow. I couldn't breathe. God, how? I'd heard nothing. Not a sound. Yet there it was, unmistakable. A glowing butt end on the grass.

Later, I realised he'd been lying slumped and out of sight behind the toilet the whole time. He must have flicked the dying fag into view. I was in such a hurry not to mess my pants I hadn't thought to check around the back before going in. The irony was that he was so pissed, he didn't even know I was there. But it was too late. For both of us. He was dragging himself up just as I was scrambling to pull up my shorts. As he staggered into view, I failed to notice that he wasn't even facing the toilet; he was headed for the kitchen. Unthinking, I grabbed a handful of the only stuff within reach and threw it all over him.

Then I bolted. Straight over the side fence and into the paddock. I heard him cursing as I flew across the paddock. A week would pass before I summoned the courage to return.

My brothers weren't any happier. We'd come from the same misery-mould. Glance back over old photos and you'll see three sullen-faced Weaver boys sporting severe short back and sides. Dad's hair policy was simple. He hated it. 'I won't have a long-haired poofter under my roof. Over my dead body.' On 'haircut days', Dad sat us on three chairs in a row outside in the sun and did us one at a time. He'd bought a pair of manual shears, figuring he'd recoup the cost in what he'd save in trips to the barbers.

He did us in order of age, eldest to youngest. I cringed when I smelled the stink of Drum tobacco as he gripped my face in his yellow fingers and twisted my head to fit the bite of the shears. He held our heads with his claw hand because he needed the good one for clipping. His claw hand was cold like a fish because the blood flow was bad. What I hated most was how his gnarled fingers pinched my face into a pucker, like I was about to kiss him. I felt my face redden and burn with shame. If you so much as blinked to keep the flies off, he smacked your head hard with the hand that held the shears, and the added weight made you see stars. I yelped when the shears nicked my skull and drew blood. Kelly and Tony flinched, not because they felt my pain, but because they could feel their own.

The cool kids at school were growing and bleaching their hair. They were suburban surfies and they had good mates and dads who took them to the footy and mums whose faces weren't swollen and bruised. And they had girlfriends. I didn't think any girl in her right mind would so much as spit on me.

Sometimes, the drama of other people's lives shifted my focus from my own misery, bringing a sense of guilty relief. What happened to our ancient neighbours is an example. Mr and Mrs Smith were in their late seventies and lived next to the McKinnons. To see their backyard, you just walked through the tomato garden and looked over the back fence. The Smiths rarely went out, minding their business and asking only the same. I never saw them unless by chance I glimpsed one of them shuffling to or from the toilet.

It was James McKinnon (or Jimmy to his friends) who told me that old Mr Smith had died. The milkman had noticed the uncollected bottles and raised the alarm. He told Jimmy's mum and they went over and banged on the door. When no one answered, they got Jimmy to scramble in through the kitchen window and open the door. They found Mrs Smith lying like a living skeleton in bed next to her dead husband. Only her eyes were moving.

Jimmy said they were wide open. He said that, through her glasses, her eyes looked like two goldfish swimming like crazy in a bowl.

Mrs Smith followed her husband a few weeks later.

Our neighbourhood was also dying. First the tractors came and started filling in the creek. It was a bloody big creek. It was our Mississippi. After heavy rain, we surged along swirling waters on rafts made of kerosene drums lashed together with rope, yahooing and whooping and wild as the wind. We fished in our creek. There were turtles in it. The Petkovitches, neighbours from Douglas Parade, even ate the fat eels that came thrashing out of it.

The workers killed our creek by degrees. They slowly choked the life out of it. As the waters bled away into a trickle, then a dribble, the eels and turtles tired of trying to find somewhere to swim. They got sluggish and fell sick and it was so easy to catch them it was sad. It got so Cha Cha and Hot Cha Cha were turning their noses up at eel for dinner. Then they bulldozed the trees and cleared the land. They were turning our jungle into a sports oval. We'd have a real footy field and netball courts right next door. Big deal.

One afternoon, the workers dropped truckloads of perfectly manicured, rolled-up lawn on the skinned ground, ready for laying like carpet the next day. When Dad spotted the bundles, he saw a brand new lawn for our backyard. He had grand visions of a golf course standard lawn, free of bindi-eyes, surrounding his tomato garden island like an emerald-green sea.

Under his direction, I hauled home bundles of lawn for hours that night. It was heavy and grubby work and the dirt mixed with my sweat and turned to mud, running down my arms and face and belly. It itched like hell and the mozzies were having a feast. When my arms ached and went feeble and light as air, I hoisted the bundles on my shoulders. When I could no longer bear the weight, I rolled them with my feet. All the while, Dad sat on the back verandah, guzzling beer and telling me to, 'Put ya fuckin' back into it, boy. Whadarya, a fuckin' pussy?'

Finally, there were three piles of rolled-up lawn stacked as high as the fence. A part of me thought I might have forced him to be a bit proud of me. To say I'd done a man's work. He belched wetly, wobbled to his feet and lurched inside without saying a word, closing the screen door behind him and turning off the outside light. I fell face down and hugged the ground, tired and aching and empty as a promise.

# ROUND 6

AGED 13, I GOT TO HIGH SCHOOL a year before Kelly. All the other kids from our primary school went to Doonside High, but Edward Street marked the entry point for Blacktown Boys' High. I arrived virtually unknown and unannounced. I was no one. Better still, I was absolutely anyone I wanted to be. Mum had primed me for months. 'You are what you think, not what you think you are. It's not how good you are, it's how bad you want it. You can do anything, Shane. You can *be* anything.' A freak incident on the first day got me off to a good start.

I was in the playground with 100 or so other kids, waiting for assembly. Hyenas from other forms circled 'the virgins'. I must have looked like an easy mark because, not knowing another soul, I was the odd one out. I caught a flurry of movement from the corner of my eye as he lunged. What happened next was pure reflex. Terrified, I grabbed my attacker in a bear hug around the chest, lifted him up and, using his momentum for leverage, smashed him into the quadrangle. All in one swift, unthinking motion. I didn't mean it, but he landed face-first and because he was quite a bit bigger than I was, he landed heavily.

'Fight! Fight! Fight!' Suddenly, it seemed as if the entire school was swarming around us like a nest of crazed bull ants. But this fight was finished. My attacker's face was covered in blood and snot and he was mooing like a poddy calf. One of the canteen ladies was the first adult on the scene and, ignoring the obvious distress of the vanquished third-former, she launched a scathing denouncement of 'foolish boys who fight'. School folklore later identified her as my attacker's own mum, and made much mileage of the fact that one of the school's best fighters had been beaten so badly even his own mother hadn't recognised him.

And so it came to pass that in a few moments I had graduated from being a bottom feeder to a great white shark. The fact that no one knew me and I kept to myself helped to perpetuate the myth.

By the time Kelly was set to enrol one year later, I'd built upon that lucky start. It wasn't that I fitted in; it was more like I was accepted for being different. For the first time in my life, I actually felt like there might be a place for me. My brother didn't respect that. The Saturday before Kelly was due to start high school, he said, 'Oi, hero, do they know you still wet the bed?'

He was lying on Tony's bed, reading one of my Superman comics. I was just leaving the room but I didn't hesitate. I spun around and fell upon him with a savagery I can still taste like rotten egg in my mouth. I punched his flailing arms until they could no longer stay up to protect his stupid face, and then I punched his stupid face until my fists were skinned raw on his teeth and bone and the only feature I could recognise was his mouth because it was wide open like a tunnel and screaming like the whistle on a steam train in full throttle. And I kept on punching and I kept on punching and I kept on punching until the train ground to a fucking halt.

Sucking in oxygen so desperately my chest was close to bursting, I staggered towards the door. First I felt the 'choof' of wind as a heavy object sailed centimetres from my ear, and then the explosion as it shattered against the doorframe, splintering into a thousand razor edges. It took me a second to realise what had happened. During Dad's sojourns in hospital, part of his physio included building matchstick ships in bottles. The hand-to-eye coordination was part of his rehabilitation. There were several of these maritime monuments beached around the house, and on a small table next to Tony's bed, in a seriously thick glass bottle, a pirates' galleon had bucked like billyo on a frozen blue ocean. If it had connected with my head, they'd still be tweezering glass splinters from my brain.

I snatched a big chunk that had formed part of the heavy base of the bottle and hurled it back. The howl that broke from Kelly's lips impaled me to the spot. A piercing caterwaul that made his previous efforts seem sissy. The neighbours didn't call the cops, they called an ambulance. By the time the cavalry arrived, the bed was dripping red, and Kelly was bone-white and shivering like a naked Eskimo. The top of his thigh was laid open in a six-inch gash so deep you could see gristle or muscle or nerve endings or all of them. They didn't remove him from the bedding; they wrapped it around him like a soggy shroud and bundled the lot in the back of the ambulance.

I sat in the front as we sped off to Blacktown Hospital, siren bawling. In the process of pitching the broken glass, I'd gashed my finger. I got three stitches. Kelly needed internal and external stitching and some plastic surgery. Dad had to burn the mattress. It took a long while to get going, and it stank like stale piss in the flames.

I can't say every fight between Kelly and me was his fault. Take the night I pissed in his mouth. When we three Weaver bastards had got too big for our room, Dad had converted Kelly's and my beds into a double-decker bunk. Being the eldest, I slept on top. Some nights, looking down the crack between the bunk and the wall, I could see Kelly's sleeping head. On this particular night, he was dead to the world with his mouth wide open like he was at the dentist's. As soon as I had the idea, it was too late. I angled my pecker, took careful aim and let him have it. The first blast hit his chin and I adjusted my sights.

Scoring a direct hit was fun, but it was nothing compared to watching him wake, wondering what on earth was going on. He spluttered and felt his face. He rubbed it. He smacked his lips to test the taste. He smelled his hands. And then he screamed blue murder when he saw me grinning like a baboon in the bed above him. 'Muuuuuuum!'

I shot out of bed like a greyhound after the bunny, bolted through the house and was halfway over the fence to the McKinnons' when a whack on the back of my head dropped me cold. Mum had worked out what had happened in a jiffy and brought me to ground with a magnificently pitched can of no-name peas.

So why did Kelly and I loathe each other so absolutely? Certainly the bottomless well of spite that poisoned our relationship ran much deeper than sibling rivalry. He had his reasons and I had mine. I was always Mum's favourite. When I was a baby I was her 'soulies of the chook' (to this day I am her 'soulies' sans the 'chook'). In a house where love and affection were rarer than hen's teeth, it must have rankled.

But the bond that was forged between Mum and me was also a yoke. Perhaps Dad saw Mum and me as the embodiment of everything that conspired to emasculate and humiliate him. The war had robbed him of the chance to compete for a woman on an even playing field. He always felt second best and living with another man's woman was proof. As her first born, and with the prominent Weaver proboscis and the name 'Patrick Shayne Weaver', I was a rude, public announcement of his inadequacy. Dad switched my first and second names. I became Shane without a 'y', not Pat, but the nose just got bigger and he himself kept the Weaver in me alive.

Kelly stood on the perimeter. He was never the one Dad came gunning for first. The upside was that he wasn't in the front line. The downside was that he was cut by flying shrapnel, but he never shared the spirit of camaraderie that bolstered the troops in the face of the enemy.

On nights when we were stuck in the limbo between daring to eat before Dad came home and trying to take the edge off the wait, Mum and I spent hours in the kitchen, drinking too much Pablo coffee (Nescafe was the ultimate luxury, but we could rarely afford it) and talking. And this is where Kelly found us when the mozzies and hunger drove him into the house. Had he joined us in the kitchen, he would have been nearer the wireless and the chatter, but it would have also put him directly in Dad's sights when the screen door flew open. Kelly went to his room and closed the door.

If anyone was close to Kelly it was Tony. They were virtually joined at the hip when we were growing up. But it was never a supportive togetherness. Kelly was the puppeteer. He jigged and Tony jerked. When he began his maddening chant of 'Nose, nose, nose', Tony joined in. It seemed they were always whispering and plotting. But I was making my own dark plans. Looking back, I'm amazed that one of us didn't kill the other. It wasn't through lack of trying.

Tony had always been a sickly child. As well as Pink's disease, he suffered from terrible chest infections and a horrid cough that nagged him through the night, making it virtually impossible for him to sleep. Mum would take him into the bathroom, shut the door and run the hot water on the shower full blast so the air filled with steam. It helped ease his breathing.

He loved birds. His pride and joy was a black chook some kid had given him. 'Blackie' ran around the backyard clucking and scratching and doing the happy little dances chooks do when no one's got their eye on them for dinner. The day the neighbour's dachshund broke into our yard and tore his chook to pieces was one of the darkest days in my little brother's life. He'd poured so much love into that silly bird.

Tony was eight when he invented the 'soup stone'. When we were so broke that Mum had nothing whatsoever to boil up to make even the most basic soup, Tony offered her a smooth stone he'd been carrying in his pocket. 'Here, Mum,' he said, 'put this in the water. The magic of the wonderful soup stone will make something beautiful for us to eat.' Mum still talks proudly about how her boy had the gift of seeing hope where others might see only a hungry stone. Nevertheless Tony was to witness an event so shocking that nothing could blunt the knife-edge of reality.

There had been a spate of reports on the tele of monks who'd burned themselves to death. Immolation was the word they used. But it's a sterile word that doesn't seem to translate the images of these men, sitting passively, engulfed in a fierce furnace of whooshing flames. Sometimes they leapt up and ran, but there's nowhere to go except into the darkness when you're a human torch.

Mum said that's where she got the idea. She thought it would be a simple, relatively painless dispatch. That's how it had seemed on TV. I don't know whether it was vanity, or if she imagined the flames would pounce up and devour her entire body and head, but she walked slowly to the bathroom and doused her legs and dressing gown with metho. Just as she threw the lighted match onto her gown, Tony came down the hall. His horrified scream was matched by her own as her skin burned and exploded in pain. Quickly, she killed the fire with a towel, but she still carries the scars, and the image of his mother that day is seared into Tony's memory forever. Of course, Mum had no idea whatsoever that Tony was in the house, and she still feels guilty for the trauma this incident caused him.

In all fairness, you couldn't accuse Dad of playing favourites. Richard was his blood son, but his head, too, was blitzkrieged with the same Gestapo haircut. He too had learned to turn from ice to running water at the sound of the Cha Cha chant. He never knew what it was to be kissed or hugged or praised by his father. When it came to wearing 'hand-me-downs', Richard was last in line. He looked like a scarecrow with tattered outsize shirts and the cuffs on his pants rolled up, with just a string between him and the ultimate humiliation. The only thing he was spared was being branded a Weaver bastard. He was a Reynard, and, God help us, for most of his life, we never let Richard forget it.

While there was no togetherness in the Brady Bunch sense of the word, there were, however, alliances of expedience. For example, being powerless against Dad, Kelly, Tony and I did whatever we could to punish his son. We didn't talk about it. We didn't plan it. We didn't even particularly like it. We just did it.

It was a mindless vendetta that began before Richard was old enough to toddle. Even when he was cot-bound, we walked past and pinched him so hard he screamed blue murder. Then we watched from the sidelines as Dad laid into him. Later, we thumped him in the head (because he had a prominent forehead we called him 'boofhead'), without the slightest warning or provocation, any time of the night or day. He became the focus of all our loathing for his father.

And his father fed the fire. He lined us boys up and paraded before us with a bag of lollies in his hand. Up and down the line, searching our faces for a clue as to which child was most deserving of a sweet. He stopped in front of each of us Weavers and paused before moving on. Finally, he stopped in front of Richard, who looked more sick than happy about it, and presented him with a lolly.

'Richard,' he'd say solemnly, 'You're my only true son.' Richard knew we'd get him for that.

Little wonder then that he jumped at his own shadow and wore a frantic expression like the world was about to explode. For Richard, it was. No one can keep the lid on that kind of pressure. It had to come out.

As a kid, Richard tortured reptiles and insects. Anything that crept or crawled or flew, if Richard could catch it, he would kill it. Eventually. He specialised in protracted suffering and slow death. A favoured method was to dig a hole and place the victim in it without water or food. He covered the hole with a plank of wood and sprinkled dirt and leaves over it. Periodically, he returned to check on the condition of the creature. Sometimes we found underground crypts with ashes and charred remains.

In spring, when the giant willow tree in our backyard exploded into a profusion of buds, literally buzzing with squadrons of bees, Richard unleashed the stinging power of thick rubber bands, embarking on his own killing spree until the ground was a squishy blanket of dead bees and the air reeked with the sweet, acidic scent of their juices. When the McKinnons' guinea pigs went missing, we shuddered.

The girls were so much younger they may as well have come from another planet. When Mum brought Beth home from the hospital, I thought, bloody hell, this is why I was condemned to live under the house, for this scrawny, hairy, screaming brat. She was born premature and looked more like a boiled chook than a baby.

As a toddler, Beth followed her father around like a faithful puppy, lost in a child's awe of the power of the parent. She'd trail after him as he worked in the tomato garden. Close as a shadow. We all thought Beth was his favourite. Beth is the only kid I can ever recall Dad holding. No one knew it was foreplay. Three decades would pass before I discovered that the abuse Dad dished out to his little girls was entirely different from anything we boys had to put up with.

Then along came Sarah. Whenever I think of Sarah as a baby, I remember 'The Day of the Rabbit'. We had a pet rabbit in a cage. Its name was Stew. I've never really warmed to rabbits. And that's the point, really; I'd forgotten it existed. The trouble was, it was apparently my responsibility to feed the thing.

I was about to learn the serious consequences of neglecting my duty. So was Sarah.

It was after school. I was lying on my bed studying Superman comics and sucking on a tomato when Richard came rushing in.

'Blood. Blood. She's bleeding everywhere.'

'Who? Who's bleeding?'

'Sarah,' he cried.

Sarah was about three years old. I sprinted out to the backyard to see her rolling around on the ground next to the rabbit's hutch. She was covered in blood and screaming. Closer investigation showed the blood was spurting from where the top of her finger should have been. Mum wasn't home, so I got Mrs Roberts from next door. She told me to run to the phone box and call an ambulance, and they rushed Sarah to Blacktown Hospital.

It seemed she'd poked a piece of grass into the cage, and the ravenous rabbit had taken both the food and Sarah's baby finger in one big, buck-toothed bite. When

Dad spilled in through the door that night, it was Kelly who told him what had happened – I was hiding in my room, listening. Dad didn't say a word. He simply turned and walked outside. He didn't rant and rave. He didn't even slam the door. So there were no clues. Only when he came back did I know something was terribly wrong.

Mum shouted 'No!' with such bloodcurdling urgency that I knew I had to get out of the house. I bolted down the hall and hit the screen door in the kitchen full force. As I passed him, Dad took a desperate swipe at me. With an axe. I found out later that he'd intended to kill the rabbit, but he was so pissed that when he opened the hutch it simply hopped off into the paddock next door. Dad figured if he couldn't butcher the rabbit, the next best thing was 'the bastard who was supposed to feed it'.

My own sense of loneliness was overwhelming and I retreated deeper into my fantasy world. The gum trees around the paddock exercised a simian influence over me, and I became an extraordinary tree climber. I could monkey up a tree trunk and disappear into the foliage in seconds. I got so close to the nests of birds I could have reached out and touched them. I went impossibly high, almost to the apex of the towering ghost-white giants, and, clinging on like a koala bear, stayed for hours, surveying the sprawling neighbourhood below. I was at one with the wind, swaying gently, rocked like an infant, caressed by the sun, breathing with the tree, joined with the sky.

I saw mums hanging out the washing, dogs chasing cats, kids playing in their yards and sometimes, when I was lucky, I saw Arnie's older sister way below, coming home from shopping or from work. She was a pert thing, about 18, and she swivelled her bum when she walked. While her undulating hips were mesmerising at ground level, her gait looked more comic and robotic when seen from a hundred feet high. I was always tempted to drop a piece of bark or a marble from my pocket, but I knew this would blow my cover forever, and I managed to restrain myself.

My method for descending from my lofty lookouts was breathtaking. Literally. I just let go, crashing through the leaves and branches and stopping my fall intermittently by grabbing hold of a branch or gripping the trunk with my arms and legs. When I thudded to the ground, my chest and arms looked like they'd been through a cheese shredder and I stank of squashed ants and beetles and crushed gum leaves. I walked home shaking, adrenaline shooting through my veins and Superman's perspective of the world helicoptering in my head.

# ROUND 7

IT WAS 1968 AND I WAS 15. As well as the insufferable heat, this Xmas (with an X, because 'Christ has bugger-all to do with it') would go down in family folklore as the time Dad disappeared off the face of the earth. Until I found him.

It was a stinker. Forty degrees in the shade. Walking barefoot was impossible and your thongs stuck to the footpath if you stood still for too long. Mighty thirsty weather. And Dad was spending more time and more money in the Hood. This was his favourite after-work watering hole (the local RSL was the weekend choice). It was handy, just opposite the train station and directly over the road from the bus that dropped him on the main road, a rolling wobble away from the fibro house across the paddock.

Dad shunned the Public Bar because it was full of 'long-haired poofters and druggies who wouldn't know a hard day's yakka if it jumped up and bit 'em on the arse'. It was also a bloodhouse; there were always blues and the cops were in and out like yo-yos. Dad preferred the relative safety of the Saloon Bar, where the veterans met and bitched about the missus and the war and the weather. Besides, you could always plonk yourself down on a stool, and when you stayed as long as he did and had a bad back and all, well, it really was a no-brainer.

On Xmas eve he'd been missing in action three whole days. Usually by this time Concord Repat Hospital would have sent someone to tell us they had him and not to worry, he was going to be okay. Or the paddy wagon pulled up and the cops bundled him out of the cage in the back. He always looked like shit. Invariably, he'd been rolled and what little dough he had left after boozing was gone. But this time we'd heard nothing. Mum had even sent me into town to walk past the pub and see if I could spot him. No Dad. We were gripped by an uneasy peace, more like numbness than freedom.

Mum said she wasn't going to let him spoil Xmas again this year, and Kelly and I ceased hostilities long enough to cut a small 'Christmas' tree from the paddock. It even looked a bit like a pine tree. We spent hours making decorations. Painted wooden clothes pegs served as candles, and Mum gave us some frayed red ribbon to wrap around the branches. Beer bottle tops sparkled like stars. For the most amazing star, hovering like a cosmic sign right at the top of the tree, she found an old green brooch that used to be her mother's, and it flashed like an emerald under the dirty yellow light in the lounge.

The wireless played a Bing Crosby Christmas Special and Mum, Kelly, Tony and I sang along. Our voices were pitched somewhere between harmony and a horror that the screen door would open like a throat, introducing a very different song. Richard was too young to sing, but he became suitably raucous for 'Rudolph the Red-nosed Reindeer'. Sarah and Beth were just babies. Ignorance was their guarantee of a merry Xmas.

That night, we slept like soldiers in a war zone. Tasting the salty sweat running in rivulets down our faces. Shallow breathing like dogs panting to keep cool. Dreading the bang of the screen door and the chilling chorus of the Cha Cha chant. We knew Mum had no money for presents and that Santa wouldn't be visiting 63 Edward Street. Someone at school told me that the words Santa and Satan were made of the same letters. I prayed to God there would be no mix-up that night.

Christmas morning unwrapped like a present, and my prayers had been answered. So far, it belonged only to the seven of us. I peeled off my wet pyjamas, showered, and changed into my yard clothes before dragging my yellowed mattress into the backyard to air against the fence. I scanned the area in grids. Tomato garden: all clear. Under the willow tree: all clear. Behind the toilet: all clear.

I could hear the three McKinnon kids over the back fence, whooping and hollering like it was Xmas. They'd woken up to freshly painted, second-hand bikes and a shuttlecock game. First the shuttlecock came hurtling over the fence. Then the yells. 'What'd you get, Reynard? What'd Santa bring ya? Go on, show us ya presents.'

I said nothing. I knew they couldn't understand. To me, this was the Xmas of Xmases. Dad was nowhere to be seen. Mum said we were lucky to have Vegemite sandwiches for Xmas lunch because that's what Santa's Aussie elves ate while they were busy bringing presents to all the good girls and boys. She said some children were so good that Santa couldn't possibly fit everything they deserved onto his sleigh. These kids would get an extra special surprise later. Something so fantastic they wouldn't believe their eyes. She didn't dare give us even a tiny hint, because if we guessed then it couldn't come true.

Later, I saw Mum in the kitchen making Vegemite sandwiches. She was sobbing into a tea towel, so we wouldn't hear her. I knew there was no special surprise coming later. It didn't matter to me. I would gladly have swapped a sleigh full of presents to see my mum happy.

It was the morning of the fourth day of his disappearance. I climbed to the top of the willow tree next to the shed in the backyard. It was a giant tree, and I was able to look way out over the paddock to the main road. I could see some kids fishing for eels in the creek with their Xmas rods. I don't know what focused my attention on the shed below. Dad had made it himself by stretching black canvas over a wooden frame. There were no windows. I didn't hear a noise. It looked the same. The door was always closed. There had been no need to lock it. This was where Dad kept his tools and tomato sprays and paint and stuff. He warned us that he'd set mantraps inside that would chop us in half if we so much as poked our bloody noses in. We believed him. Absolutely.

But now the shed was a magnet. The pull was overpowering. I felt sick to my stomach, but I knew I had to see inside. I climbed down from the willow tree and opened the door. A blast of hot air smacked me like a furnace. Then the stench. At first I thought he was dead. He was sprawled back in an old deck chair. Flies buzzing. Wine and beer bottles strewn on the ground. His arms flopped by his side. His head was thrown back and his mouth was open. His face was grey plasticine. His glasses were missing and he looked different without them. I stopped. Time stopped. And then it jump-started again like a heart leaping under a fibrillator. 'Dad?' Slowly I moved towards him. When I got closer, I knew he'd shat himself. He'd vomited over his shirt and there were maggots seething through the mess. Even the gunk in his nostrils was flyblown.

It happened in a blink. Suddenly, he wasn't a man any more. He was a slab of contaminated meat. Obscene. Something to be removed. In my mind I could see myself grabbing the garden shovel and smashing his fucking face in again and again and again as hard as I could. I'd smash it till it was mash. I'd do it for Mum. I'd do it for all of us. I'd do it for me.

Ironically, sometimes it is the things we do *not* do that are the defining moments in our lives. 'Oh, God help us,' said Mum. She had come up behind me and put her hand on my shoulder. Together we walked to the phone box halfway up the street and phoned Concord Repat Hospital. We walked with our heads bowed and in silence. There was nothing to say.

The ambulance pulled up with the light flashing but no siren. Two bored men in white carried Dad off on a stretcher. A couple of doors down, the venetian blinds in the Laurel's main bedroom parted a crack. My face flushed with shame. We looked like a ragged funeral procession with Mum and me following the pallbearers as far as the letterbox. Cha Cha and Hot Cha Cha brought up the rear. Cha Cha coiled himself around my legs, snaking in and out, and purring like a lawnmower.

After a month in hospital, Dad came home like he always did. He brought two ships painstakingly crafted from matchsticks and encased in glass bottles. It took me years to understand how he managed to navigate the ships through the thin necks of the bottles. I imagined that he'd somehow 'grown' the glass around the galleons. Later, I read in a magazine that the ships were inserted with their masts collapsed. Only when they were firmly affixed on their blue waves of plaster of Paris were the strings pulled to raise them and unfurl the canvas wings, moulded, as they were, to billow in a phantom wind, propelling the craft on a never-ending voyage to nowhere.

Meanwhile, my brother Tony had also set sail for a strange land from which he'd never fully return. Tony was around 11 when he met and befriended a strange young man named Edwin. Edwin didn't seem to have a home or parents. He was another of Blacktown's lost boys. Edwin was psychotic. I had read in one of the *Reader's Digest*s lying around the house the difference between psychosis and neurosis: 'Neurotics build castles in the air, psychotics live in them. (And psychiatrists take the rent from both).' Edwin had definitely set up residence in some place that existed only in his own mind. He was still just a kid, but he'd been tripping and hitting up for so long he'd at last managed to exile himself from reality. He introduced Tony to his recipe for escapism, and because anywhere was better than here, Tony followed him.

That's when the tattoos started. We found out one summer, when, despite the oppressive heat, Tony insisted on wearing shoes and socks and long-sleeved shirts. They hid his cartoon skin from Mum. Over the years, almost every part of his body, from his fingers to his elbows and even his feet, became a canvas for some drunken or drugged Andy Warhol.

These were probably the worst of my Edward Street years. I was old enough now to know that what was happening in our lives wasn't normal. I was old enough to feel guilt and shame and frustration that while I was 'Mum's little man', I was powerless to protect her. My love for her was unquenchable.

We had a set routine to keep our fears from eating us alive from the inside out. Mum and I sat together in the kitchen and we talked for hours, driven by adrenaline and cheap Pablo coffee, escaping across desperate bridges built of words. We did whatever we could to distract us from the Cha Cha chant we knew was on its way. It was better to be caught together in the kitchen. Better than being shocked from sleep and not knowing whether the other was okay.

I felt guilty as sin, but I had these deliciously disgusting fantasies where Mum and I were together in a crisis situation from which escape was impossible. Rather than allow me to die without tasting the candies of carnality, she gave herself to me. My face burned with shame. I was gripped by the exquisite terror that she'd see the bulge in my shorts. If she did, she never said.

Sometimes, when we went out together, passersby would mistake us for boyfriend and girlfriend. 'There aren't really that many years between us, Shane. And you're so big and strong,' she'd say. One of her favourite stories was about a time we were taking the bus into Blacktown. Suddenly it stopped abruptly and she crashed into me. 'It was just like smashing into a brick ball,' she gushed. We made a grand couple, especially when Mum didn't have a black eye or a swollen mouth. And I held her hand tighter, letting her know I thought I was the luckiest man in the universe.

'I've got to write an essay that features a cat, seven wheelbarrows, a train and a house on a hill,' I said. We were sitting in the kitchen again, waiting for Dad to pour like poison through the screen door.

I could tell by the light in her eyes that Mum was already pulling together the threads of a fantastic story from whatever secret place she stored them. Over the next few hours, we forgot that the night was a black book that would open to another story we didn't want to hear. Instead, we lost ourselves in a crematorium on a hill where the caretaker, incensed by an old woman who'd kicked his beloved cat Issiah, strangled the life from her. We watched in horror as he carried her body to the oven in one of seven wheelbarrows. The mournful whistle of the passing train muffled the awful clanging of the heavy metal door.

Stories were a key to distant kingdoms where Mum and I made the rules. We were boss. People behaved as we told them to. Events unfolded at our bidding. We were in control. I loved the rhythm of words. I loved the way their music made my heart sing and soar far away from Edward Street. I'd found a book with poems by William Shakespeare in the school library, and even though I hadn't understood all the words, I understood their sentiments from the way the words rose and fell and danced and skipped across the pages.

Although my own library was somewhat limited, an opportunity to change that soon came along. A school friend had heard about a retired teacher who lived alone near Riverstone and who had died recently. The news came from the 'milkman of death'. He'd been the one who alerted us to the death of Mr Smith. Again, he'd noticed that the bottles of milk had turned into yogurt on the verandah. Apparently the teacher had owned a big library of books, and since I loved books and my friend loved an adventure, one hot Saturday morning we jumped on our bikes and made the marathon journey to a run-down, weatherboard cottage stuck out on its own in the bush.

We found an unlocked window and climbed in. I went first. I never said anything, but I was scared shitless. The window was high up and I dragged my belly over the sill before dropping headfirst to the floor, breaking my fall with my hands. The first thing I saw when I stood up and adjusted my eyes to the thinness of the light was a full-length painted portrait of a middle-aged man. He was bespectacled and angular with dark, greased-back hair, long at the back and sparse at the front. He had a prominent forehead and narrow nose, his face long and sallow like he'd spent his whole life indoors reading. He was wearing a baggy grey suit with a white shirt and a blue kerchief knotted round his neck. He looked down at me steadfastly and dispassionately, reminding me of a hawk. I knew he was the dead teacher.

They had been right about the books. A vast, towering bookshelf skirted the walls and was bursting with books. You could smell generations of learning. There were weighty tomes, sets of encyclopaedia, limited editions with hand-painted flowers protected by rice paper, foreign titles, books with leather covers, some dog-eared and some brand new. More books than I'd ever seen anywhere in one go. All had obviously been cherished. I couldn't believe my luck when I spotted the *Complete Works of William Shakespeare*.

We hadn't thought to bring anything to carry our loot in, and after ransacking the house all we found were some sheets. We tied these into bags and filled our makeshift carriers with books. But we were too greedy and, unable to manage the ride home, we were forced to hide our booty in a ditch. We resolved to come back in a few days. I stuffed the copy of Shakespeare down my shirt and took it home with me.

When we returned a week had passed and it had rained in the interim. The books were ruined. The hand-painted flowers had run, smudging the printed words with tears of pink and green and crimson and purple dying to lilac. The leather covers had warped and buckled in the rain and sun. I rescued what I could and wheeled home with a big hollowness in my heart.

I hid the books in my cupboard. A few days later, Mum stopped me in the hallway. She spoke in whispers, like she had a secret and was worried someone else might hear her, even though we were the only ones at home.

'Shane,' she said, 'I was cleaning your room when I felt someone else was in there with me, watching me. I looked up and there –' and she was pointing now, and her arm was shaking '– standing in the light from the window, for just a few seconds, I swear I saw an elderly gentleman with glasses. It seemed like he was looking for something.' She went on to describe the dead man in the portrait.

I believed her wholeheartedly, mainly because Mum obviously believed unequivocally that she'd seen him, but also because her description fitted the portrait to a T. It seemed right to me that because she'd been condemned to suffer so much, she should be recompensed with a gift of discernment denied to 'normal' people. Or maybe her belief in such things was part of a desperate quest to find meaning in her life.

Looking back, I can see that Mum was driven to find a bigger reason than her boys to go on living. I don't know how long she'd been looking for Jesus, but I joined the search party when I started high school. Although she was born a Catholic, she had 'philosophical problems' with the Pope's supposed infallibility. One of her favourite examples was the Papal stand on contraception.

'If he's infallible,' she asked, 'how come he changes his mind so much? Do you know what "Catholic" means, Shane? It means universal. Now, I ask you, how intolerant, how presumptuous is that. Eh?'

I think the fact that her parents were Catholic was a contributing factor, too. After all, their brand of spirituality didn't include an iota of Christian compassion for their daughter. She must have felt like a sacrificial lamb on the altar of their hypocrisy.

So she wrote down Church of England on any forms that asked for religion. Later she found a Methodist church she liked because 'the hymns are so much happier than the tired old songs they sing in the Church of England'.

Then, Egyptology was the way, the truth and the light. Mum devoured everything on the subject that she could find. She was convinced that in one of her earlier lives she had been a handmaiden in the court of Cleopatra. When I was 16, *The Third Eye* by Lobsang Rampa became the bible. She once took my hand and guided my fingers reverently to the mystical site directly above the bridge of her nose and between the sea-green windows to her soul. But my cynicism was even more brazen than that of

Doubting Thomas, disbelieving even while my fingers found their mark. She was outraged the day I told her, 'Hey, I've got a magic third eye, too, Mum, but I can't show it to you, eh; I'm sitting on it.'

She found a small but robust Lutheran church near Blacktown Boys' High. The pastor was a cherubic-faced Lithuanian named Munsinskis and the love of God shone from him so radiantly that, high in the pulpit and framed by a huge stained-glass window, he looked like a da Vinci painting come to life. I was confirmed in this church, and we continued to worship there every Sunday for two years.

During this period of God hunting, Mum decided she should marry Dad. Maybe she thought things would change. Maybe she thought holy matrimony would make a difference. Richard, Beth and Sarah had been born, and Mum said Dad insisted they marry so his kids wouldn't be bastards and could legally be called Reynards. Shit, she never had to marry him for us Weaver bastards to be called Reynards. Mum looked nervous but pretty on the big day, wearing a flowery summer frock and tiny black shoes. She had her photo taken in the front yard, and before they left to take the bus to the train station, she said, 'Don't worry, Shane. Everything's going to be much better now.'

But I knew her well enough to know a part of her was dying that day. It was the part of her she'd never surrendered to Dad; the piece she'd always kept to herself. He'd never had a bit of paper that said he owned her. To Mum it didn't matter that everyone knew her as 'Reynard', there was no legal document that said it was so. She had always been a Howe, which was her maiden name, until that day. Years later I asked her if she remembered the date she married Dad. She said, 'I don't want to think about it, dear.'

They caught a train to Central and did the business in a registry office. Mum told me how she asked Dad if she could duck into a cathedral that was close by. He said to be quick. The cathedral was empty and as she knelt to pray, the most astonishing thing happened. On her knees and lost in communion with God, she heard a scream pierce the silence and reverberate around the stone walls. She was startled to realise that the sound had broken from her own lips, as if God Himself was expressing divine rage.

When she told me this story, I felt an overwhelming sense of foreboding so pervasive that it crushed my spirit like a dead weight, flat-lining any furtive thoughts of a normal life. If heaven itself revolted at their union, then what possible chance was there?

If we were at last a nuclear family then the clock was set a minute to midnight and we lived with the harrowing certainty that the end of the world was nigh. We were in the most invidious of positions, unable to draw strength from each other, and isolated from our neighbours who had their own problems, thank you very much. But it went deeper than that. The Weaver–Reynards were people you just didn't want to know. We were an embarrassment. We were a stark reminder of just what a shit hole Blacktown was, and what it could reduce you to.

They reckoned Australia was a classless society, and I fell for it once. But I was just a kid then. By now I could see it was a crock of shit. I saw that people everywhere were sorting themselves out according to who had what or who worshipped what or who wore what or who earned what and that it came with the skin. And while dinner parties and soirees were hardly de rigueur in Blacktown, there were those people you'd have round for a barbie and a beer, and those you wouldn't, even to clean up the mess.

With the exception of the McKinnons over the back and the Roberts family next door, the good folk in our neighbourhood variously feared, hated or felt sorry for the Reynards. It was no mean feat to be deemed the least worthy pieces of shit in a sewer teeming and steaming with turds.

Little wonder then that Mum found comfort in another deity. Brandivino was a cheap brandy substitute that answered her prayers for escape and peace, and even love. The god of grog came upon her and I watched in fascination and in fear.

So how did this conversion take place? It was our next door neighbour, Mrs Roberts, who gave Mum her Brandivino baptism. Her husband was a labourer, and they had two kids. The eldest was a boy named Jimmy. Everyone called him 'Little Jimmy', to save confusion with 'Big Jimmy', Jimmy McKinnon, who lived over our back fence. Little Jimmy was one of those kids euphemistically referred to as 'slow learners'. Mum reckoned his difficulties stemmed from the fact that whenever he got out of line, his mum would clip him over the ear. Hard. The poor bugger's ears were always crimson, and they stuck out like he was about to do a Dumbo the elephant and fly off. I wondered if this physical exaggeration was also on account of his mum's heavy hand.

Dad despised everyone, but he reserved a profound contempt for Mrs Roberts. The Roberts family was just as poor as we were, but somehow Mrs Roberts could always afford the trendiest clothes, loads of make-up and she owned several spectacular wigs. Whenever she went out, she wore a giant blonde, black or brunette beehive, amazing earrings that hung halfway down her face, and cherry red or even purple or orange lipstick. She smelled good enough to eat. Her miniskirts were so tight she had to take tiny steps like a Japanese geisha. I can still see her bum wriggling as she flounced past our house to catch the bus into Blacktown.

All the teenage boys in the neighbourhood used to whack themselves off with a picture of Mrs Roberts in their heads. Dad said she was 'a fucking Barbie doll whore' and warned Mum that he'd chop her tits off and make her eat them if she had anything to do with the slut.

Mum kept away from Mrs Roberts on weekends, but when Dad was at work she was next door like a shot. Mrs Roberts loaned her make-up to cover the bruises on her face, and she was always happy to listen. That's when Mum started drinking. What began as a couple of drinks with Mrs Roberts became a daily sacrament, and Mum always had a bottle of Brandivino hidden in the house.

When Mum was out of it I looked after the kids, made dinner and put them to bed. I didn't mind. But they did. I ran a tight ship. Like Dad, I organised emu-bobs, where the kids lined up and walked the distance of the yard, picking up everything that wasn't grass or dirt. Every speck, back and forth, until there wasn't an alien particle in sight. I made them clean their rooms till they were spotless. The beds had to be absolutely wrinkle-free. Mum never noticed, and Dad had other more pressing domestic considerations. He had to deal with a Mum he'd never met before.

The funny thing was that Dad was so pissed himself, he didn't even know Mum was stonkered at first. Soon, however, primed with piss, Mum talked back to Dad. In the days before the bottle-fed bravado, she copped all sorts of shit, as long as he left us kids alone. Now she gave him lip. She called him a nazi and for the first time in my life I heard my Mum swear; she told him he was a fucking kraut. He whaled into her something fierce. I watched from the sidelines, hating myself because I was too afraid to step in and help her. He knew exactly how I was feeling. When she lay battered and bleeding on the floor, he smiled and called me a fucking gutless wonder. And his words stabbed me in the heart. Because I believed him.

# ROUND 8

'IF IGNORANCE HAS DEPTHS, REYNARD, you have plumbed them.' TJ Kavenagh was my Ancient History teacher, and he had his own proprietary way of making you feel like shit. He was also the most inspirational teacher I ever had. Even his put-downs were imbued with an eloquence that made them somehow more edifying than demeaning. It was like calling someone a moron in Latin: if they understood you they were hardly moronic. In his inimitable, backhanded way, TJ was telling me I was destined for greater things.

Pre TJ, however, my first four years in high school were spent with the 'losers'. Kids with names ending in 'opolis', 'owlski' and 'inski'. Kids who ate salami for lunch and whose mothers, Dad said, looked like they needed a damn good scrub, delousing and a shave. No allowance was made at school for the fact that no one at home spoke English to these kids, we were all simply placed according to our primary school results. Since my record at Marayong was distinguished more by my absences and body odour than by academic promise, I was in the bottom class.

My first day's encounter with the school bully had marked me as an unknown quantity. Keeping to myself added to the mystique. By the time Kelly turned up in my second year, the other kids steered clear. General consensus held that Reynard was as mad as a cut snake.

By then, Kelly and I hated each other with a rage that was volcanic, erupting into episodes of violence so extreme they literally drew crowds. It became a ritual. 'Come and watch the Reynards kill each other.' A Ku Klux Klan of kids would dog us after school. Almost every afternoon, we stopped by the railway tracks and fell upon each other like gladiators in a death match. Because we were fairly evenly matched there was rarely a clear winner and the brawling lasted until we lay battered and bleeding and unable to throw another punch. The other kids went home laughing.

But the balance of power was set to change. Two events would give me the upper hand once and for all – over Kelly and Dad and any other bastard who ever stood in my way. The first was the appearance of Todd Jones, who showed me the rancid heart of hate. The second was my discovery that I could use words to rewrite my life. These were polar extremes that would vie for precedence in my life for more than three decades.

I first met Todd on a hot Saturday morning in 1969. I was 16. The usual neighbourhood gang was out on the paddock for one of our marathon rugby league games. It was supposed to be touch football because of the differences in our sizes and ages, but our heroes, Johnny Sattler, Graham 'Changa' Langlands and Bob McCarthy and co., would never have approved of anything too wussy. Inevitably, 'touches' turned into full-blooded thumps and teeth were sometimes lost along with tempers.

There was myself and Kelly, Chuckie Williams, Fred Little, Jimmy McKinnon, Arnie Dragoman and Davy Petkovich. The not so magnificent seven. Me, Kelly, Chuckie, Fred and Arnie lived in Edward Street. Jimmy's place was directly over our back fence in Block Street. Petkovich lived in Douglas Parade, his backyard a cooee away on the other side of the creek, facing our front yard. His family had about an acre of land for their backyard, and I used to see Davy's father tending his pumpkins, grapes and melons. He was easy to spot because he was big as a bear and wore overalls and a red and white spotted handkerchief knotted in three places on his head. He never spoke a word of English, as far as I know, but he was a tireless worker and his garden fed his family and earned them extra money on the side.

Under normal circumstances, Davy would've been put in the 'wog bin', but he was a damn fine football player who threw a mean dummy and had a deceptive side step. And Arnie would have joined him there, too, except he was the fastest sprinter of any of us over the distance of half a footy field. Nevertheless, there was no need to extend the civility we showed them on the paddock to our school life, and, generally, we didn't.

The teams were me, Jimmy and Petkovitch versus Kelly, Chuckie, Fred and Arnie (Chuckie was the youngest and such a useless dip-shit whinger that he didn't really count). There was no referee, no rules, no boots, no time-out, and no how-do-you-dos. Our games often ran from midmorning until we dragged ourselves home in the dark.

Most times, we never even stopped for lunch. Our front yard was the closest, and we'd cool down and fuel up with long camel drinks of water straight from the tap. If you were first in, it was smart to let the water run for a while before wrapping your laughing gear around the tap – spiders loved the cool of the pipes and sometimes crawled inside, making a most surprising hairy meal for unsuspecting mouths.

Todd appeared from nowhere. 'What's the chance of a game?' His hair was sandy, his chin stubbled and he was wearing ridiculous sky-blue, terry-towelling shorts that were hitched up way too high. When he walked, you could see the white flash of his underpants through the gaps. This earned him the name 'Ballsack'. Until we learned not to call Todd names.

Todd's massive chest seemed in contempt of the white singlet that strained to contain it. His arms parodied Popeye's after he'd just poured a truckload of spinach down his throat. Arnie piped up, 'No. You're too old.' Loosely translated, this meant, 'For fucksake, pal, you look like you could do some serious damage. And enjoy it.'

I don't know whether I had an inkling of the difference Todd would make to my life, but I threw the ball to the newcomer and said, 'Let him play. He can be on our side.' He caught it. It was the beginning of a fierce friendship that lasted ten eventful years.

It turned out that Todd was a few years older than us, nearly 19. He'd specialised in wagging school and general ratbaggery, and everyone had had a gutful. He'd just been released from a Boys' Home into the care of his blue-haired granny and her wino brother. They lived in the only brick house in Edward Street, up the hill near the railway line, and all we fibro people thought they were dead-set posh. His parents were in the throes of a messy divorce (these were the days you had to prove your partner was banging like a dunny door) and the plan was that a change of environment would give Todd a chance to break with bad influences and get his life in order. Blacktown was probably not the best location.

Todd introduced me to lifting weights. He was obsessed with turning his body into a lethal weapon, and he had converted his granny's garage into a gym. Railway sleepers and bricks doubled as weights, and we spent hours doing repetitions in front of a highly polished but cracked mirror. Todd hated the world with a ferocity that was viral and it fuelled a strict and unrelenting exercise regime. He gritted his teeth and screamed in rage for more weight, more pain, and more firepower against a universe he was convinced was out to crush him. Todd gave muscle to my misanthropy, and right at that time, I had a raft of reasons for hating the human race – and myself.

My bedwetting embarrassment reached high tide when I was 16. Dad insisted I join the school cadets. It was free and he said that maybe the army would be able to kick the Weaver wanker out of me and turn me into a man. Every year, Blacktown Boys' High cadet unit went to Singleton Army Camp for two weeks. We slept on wooden boards under huge eight-man tents. I was terrified that my bedwetting would be discovered. I brought my own waterproof sheet and I used my sleeping bag as a blanket rather than risk snuggling inside and fouling my nest. I trained myself to wake early and I stuffed the pissy garments into plastic bags and sealed them with rubber bands before stashing them in my pack. Everything was fine until the last day of camp.

We stood at attention, dressed in our 'jungle greens' and lined up in platoons. Our commander (and music teacher), Lieutenant Gormly, dropped the bombshell. 'Okay, lads, kit inspection. On the count of three, you will empty out the contents of your kit. One, two, three!'

Everyone proceeded to do just that. Me too. I watched in sick disbelief as the platoon sergeants walked up and down the ranks, prodding and poking and perusing everyone's gear. Finally, Sergeant Philips stood in front of me. Sticking his baton into my gear, he began rummaging around.

'Hello, what's this then?' he said, seeing the sealed bags. I stood there, guilty as a silent fart, unable to speak.

'What, Private Reynard, is in this bag?'

'N-n-nothing, sergeant,' I stammered.

'Great, then you won't mind opening it. Now. That's an order, Reynard!'

A hush fell over the parade ground as I stooped to undo the sealed bags. Forty pairs of ears were pricked and tuned to the drama that was unfolding. I found out later that kit inspections were meant to catch cadets trying to smuggle live ammunition or other army property off the base. I wished to God that I had only been concealing a nuclear bomb.

Having undone the offending bag, I stood back to attention. I watched in horror as the sergeant stuck his baton into the opening and lifted the bag high into the air, shaking it vigorously until the fetid contents spilled out like intestines.

What happened next will stay with me till the day I die. 'Peee-yew!' The sergeant's face contorted in disgust and he clamped his hand over his nose and mouth. Cadets on every side convulsed up and down the ranks like a great, green Mexican wave, those closest to the epicentre of the stench most affected.

I told Mum I was quitting cadets. She said over her dead body. She said what had happened was a stroke of luck. It gave me the opportunity to prove to myself and to her and to everyone else that no matter how tough the going got, I was in there for the long run.

A year passed before everyone forgot 'The Day of the Piss Bomb'. I still remember. It was policy to leave cadets at 17 so your final year could be spent studying for the Higher School Certificate, the exams that decided if you went to uni or not. I was honourably discharged as a corporal, but other extracurricular activities were taking up more of my time.

On Friday and Saturday nights, Sydney's west became a suburban version of the American Wild, Wild West. Fists and feet and the occasional knife replaced guns, and the quickest draw was the first in with a king hit or a head butt or a knee in the cods. Walking the streets after dark was like wearing a neon sign that said you were in the market for blood. Some parts of town were worse than others. Blacktown Railway Station after midnight was no-man's land. The 500 yards from the Robin Hood Hotel to the West End Milk Bar were like running the gauntlet; you knew sure as sharks you'd get a smack in the head unless you were one of The Untouchables.

Like Paddy. He was the leader of an elite group of shaven-headed savages who no one dared to give so much as a sideways glance. One night, Todd and I saw why. We were sitting in the West End, stoned off our faces on piss and pot.

Through the plate glass shop front, we watched a stocky bloke with a shaved head and a skin-tight green T-shirt swagger up to three longhairs on the footpath. His entourage of six mean-mouthed, hair-trigger hooligans (as Mum referred to this type) circled the perimeter. Not that Paddy needed help. Everyone in the milk bar sensed at exactly the same time that something cataclysmic was about to happen.

It was over in a flash. Six punches, two apiece. Body and head. Left rip, right cross. Left hook, right cross. Left jab, right cross. The most impressive thing, apart from the dazzling speed and dynamite dispatch, was the loud hissing sound Paddy expelled when he exploded. Psssst. Psssst. Psssst. Like jets of ultra-high-pressure steam shooting in short, controlled bursts, from an extremely large and very pissed-off kettle.

The damage done, Paddy and the boys sauntered into the West End, and Paddy caught Todd's eye. Neither looked away, but nor was there that unspoken spark that precedes a lit fuse. Maybe Paddy had had enough action for one night. Maybe the bulge in Todd's biceps told him it might be smart to find out a bit more about the new kid in town.

Todd wanted to know where Paddy had learned to fight like that. He asked around and wrote down the address of Eddie Raye's boxing gym on the lid of a packet of Marlboro. We lobbed at the gym a few days later and found out that the 'pissed-off kettle' effect was part of the technique taught at Eddie Raye's boxing gym; apparently, the expulsion of air minimised the chances of getting winded if your opponent slipped a sly one into your guts.

Eddie Raye was a short, fat, sweaty man with florid cheeks lit up by a network of tiny red veins. His glasses perched precariously on the edge of a stub nose. He spoke so fast he stuttered and it seemed as though his words were always racing to catch up with what he was trying to say. For obvious reasons we called him p-p-porky pig. He explained that he didn't have time or p-p-p-patience for amateurs, that he only trained p-p-pro's and that he took 25 p-p-per cent of every fighter's p-p-p-purse. He took an accountant's look at Todd's arms and shook his hand. He looked at me and asked if I was serious. 'Don't worry about him,' Todd said, 'he'll be doing lots of extra work with me.' He wasn't kidding.

Overnight, the weight-lifter's gym at Granny's became a shrine to the legends of the square ring. Cassius Clay, Johnny Famechon, Jeff White, Charkey Ramon, Hector Thompson and Smokin' Joe watched us impassively from the walls. A stack of tyres piled up head-high against the brick wall became an immovable boxing bag. (This was later blamed for Todd's inability to fully extend his arms when he punched.) Unable to afford gloves, we bound our fists with tea towels and sparred round after round in the backyard, keeping one eye on a clock under the clothesline to gauge the time. Todd sometimes dropped his guard, inviting me to smash his face again and again and again. I was reluctant until he told me what he'd do to me if I didn't give it all I had. 'Fuckin' hit me or so help me God I'll knock your teeth so far down your throat you'll have to stick a toothbrush up your arse to clean them.' He didn't mean it, though. I loved Todd and he felt the same about me. Later he said he was sorry, but he had to be sure he could take it as well as dish it out.

Between rounds we rinsed the blood from our faces with the garden hose. Lengths of thick hemp doubled as skipping ropes and the coarse fibre tore at the flesh of my hands as the rope spun. Every morning, before I went to school or Todd went to work, we ran for miles. I rode on his rage. I peaked on his paranoia. I honed an edge on his hate.

It became my life. Wake and run. Monday to Thursday nights at the gym. Saturdays and Sundays at Todd's place. Friday and Saturday nights prowling the streets. This was the skinheads versus the longhairs era. Gangs on trains from Parramatta and Granville invaded our streets like hordes of marauding Vikings. Todd and I both had our hair shaved short, but it meant nothing. I wasn't prejudiced; I'd bash anyone. Well, not quite anyone. When we passed Paddy and the boys in the street, we never acknowledged each other, but they never failed to let us pass. It had nothing to do with me; Todd was our key to the city.

Poofter-bashing was a popular sport in the 1970s, and units were deployed to Kings Cross from the suburbs. 'Let's go get a Nancy,' Paddy egged the boys on. 'Let's give those pillow-biters a taste of the old ultra, eh,' he sneered, doing his very best Alex from *A Clockwork Orange*. He and his droogs would pile into a car and burn rubber to the Cross. They used a cute little guy with the heart of a cobra as bait. Johnno was 17 but looked like he was 12. He'd sit outside the gay bars and smile and bat his eyelashes at the fairies. When one of them responded to the come-on, he was led down an alley where the passionate fucking of drag queens was done with iron bars and steel-capped boots and the only time the boys got their dicks out was to piss on the mess they'd made.

I didn't hate queers any more than I hated anyone else, and saw no reason to go out of my way. I was relieved that Todd shared my feelings because, deep down, I knew it would've made me puke to bash someone who was 'girly' and unable or unwilling to fight back. Another reason Todd and I got on like a house on fire was because while he hid behind the 'Fuck, I hate 'em all' attitude, I knew damn well he wasn't into bashing someone just because he 'walked funny' or had 'soft skin' like a sheila.

I was amazed at how indiscriminate the violence was. For example, while Paddy was the prime mover in some of the more gore-spattered poofter-bashing excursions, he also facilitated the boys' trips to Mascot International Airport where a raving queen who managed the bar served a free flow of whatever they fancied in return for a bit of what he fancied later.

I never commented on the savage injustice of it all, however. I wasn't as stupid as I looked.

Todd had his first fight at South Sydney Juniors with just a few weeks' gym work under his belt. I went along to watch. He became a regular club fighter and it didn't take him long to work his way up to six-rounders. One night, the promoter told Eddie Raye that one of the four-round boys had pulled out. 'He's got stomach trouble,' he said. 'He's gutless.' Everyone thought that was hilarious. Except for me. I knew exactly how the poor bastard felt. 'Don't s'pose you've got a boy who'd like to glove up,' he asked. 'It's worth 25 bucks.' He was looking directly at me.

No way in the world was I going to squib out in front of Todd. 'Yeah, I'll 'ave a go,' I said, regretting the words as they bumbled from my mouth. So I had my first pro fight aged 17 – before I was legally allowed into licensed premises. Fighting in the ring in front of a screaming crowd wasn't anything like sparring in a gym, or even mixing it with Todd in the backyard. My legs were rubbery. It was like fighting on a boat pitching on the ocean. I got the living Jesus punched out of me. But the crowd clapped and Eddie thumped my back and said, 'Good boy,' stuffing 25 quid, minus his 25 per cent cut, into my aching hand. Todd grinned at me and my boxing career was off and running.

At the same time, my essays and flair for English had begun to distinguish me at school. I was addicted to writing. I slept with a pen and paper under my pillow and learned how to write in the dark. It was my English teacher, Mr Blake, who suggested it was time for me to 'move from the relative passivity of the written word into the bolder dimension of the spoken word'.

He made me the third speaker, or 'whip', in the Blacktown Boys' High debating team. And I loved it. Speaking in public was like releasing words from cages. Once you let them loose, you couldn't be sure what mischief or havoc they'd wreak. Nevertheless, before I stood to address the audience, I was always sick with nerves. Mr Blake said, 'Everyone gets butterflies, Shane. The trick is knowing how to get them to fly in formation.'

My butterflies became a squadron of spitfires the second I opened my mouth. Suddenly I took control. I was 'the whip'. I poured vitriol like scalding fat on my opponents. I made the audience wince and my adversaries wither. My favourite tactic was to turn my opponents' words back on them, stabbing them with the sharp end of their idiocy. I listened intently for anything they might say that actually supported our argument, and then I went straight for the jugular. I began my rebuttal with a magnanimous word of thanks. 'Thank you, Mr Wilson, thank you, thank you, thank you. A thousand thank yous. On behalf of our team and everyone here, I applaud your intellect and your skillful rhetoric, for indeed you have made our case far more concisely, far more eloquently, far more robustly, than ever we could have hoped to achieve.'

I particularly loved watching the smug, private school ponces squirm as I listed the inconsistencies in their case and demonstrated the myriad ways they had succeeded in building an irrefutable argument for our side. I did it with a sneer. I had turned condescension into an art form. I was establishing a reputation as someone who could cut opponents to pieces, wielding words like razors. At the same time, I was training like a madman and fighting four-rounders and learning how to respond when words weren't enough. But I wasn't living under any illusions. I knew my place. There was always someone ready to remind me.

Dad knew my final exams were coming up. 'You're wasting your fucking time. You should have a job. I'm paying to feed you and you've got your nose stuck in books you'll never understand. Who do you think you're fooling? You're a chip off the old block. You're a fucking loser.'

Nor was the gym a morale-booster. My official title was 'Spit Bucket Boy'. Between rounds, I removed mouth guards and pressed the water bottle to the lips of boys who were sparring. I held the heavy bag for Todd while he literally beat the stuffing out of it. And I was a life-size dummy when Paddy needed me to rest my head on his shoulder in close while he rehearsed dropping and smashing his shoulder upward into my face, nearly breaking my nose and setting him up for a salvo of blows to my body and head. He'd earned the nickname 'The Shower King' because after the final bell, the audience would scream in appreciation and rain the ring with coins.

I was different. My whole life I'd been told I was a useless, stupid, gutless bastard. I was still hiding under the house. I was still hiding under the bed. Fuck, I was 17 and still wetting the bed. And I was the only one at the gym who was still going to school. My bus stop was right opposite the public bar of the Robin Hood, and on those rare days I took the bus, I saw Paddy and the gang smouldering on the steps, sinking beers and glowering at the 'schooly'.

# ROUND 9

THE POOR SODS NEVER KNEW where to look. They'd be walking along, cocooned in their smug, self-satisfied routines. Some of them even dared to be overtly happy, sharing a joke with their friends and laughing or smiling. That really lit my wick. The last thing they expected was a pimple-faced 17-year-old with a big hooter and a chip on his shoulder the size of the Opera House to look them straight in the eye. And bark.

It was the expression of sheer unadulterated rage. I began growling deep in my throat when they were about twenty yards off. Some crossed the road immediately. I felt a surge of power, like I was a cyclone of hate, blasting the enemy away. Others toughed it out, determined to stand their ground, like they had a right. And the braver they were, the more viciously I snapped my teeth and the louder I barked, never for a second taking my eyes off theirs. I hated them. I hated them all. I hated them almost as ferociously as I hated myself.

And then the worst possible thing happened. I found my real father again. I'd posted a 'got nothing to lose' letter via an old Queensland address Mum still had for my grandparents. They passed the letter on to him and he wrote a short note back. He'd married Liza and was happily living in Cairns. He felt he'd already given me a chance to be part of his life and I'd chosen Mum instead, but he agreed to see me, he supposed, if I could find my own way.

I needed to talk with him. I needed to ask him why he'd left us behind in the first place, and then why he'd never kept in touch with Kelly and me when we'd left Queensland, why he'd never sent so much as a birthday card. I wanted him to see that I was a man. A professional boxer. I stuffed some of my school essays into my carry bag. It was important to me that he saw I was quick with my mind as well as my fists. I was ravenous for his love and approval. Mum was worried. 'So much time has passed, dear. My heart would break if you were disappointed.' I told her I had to go and that I'd be back in a month, six weeks at the longest.

It was school holidays. I hitchhiked for eight days. When I knocked on his door, I smelled and looked like what I was – a filthy beggar with no place to go. He let me in. His old lady, Liza, pulled a face like they'd just adopted Rosemary's baby. I shivered in the ice storm of their hostility. I resented the fact that they had a nice home with a phone and carpets and pictures on the walls and photos on the shelves that never even hinted that the Weaver bastards existed. I didn't know what to call him – Dad, Ryan, Sir, Cunt. I called him Dad and it felt awkward. It didn't fit. I didn't fit. Nothing fitted.

I didn't see much of Ryan or Liza during my short stay. They worked shifts and when they were home of a day,

I was out, ostensibly looking for work. In fact, I'd bonded with a tribe of hippies who'd turned me onto mushies, and most of my time was spent bouncing slow-mo on the dark side of the moon. I'd met them at a disco called The House on the Hill where one of Ryan's mates worked picking up glasses. He suggested I apply for a job in 'crowd control'.

'Earn yourself a bit of pocket money, eh. Save ya having to put ya hand out to your old man all the time.'

It didn't take Einstein to figure out where that idea had come from. Tough luck, work wasn't on my list of priorities.

Instead, I'd become a space cadet and I was seeing and writing some pretty weird shit. More and more, writing was becoming an integral part of my life. Just like a song can take you back to a specific time and place, so my poems were like magic carpets, although rarely were the destinations enchanted or illuminated by hope.

One acid-distorted night, looking out over the ocean with eyes that would not, could not, close, I wrote of 'Eye-sore sirens, sailing savage seas', of Ophidian whores, 'Tits withered and white as anaemia, thighs wasted by embraces familiar of grey men drifting across ocean floors.' I hadn't slept in 48 hours, I had lockjaw from the arsenic in the trip and my pulse was racing like a hare one snap away from the drooling jaws of the hound.

I wrote of my life in suburbia and echoed a story I'd heard in the schoolyard about a father's inappropriate behaviour towards his daughter. And I wrote about the smiling faces and staged happiness represented in the everyday picture chronicles of suburban life. We never had to worry about such hypocrisy.

> *Dead people never smell*
> *In the incorruptible hell*
> *Of their fleshless*
> *Photo tombs.*

Ryan was a cook by trade, and he used words like a spatula or a rolling pin. They were practical tools for getting the job done. His messages were served without the garnish of wit or irony. His most poetic pronouncement during my visit was, 'I think you'd better clear off.'

He'd graduated from '20 years' slaving over a hot stove' in the mining towns in northern Queensland, to managing a small cafe-cum-restaurant in the main street of Cairns. He objected to me smoking pot and drinking his piss while he was at work. One night, as he was leaving for the cafe, he said, 'You're not pulling your weight, son, and you show no respect whatsoever. It's upsetting Liza and that's something I will not, I repeat, I will not, stand for. You'd better clear off by the time we get home or I'm calling the police.'

I sat outside on the back verandah in the dark, fuming. I drank all his beer. I drank his Scotch. I smoked the last of my dope and I stubbed out the roach on the slimy back of a huge cane toad that hopped up to the house every night to eat dog food from a dish they'd left out for it. I'd show the mongrel exactly, I repeat, exactly, what I thought of him and his precious fucking Liza.

I went inside and selected a large butcher's knife from the kitchen drawer. I took it outside and sharpened it on the concrete steps. Backwards and forwards across the step, again and again, methodically, with the tired, sure rhythm of inevitability, until the starving blade glinted.

Then I went back in and slashed my wrists. Very slowly and very deliberately. It was easy. Like slicing liver. The plan was to fill a glass with blood. When he walked through the door, I'd toss it over him and say, 'So you want blood, you fucking cunt.' But I passed out well before they got home, bleeding like a stuck pig all over their expensive and oh-so-tasteful shag-pile carpet. They bundled me into the back of the car and rushed me straight to the cop shop. Apparently, the cops took one look and said, 'Hospital. Fast.'

Two days later, I woke up in the closed ward of Cairns Base Hospital with my wrists bandaged. It was a zoo. There were guys going through the d.t.'s. There was a hippie coming down from a 'blue meanie' trip that had done his head in like a Roman Polanski movie. There were two other failed suicides and a mixed bag of depressed, catatonic or manic men and women. When the nurse insisted I join in the morning exercise routine to the tune of 20 push-ups, I made a mental note of where my street clothes were and a firm decision. As soon as the opportunity presented itself, I got dressed and went for a brisk walk. I kept on walking.

When I reached the old man's, no one was home. But my bag was packed and waiting outside the garage door. Thanks to the push-ups, blood was seeping through my bandages and my wrists were throbbing. It hurt like hell but I managed to pitch a brick through the front window. I wasn't able to carry my bag, so I tipped out all my stuff, festooning the garden with underpants and singlets and socks before setting out for the highway. I took my essays and poems. And I got lucky. A beer-bellied truckie with a razor stubble, green teeth and tobacco breath gave me a ride all the way to Epping in Sydney. He fed me hamburgers and Cokes and he didn't make me talk too much. In return, I only had to kiss him and suck him off a few times.

It wasn't the first time I'd been privy to life's dirty little tradeoffs. Doing the business in the cabin of the truck, I recalled an incident that I'd all but banished from my mind. I'd become adept at burying rotten memories too deeply to exhume, but sometimes, despite the depth and the desperation to forget, volcanic forces thrust them up from their subterranean sleep and, as they broke through the surface, I was startled by their size and shape.

I was 12 when Mum had finally managed to get me into a charitable refuge on one of Sydney's beaches where battered and abused kids went to swim and forget and heal until it was time to leave the sunshine and go back to their own private hell. We three Weaver boys all had our turn there.

The first thing I'd done was find out where they stored the bed linen and devise a plan to keep my bed-wetting a secret. I slept naked so I didn't have to worry about replacing my pyjamas. I rose before the sun, peeling the wet sheets from the bed, and putting on my swimmers before sneaking out. I made my way down to the beach, wading out waist high and wedging my pissy sheets between the rocks. By the time everyone was awake, my bed was made, I'd showered and was ready for the day. Thinking about it now, someone must have known what was going on, but no one said a thing. It wouldn't have been therapeutic.

Most nights after lights out, our religious instructor came and sat on the side of my bed. Bill was a tall, skinny guy with a long face, horse's teeth and a big Adam's apple. He reminded me of Goofy, only he wasn't funny. He asked if everything was okay and told me to shut my eyes while we prayed together. When my eyes were closed, he slipped his cold hand under the sheets and pulled me off. I think he interpreted my lack of pyjamas as an invitation. I was scared and ashamed. Partly because I knew it was wrong, and partly because I liked it.

He wrote to Mum months later, asking if he could take me on a skiing trip to the Snowy Mountains. When Mum told me, the look in my eyes must have said it all. I'd felt safe surrounded by the other kids in the dormitory, knowing I could scream if things looked like getting heavier than a hand job. It would be different on my own. Two weeks later, when his car pulled up outside 63 Edward Street, Mum met him head-on at the gate. She smacked his face so hard I could see her handprint on his cheek and hear his ears ringing from my peeking place behind the venetian blinds.

After my two-week father and son reunion, I went back to school. The wounds on my wrists had become infected, and Mum bandaged them with torn sheets. 'They might look raggy, love, but they're clean. I double-boiled them myself.' I wanted to stay home until my cuts had healed, but Mum said I had to go because school was the 'only way out of the lousy, dead-end life I'm stuck with'.

So I went, but I felt like everyone was staring at me. I felt they all knew what I had done. I felt their eyes fasten and cling like another set of bandages around my wrists. I felt like Frankenfuckingstein's monster. I felt like a misunderstood mish-mash of body parts, roughly assembled and blundering oafishly among the good citizens of the world, who I could only despise for their normality. I felt pitied and pitiful.

A lot of us knew that Blacktown Boys' High was either an escape route or a toilet bowl. So some of us slaved like Trojans to get to university. Boys, however, will be boys, and along the way we were capable of unspeakable acts of barbarism against anyone we judged as not being 'one of us'. The handicapped and the ethnically typecast were fair game.

But it was by no means just we students who were practitioners of the cruel put-down. One Ancient History lesson, we were studying a play called *The Frogs* by the Greek playwright Aristophanes. TJ Kavenagh figured that the best way to understand it was to read it aloud, and he set about attributing roles to various members of the class. Seated among us were twins, Greg and Glenn Summerhayes (named, incongruously, after Gregory Peck and Glenn Ford).

The Summerhayes twins were inordinately quiet, and arguably the least disruptive students in the entire school. Which is hardly surprising when you consider that they stuttered like machine guns. The more embarrassed or distressed they became, the redder their faces blazed and the more furious – and excruciatingly funny – the stuttering. When it came to nominating players for the role of the amphibians that lined the banks of the River Styx, TJ cast the twins. Without hesitation. Maybe he was bored. Maybe sometimes he was capable of being just as puerile as the rest of us. The words uttered by the slimy hoppers included a few choruses of 'Brek-a-kek-kek'. Not easily articulated by linguistically challenged students in the company of their pernicious peers. The embarrassment of that occasion stuck with the twins like warts. From that day, they were known and addressed as 'The f-f-f-frogs'.

Frogs are, of course, relatively innocuous creatures, especially when compared to the predators that prowl the quadrangles of schoolyards.

All schools have a scapegoat. Someone who is democratically appointed to atone for every injustice that was ever perpetrated upon anyone at all. Our sacrificial lamb went by the name of Valesini. He was thumped, harangued, ridiculed and lambasted every school day of his life. It didn't matter how low you were ranked in the school hierarchy, you could do whatever you liked to Valesini with complete impunity. Even if he was bigger than his tormentor, poor Valesini knew better than to so much as defend himself by covering up, let alone to resist. His raison d'etre was to be punished, regardless of his innocence of any crime.

One day, his ancient parents came to the school. They were stooped and walked unsteadily, as if they were carrying an incredible weight on their bony shoulders. They were on a mission, and complained bitterly to the headmaster. A crisis meeting of department heads was convened and it was decided that the primary reason for Valesini's plight was his name. If this were changed, they reasoned, then his peers' attitude and treatment of him would also change.

An extraordinary assembly was called and the entire school was summoned. Valesini stood on the dais next to the headmaster as he addressed the students. He hung his head like he was awaiting the executioner. There's no doubt he wished he were dead.

'This young man you see before you is not the young man you knew,' he spoke with conviction. 'Nicholas Valesini is no more. Allow me to introduce you to the newest member of our school, Nicholas Johnson. You will receive him into your classes, and indeed into your hearts, with courtesy, kindness and respect. I will be giving this matter my continued, close, personal attention.'

Then he put his arm around the hapless figure by his side, and we watched our new classmate wither like a flower in the face of an inferno.

That afternoon, we bundled Valesini into a waiting shaggin' wagon and drove him about 200 miles out of town. Along the way, we tortured him with stories of what we intended to do to him. Arriving at a desolate spot, we stripped him, gagged him and tied him to a tree. Then we drove home.

Fat boys were easy targets. The in-crowd played footy and we were all fit and hard. I was fighting regularly, and not carrying an extra ounce. We abhorred lard and the lazy pigs with bloated faces and sheila's hips and waddling arses. I remember when one of us drew a pair of tits on the back of a fat boy's white shirt. It was hilarious for two reasons. First, the ample folds of flesh on his back actually resembled tits (the drawing dramatised the effect beautifully, lending a lewd wobble to his dorsal mammary glands when he broke into a trot, frantically trying to lose his antagonists). And secondly, because he was so ashamed of his body, the poor bugger would never remove his shirt. For the duration of the day he was condemned to shake his faux titties wherever he retreated.

I guess we all had our own motives for this vigilante persecution. I won't speculate about the others, but my own complicity was underwritten by a pathetic attempt to align myself with those I considered to be 'normal'. Kids whose fathers never beat the living shit out of their mothers. Kids whose fathers watched them play footy and yelled encouragement from the sidelines. Kids who weren't afraid to laugh out loud and mean it. Kids who didn't wet the bed.

And, even while I cringe with shame to admit it, I liked being the one who was inflicting the suffering for a change. I liked the control, the power to influence another person's happiness or pain. I liked it and I hated it, because deep down, so deep no one could see it, but not so deep that I was ever allowed to be unaware of it, my heart bled for the victims. Because they were me.

With a drink in hand I could forget about being a victim, for a little while. And incongruously, school afforded the opportunity for a 'legal' drink. I felt like one of the cognoscenti in the company of the coolest students, meeting up with a few of our younger, more liberated teachers at the East Blacktown Hotel for a beer on Thursday nights.

There was big Dougy Blake, our English teacher. He had a huge Merv Hughes-type handlebar moustache, twinkling blue eyes and a deep, generous laugh. And Dave Robilliard, our PE teacher. He always wore a tight-fitting T-shirt and shorts that showed off his muscular legs and the curvature of his arse. These guys were 'the last of the Mohicans', the final issue of the NSW Education Department's Wyndham Scheme, and they were only a few years older than we were. For obvious reasons, the system was changed to widen the gap between teacher and student. At any rate for me it wasn't going to be an issue. My school years were coming to an end.

# ROUND 10

IT WAS 1972 AND THE FINAL year of school. The year we sat for the Higher School Certificate, the exam that would decide who went to university and who was condemned to a treadmill job. It was also the year TJ rescued me from a fate worse than failing an exam – failing to even turn up. We'd just finished the English paper and were shuffling out of class to go home and either swot up on Thucydides or relax and chill, depending on our state of preparedness for the next day's ordeal by paper. I'd developed a silly habit at the time, which almost proved fatal. Rather than check the noticeboard personally for the exam schedule, I'd ask my mates what time the next exam was on. 'One thirty,' was the unanimous reply.

That night I slept the deep, grateful sleep of the reprieved. I knew English had gone well, and I was supremely confident of coasting through Ancient History. There was a loud knock on my door at 9.30 the next morning. Mum was grim-faced. 'Your teacher, Mr Kavenagh, is at the door, Shane.' I met him there, rubbing the sleep from my eyes. He looked at his watch and shook his head.

'The exam started just over half an hour ago,' he said. 'They'll let you sit it if you're no more than an hour late. Dress quickly. I'll wait in the car for you.'

The dirty, rotten bastards. They were probably snickering even as I was putting on my shoes in TJ's speeding vehicle. I sat the exam and afterwards pretended not to care. But I did. I cared very much.

On the last evening of school, the sixth-formers were given special dispensation to hold a sausage sizzle in the school courtyard. It was strictly a 'No Girls' zone, but the teachers turned a blind eye to a few cans of Tooheys. They drew the line, however, at overt pot smoking. It was a let your hair down and let it all hang out celebration of the last six years of toeing the line and playing the game. We were the survivors. Daddy Cool was all the rage and we were 'doin' the Eagle Rock'. Emotions ran high, but it was harmless, if mindless, fun. A few kids got pantsed (held down by a group of screaming savages while their trousers were ripped off and ripped up). A few got flushed, which entailed being grabbed by a posse and dragged off to the toilets where their heads were unceremoniously inserted into the bowl before the loo was flushed.

When I saw an army of 20-odd kids banding together like a platoon of conspiratorial baboons, whispering and stealing looks in my direction, I knew what was afoot. They surged towards me in a bum's rush of arms and legs, overwhelming me with sheer numbers and forcing me through the toilet doorway.

Once they had me inside, however, the numerical advantage was negated by the fact that only two or three could follow me in through the narrow doorway at a time. No one was keen. I was a pretty handy four-round pro fighter at that stage. They piled up on top of each other at the entrance and stood there panting and wild-eyed. I looked back. And then I exploded through the doorway like a bucking bronco from the stalls, scattering my would-be tormentors like chooks. My heart still quickens to recall a time when my presence was a force so powerful it would literally sweep opposition away.

Happily drunk and secretly stoned, and feeling like a huge weight had been lifted from us, no one wanted to let this evening slip away. It marked the end of a chapter in our lives that would stay inscribed in our minds, and indeed in our destinies, forever. Someone said he knew where TJ lived, and in the early hours of the morning a war party drove out to his home in Baulkham Hills. This was a relatively up-market suburb some 40 minutes from Blacktown, where TJ lived with his elderly mother and, as we discovered, one very old, very redundant watchdog.

Along the way we collected every sign we could find. A homemade effort, proclaiming 'Kittens for Sale'. Another in red paint offering 'Fresh strawberrys' (we chuckled, knowing the misspelling would rankle). By taking it in turns, two at a time, we were even able to dislodge a street sign. There were shop signs, traffic signs and 'Men's' and 'Women's' signage ripped off from a public toilet.

The plan had been to decorate TJ's yard with the purloined signs, but it was a balmy night and, scouting around, we noticed the back door was open. It was obvious where the signs should go. The screen door was unlocked (you could tell this wasn't Blacktown), but there was resistance. Something was barring the way. I reached my hand behind the door to ascertain what the obstruction was. And I ripped it back out like I'd encountered a flame. Something big, heavy and hairy was lying there, and whatever it was, it had slobbered all over my arm. My reaction certainly commanded the attention of the troops, and they stepped back as one, our hearts thumping in collective paranoia (exacerbated by the fact that we were stoned off our faces).

After a few tense, nay terrified, moments, I realised that whatever was behind the door wasn't coming after us. I took a cigarette lighter and investigated. A dog. In fact, an obese Labrador that had promptly fallen asleep again. We stepped over its snoring body and commenced installing our stolen signs throughout the living room and even up the hall of TJ's residence. In an episode of breathtaking courage, I delivered the coup de grace, slipping into the bathroom and leaving a message scrawled in his mother's (I hope!) lipstick on the mirror: Brek-a-kek-kek.

And suddenly school was over. Now, the three-month wait till the results. I veged. I got very, very stoned. I drank lots of piss. Anything to take the edge off the uncertainty. When the postman finally arrived with my official marks, it turned out that I had graduated from Blacktown Boys' High with Level 1 passes in English, Ancient History and Modern History, despite starting the first question of my Ancient History exam almost an hour after everyone else. TJ called it 'The most remarkable First

Level pass I have ever witnessed.' His praise felt like rain on a bone-dry desert. My English mark put me in the top ten per cent in the State. I had matriculated with scores sufficiently high enough to qualify me for entry into every university in New South Wales. More than that, I was able to choose from a variety of scholarships.

Mum was beside herself. She was speechless. But when she hugged me I felt the relief and gratitude and pride in every silent sob. She'd surrendered so much for this moment, never doubting, not for one second, that it would arrive and that her faith in me would be vindicated.

The tide was changing. I may have been petrified every time I jumped in the ring, and I may have lost my first seven fights, but I'd climbed in anyway and I'd never dogged it. I'd always given it my best shot. And I may not have been Mark Antony when it came to public speaking, but I was transformed into someone else when I stood before an audience. Someone confident. Someone who was learning that words and the way in which they are delivered can change people's perceptions in a heartbeat. Nevertheless, it wasn't the power of the spoken word that was about to change my universe; it was unbridled, brute force. I thumped Dad.

I don't know what made this fight any different from a lifetime of others. Dad had Mum shoved up against the fridge in the kitchen. 'You fucking slut.' His claw hand pressed to her throat. I'd come out of my bedroom and I could see them from the lounge. The fridge handle was digging into Mum's back and her eyes were clamped shut against his snarling hot breath. Her head spun from side to side as he beat her face like a drum with his good hand, this side then that, over and over.

I came running from the eye of the hurricane. I came from a thunderstorm that had been brewing so deep within me I hadn't even known it was there. I came screaming in a tsunami of fire and ice. He started to turn as my fist caught him flush on the side of the jaw. The glasses flew from his face and he fell against Mum in a parody of intimacy that fuelled my fury. I grabbed him by his shoulders and wrenched him off, picking him up bodily and flinging him all the way across the kitchen into the lounge. And then I was on him. A feral dog, tearing his white work shirt off his back, ripping at his face as he tried to crawl away, screaming in uncontrollable, inconsolable rage.

'Who's a gutless wonder now, you fucking cunt? Tell me, cunt, who's a fucking gutless wonder now?'

If Mum hadn't stopped me, I would have decorated the walls with his brains. Later, she said that this was why she had thrown herself between him and me. To stop me murdering him and wasting my life. My throat was shredded and my chest was a heaving bellows that tasted of blood and iron. 'If you ever lay another finger on her, so help me God, I swear I'll kill you, Saul,' I said. 'I'll fucking kill you.' That was the first time I'd ever called the bastard Saul. I never called him Dad again. And from that moment on, I never again referred to myself as Reynard.

It was also the night Mum said she knew we were finally leaving Edward Street.

We packed up what little we owned the next day while he was at work, and moved to a friend's place for a few weeks. Mum managed to find a job as a factory-hand, working night shifts at Arnott's Biscuits in Homebush, and we moved into cheap digs on the other side of town. This was the first in a succession of what Mum called 'very basic but clean, honest houses'. Even though Saul was no longer in the picture, we still sneaked around the house, talking in whispers and afraid to laugh or cough or even fart too loudly. Some habits last a lifetime.

I elected to take a Teacher's Scholarship and study for my Bachelor of Arts at Sydney Uni. I was Shane Weaver now. Reverting to my real surname wasn't difficult, as Saul had never adopted us. Legally, I'd been a Weaver all along.

I would be like TJ, at once sardonic and inspiring. Unfortunately, it wasn't easy to simply shuck off a lifetime of being told how stupid and useless I was. I blustered around campus like I had a sign on my forehead emblazoned with 'The Bastard Boy From Blacktown'. Surrounded by the trendoid sons and daughters of professionals from Sydney's more salubrious suburbs, I felt like Kmart next door to Harrods. Like a self-fulfilling prophecy, my bargain-basement behaviour earned me contempt and condescension in equal parts.

Even though there were several of us from Blacktown Boys' High and my mate Jimmy from Doonside High, the difference in our subjects, the sheer size of the place, and my increasing participation in the world of boxing, kept us apart.

The funny thing was, although boxing was consuming more of my time, I never really felt at home in the gym, or the ring either. Nevertheless, I was locked in. Even with the scholarship, Mum was the sole breadwinner and the only way I could afford to go to uni was to get a job.

Boxing in the clubs at night gave me money for board, and freed me up for uni during the day.

My natural weight, fit as a flea and not carrying an ounce, was ten-and-a-half stone. But because I was five feet seven inches short, Eddie Raye insisted I sweat down to below ten stone. So I took urine tablets a week before fights and limited my liquid intake to one-and-a-half glasses daily for three days before the event. When I climbed into the ring, my lips were cracked, my tongue was parched as a cuttlefish and my throat was a desert. My body coped okay for four rounds, but I collapsed like a rag doll at the final bell. Although I won a few fights, I lost most and copped a few cruel hidings. Post-fight celebrations were always the same. 'Poor me, poor me, pour me another drink.'

It made sense for Eddie Raye to have as many boys as possible fighting on the same night. Twenty-five per cent of three or four purses was better than a cut from one. There was usually a troupe of us. Paddy fought the main event; Todd featured in a six-rounder, and then there was me and any novice stupid or broke enough to glove up. They called us 'four-round fodder'. I didn't care. I was a minor player, but I basked in the reflected glory of the other guys' achievements. They made me get up and buy the jugs, they made me get the change for the pokies, they made me carry their bags, they made me the butt of their jokes, but it was better to be the clown in the circus than to get left outside the big top.

I didn't go to uni for days after a fight. My head ached. And I was still pissed. And even when I did eventually arrive, I'd spend more time in the music booths, smoking pot and tripping to the Velvet Underground and Leonard

Cohen. I loved the music booths at uni. They were free and you could book them for up to two hours. I never missed English lectures, however. I was in my element sitting anonymously among a hundred or so students, listening to eloquent cynics dissect antisocial butterflies like J. Alfred Prufrock with deftly wielded scalpels of insight. But I dreaded tutorials; you can't hide a black eye, a fat lip or a western suburbs attitude when you're one of eight people. 'I have heard the mermaids singing each to each, but I do not think they will sing to me.'

I got my first tattoo while I was at uni. I jumped on a bus to King's Cross and asked an old guy selling dirty magazines where I could get a tat. He directed me around the corner to a small, sweat-stinking room hot with too many bodies in various states of undress. A 15-stone bear of a man, his tree trunk arms writhing with snakes and his barrel chest a hairy playground for fire-breathing dragons, pointed a finger marked 'L' for LOVE to a chart on the wall and lisped, 'Pick a picture thunnyjim.' I strutted out with a gauze bandage over a butterfly bleeding prettily on the top of my left arm.

I walked around uni with one shirtsleeve rolled up high and my tattoo screaming 'Fuck you' to all and sundry. My boxing, my academic success, my speaking and writing prowess, all of it was fuelled by an all-consuming paranoia that I might actually be the 'gutless, witless wonder' Saul had seen whenever he looked at me. The clue is in the delivery: look closely and you'll see my performances and victories are always, even to this day, underscored by a desperation so keen it's almost palpable.

Saul was always limping close behind me, and the desire to torment his son as he had tormented me was sometimes irresistible. Even when I made it to Sydney Uni and should have known better, Richard-baiting was still a favourite sport. The day of the corpse is a notable example.

A classmate from Blacktown, Andrew Johnson, whose aggregate mark had been sufficiently high to win him a coveted place as a first-year Med student, had deigned to take me, a lowly Arts student, into the closed room where they keep the cadavers.

We passed a glass cabinet with three huge jars mounted on shelves. Inside were three human heads, suspended in clear liquid. It was unnerving because they were at such a height that I was looking directly into their eyes. They gazed back cloudily. The head in front of me was brutish with thick lips and large fleshy ears and a stubbled, lantern jaw. The mouth was slightly parted as if its pickled owner was about to speak. The hair was shorn and a serial number carved into the skull. Apparently, the State had donated the bodies of executed prisoners to medical science. These guys got more than the death penalty; they had been sentenced to be Medical exhibits A, B and C for eternity. 'Follow me,' Andrew said, 'the real action's in here.' He was right. Andrew's assignment was to dig around to find the fallopian tubes in some poor woman who had left her body to science.

The thick formaldehyde smell of the room overwhelmed another odour I knew had to be worse. Each body was covered with a heavy waterproof sheet and the heads were bagged. This, said Andrew, was for two reasons. One, to prevent the unpleasant occurrence of recognising someone, and two, as fledgling first-year students, their business didn't take them into the sanctified sphere of the human head.

When Andrew removed the sheet, I saw that time, embalming fluids and the invasion of countless hands and sterile instruments had rendered the subject more of a lump than a lady. The stomach cavity had been opened so often that he simply pulled aside the flaps of skin like leathery curtains to view the visceral architecture. The organs had been removed and replaced again and again like pieces of a 3D jigsaw.

His quest for the fallopian tubes took him to the furry nether regions and I watched him probing.

What I did next surprised not just Andrew, but me too. I leaned forward close to where Andrew was working, as though studying the procedure intently. And I reached out and plucked a few pubic hairs. I enfolded them into a tissue and put it in my pocket.

When I got home that afternoon, Richard was playing in the backyard. 'I'm making a Vegemite sandwich, mate. Want one?' Of course he did. Like all of us, Richard had gone hungry so often that saying yes to food was a reflex action. Indeed, being the last boy in the food chain, he was more wolfish in his eating habits than any of us. He had earned another name, 'Guts-ache', by virtue of his insatiable appetite. As he chewed, I asked him with a sick smile, 'So, Richard, how is it? Does it taste kinda . . . dead?' Ripping the sandwich apart, he spotted a few hairs in there, and as he fished them out I explained their origin. I laughed like a drain while he puked until he dry retched.

I had become an uncomfortable synthesis of sadism and sensitivity. I say 'uncomfortable' because what I did to others and what I saw people doing to each other invariably filled me with dismay and disgust. I had developed a radar-like sensibility for misery and injustice. Having been the victim so often, I was attuned to the plight of the underdog. Sometimes, as with the pubic-hair incident, I'd abuse this gift for insight by spotting the chink in a person's armour and thrusting a knife up through the breastplate and twisting it. Other times, I felt so strongly for those who were treated unfairly that I was reduced to tears. My trips to uni filled me with a sense of mourning.

To get there, I caught the train from Blacktown and got off at Redfern, walking the rest of the way. That was an education. Redfern was an Aboriginal ghetto. I passed crumpled men and women sleeping it off, hugging their flagons with the desperation of lovers. It was like walking through the post-apocalypse of the first *Mad Max* movie, the set all sucked dry of colour, the people all sucked dry of hope. There was never much movement in the grey midmorning, apart from a few mongrels feeding on garbage and the occasional gust of wind playing hide and seek with scraps of paper.

The 'boongs' (as I'm ashamed to say we called Aborigines back then in the 1960s and 1970s) I trained with in the gym, the boongs I fought in the clubs, the boongs I went the knuckle with in the pubs, they were all trying to claw their way out of dumps like Redfern. I always thought the real lesson was in the fact that to get to the highest seat of learning in the country, I had to literally step over the bodies of the indigenous people.

There were no roll calls at uni. The only measure of success was exams. My claim to fame was writing an essay on Chaucer's *Canterbury Tales*, comparing the plot to a popular TV sitcom of the time called *Number 96*. It centred around the lives of residents of a fictitious but familiar apartment block in Sydney, and was considered groundbreaking for dubious reasons – it featured Australia's first homosexual TV character, and the entire country tuned in when a buxom, blonde beauty named Abigail flashed her tits in one well-publicised episode. My topical interpretation of Chaucer's bawdy story hit a nerve and my paper came back marked 'See you in Honours'. But that wasn't going to happen. Lou Myers was about to enter my life.

He walked into Eddie Raye's gym one night with a skinny, red-haired kid about 14 years old. A few guys were shadow boxing. A few were doing their 'groundwork', push-ups and sit-ups and on-your-back-bike riding. I was skipping rope and watching Paddy humiliate the punching bag. He snarled and spat at it, throwing vicious combinations, and every now and then whacking it with an elbow or smacking it hard with the top of his head.

The rhythm in the gym slowed like breathing as the strangers walked in. The older guy, obviously the trainer, dropped his bag to the floor, grinned and spread his arms wide as if to embrace us all in the warmth of his bonhomie. It was like he'd just come home to the bosom of his family after a long absence. He seemed entirely oblivious to the fact that he was about as popular as a leper at a public swimming pool. When he announced that the young lad was available for sparring, the gang was unanimous. 'Feed him to Reynard. Ha. Ha. Ha.'

So I gloved up and went a few rounds with the kid. It was like being brutalised by a vicious carrot. He was lightning fast and packed thunderbolts in both hands. When it was over, I couldn't see out of the swollen slits in my face. Even Paddy and co. watched the show like stunned mullets. I asked around and found out where Lou Myers lived.

The next night, I knocked on his door and through sausage lips begged him to take me on. 'Can you teash me to do what that kid done to me?' I asked in my most Blacktown voice. Although my grammar was perfect, I'd learned that when in Rome it was smarter to not be smarter than the Romans. He smiled like he'd been expecting me, and said to be there the next day, ready to train at six sharp. 'And bring ya sandy-haired mate with the muscles, eh.' So it looked like both me and Todd were in.

The anti-macho truth about my boxing years was that I was terrified every time I got into the ring. The only way I kept punching for so long was by swearing to myself that every fight would be my last. Every fight was preceded by my 'never again, never again' mantra. So why did I keep doing it? Because I needed the money and I needed the applause. And I don't know what I needed most.

I didn't know it then, but the following week I'd find my most dangerous opponent. This would be a fight that would last for 15 years.

# ROUND 11

THE FIRST PART OF CHARLENE I ever saw was her arse. It was 1974 and I was 21 years old and on 'perve patrol' at the Mount Druitt Shopping Mall with my mate, Mike. Lou had wangled me a part-time job on the Metropolitan Water Board, where he was a foreman. But I didn't work much. No one did. I spent my mornings galloping around the trotting track at Blacktown Showground. Mike and the rest of the gang sat in the Water Board truck, smoking and watching me do lap after lap. When I'd run far enough to please Lou, they dropped me at home for a sleep. A few hours later, they picked me up and we spent the afternoons cruising the local shopping centres and looking for talent.

'Fuck me dead,' I said. 'Get a loada that!'

The checkout chick was bending to pick up a bag of groceries and her skirt was so short it had made the happy journey up around her waist. She had on a pair of white panties that looked like they were trying to do a Houdini and escape up the crack in her arse.

'That's my next door neighbour,' announced Mike with a proud Liverpudlian leer in his voice. 'She's a right little corker, int she!'

He organised a barbie at his place for the next Friday so I could meet her. It was lust at first night. She was a 17-year-old Pommy peach with bleached blonde hair and the biggest tits I'd seen outside of Todd's stick magazines. Poor Charlene must have thought she'd landed the perfect catch – university student, up and coming professional boxer, and a sensitive young man who loved his mum.

She played hard to get and it took me 48 hours to get into her pants. She was actually a redhead. A month later she was up the duff. I resisted the pressure from her parents to walk down the aisle, but 'did the right thing', staying faithful and feeding her sausage. Mum said girls didn't get pregnant by accident any more. Maybe not, but I felt like an accidental father.

Eight months later Charlene and I were dancing at a New Year's party at Lou's house when Charlene hit the deck, doubled over with contractions. I got a mate to run us to Blacktown Hospital. Those were the days when a bloke was considered a dead-set pervert if he wanted to stay with the missus during the birth, and I left her in good hands and went back to my mates and the keg.

I called my first daughter Talullah. I was high as a kite on 1 January 1975, the night she was born. Charlene and I weren't even living together. She was living at her folks' house and I was living in a daze at 15 Swinson Street. Talullah's birth barely registered.

Mum had found herself a new man. James was born in Yugoslavia, I think, and had thick black hair, a Jesus beard, olive skin and flared nostrils. They had met when

James was at Rydalmere Hospital undergoing treatment for manic depression. Some days he looked like he'd hit rock bottom and started to dig. Others, he was deliriously and capriciously happy, flinging his unopened pay packets out the window of his car 'for the poor people'. James drove a bright orange Cortina with fat wheels and a sound system that throbbed so hard you felt the music pulse through your body like electrified blood. After Mum, he loved that beast more than anything else in the world.

Even before Mum had introduced me to James, I'd seen him around. The first time, I had been sitting at a table with Todd and a few of the local spunks at the Miller's Hotel in Shannon Road. James was playing pool and had just finessed the white ball onto the black to try to wrap up the game. It was looking good. As he stood back to watch the eight-ball glide then dribble towards the centre pocket, Chris Dylan moved in from the blind side and smashed him several times in the face. Dylan had a reputation as a bother boy. Actually, he was a skinny streak of pelican shit who always picked his mark.

James, medicated and with a few grogs under his belt, hadn't been just low-hanging fruit, he was a badly bruised peach scraping the ground. Dylan punched like a sheila, but his trademark was the sharp-edged rings he wore on both hands, and he had sliced up James' face. The poor bugger literally didn't know what had hit him, and he had stood there in wide-eyed, open-mouthed amazement with blood pouring down his face and onto his shirt. Then, when the penny had dropped, he'd started crying. First, in polite little sniffles, and then, as the hopelessness of his situation dawned on him, he had began bawling like a baby.

I had felt sorry for the bastard and I always thought Dylan was lower than a snake's belly, but it wasn't our fight. Two burly bouncers escorted James outside and told him he was a cunt and he was barred. Of course, I didn't have a clue that he would one day be Mum's husband.

Stepping into their home in Swinson Street was like getting on board the peace train. It was far out, man. James had a mate who was a tattooist and he'd drawn the outline of a huge dragon on one of the walls. He was always promising to come round and colour it in. James had installed a disco light in the lounge and it added a psychedelic dimension to tripping. This was probably the last place in the world where Mum should have received her long-lost father. But that's how it happened anyway.

I'm not sure how he got the address, but a telegram announced his arrival the next day. Apparently he was taking an ocean cruise and as the cruise liner was berthed at Sydney Harbour for a day he'd deigned to pop round and visit the poor people. Mum went into panic mode. She weeded the garden, scrubbed the place inside and out and hid the dope. She even bought an expensive packet of dark chocolate biscuits, recalling some distant occasion when he'd said they were his favourites. She invited me around to meet him because she considered me her crowning achievement. 'He's bound to appreciate the fact that you're going to uni, dear, and that you're a professional boxer.'

When the taxi pulled up, out stepped a short, pot-bellied, red-faced man with three chins, all of them weak. He was wearing cream slacks with matching jacket, a captain's hat, a pale, sky-dyed shirt and a startling Prussian blue scarf with white polka dots, for fucksake.

He looked as much at home in Swinson Street as a fat funnel-web spider on a baby's nappy.

His sole topic of conversation was himself, and when there was a lull in the flow, lo and behold, he produced an album of his 'greatest hits'. He handed it imperiously to James who took it in both hands and placed it reverently in his record player. Poppa's presence (I was instructed to call him Poppa and, suspecting there might be a quid in it, complied without a murmur) sent James hurtling back into a second childhood. He was completely overawed. Not that Poppa appeared to notice. He pointedly avoided speaking directly to the man of the house the whole time he was there.

When he left, we let out a long, heart-felt sigh of collective relief and broke out the dope. Mum suggested we listen to the record he'd left with us as 'a little something to remember me by'. We all missed it at the time, among the tinkling of the ivories and the teacups and the Poppa-centric conversation, forced titters and awkward silences, but, replaying the album, we distinctly heard the sounds of a postman's whistle and a dog barking. He'd obviously recorded it in his own lounge room. Poor Poppa.

Things returned to 'normal' about two seconds after he left. You could be forgiven for thinking that James had a beanbag growing out of his arse. He was always slumped in it, strumming his acoustic guitar and murdering Cat Stevens' 'Sad Lisa' or 'Wild World'. But no one gave a shit because we were so stoned we could barely scratch ourselves and reality was only a concept, man. James even looked a bit like the Cat with his swarthy skin, black beard and wavy hair (except he invariably had a bit of snot in the mo or some food in his beard).

Officially, the Swinson Street household comprised Mum, James, Beth and Sarah. I'd moved out when Charlene got out of hospital following Talullah's birth, and we'd set up house in a dump opposite an egg farm on Shannon Road, about ten minutes' drive away. The floor in the kitchen was built so it sloped to give the water from the terminally leaking roof somewhere to drain. In fine weather you could see the sunshine filter through the cracks where the walls joined. In winter, we wore singlets and jumpers and sucked bongs and cans to warm up from the inside out.

Kelly was by now married to his second wife and living, together with her five-year-old son from a former relationship, in Seven Hills, the next suburb on the way to Sydney. Tony was sticking close by his alien friend, Edwin, and bunking with a pot-pourri of dope fiends on a round-robin basis. I didn't have a clue where Richard was.

But 15 Swinson Street was always an open house, and you'd more than likely find a few of us there any time, night or day. When I was fighting with Charlene about drugs and booze, which was the rule rather than the exception, you'd find me there, too. This was the era of free love, and it was Rafferty's Rules at 15 Swinson Street. Except for Mum, everything went, from rooting like rattlesnakes to toking on joints, tripping and the drug of the moment – smack.

Mum had one go at pot but it wasn't her bag. She got paranoid and thought we were all cold. She ran around trying to make us comfortable with pillows and blankets. We thought it was hilarious, but it was no joke for Mum. She was convinced that we'd suffer if she failed to administer the right care. It was the one and only time she tried weed. Besides, she didn't need it. She was the happiest I'd ever seen her. I guess she needed someone to mother now that we'd grown up. Or gotten bigger, at least. And then there was her job. From the moment she left Saul, Mum had worked. She had no choice, but as she had no qualifications either, this meant working shifts in factories. First, there was Arnott's Biscuits and then Lifesavers. Swinson Street, however, marked a step up in her professional life, and she was delighted when she scored a job at Kmart, working on the floor.

She wandered around asking people who were lost in the aisles, 'Can I help you?' and directing them to underwear or shoes or toys. Part of her job was to keep a lookout for shoplifters. If ever she spotted someone who looked like they were down and out, however, Mum turned a blind eye. It was her only dereliction of duty.

Whatever job she had, she never missed a day and she gave it everything she had. She paid the rent, fed us and clothed us. And now she was free of Saul, she put a lid on drinking and any thoughts of killing herself evaporated. At last, Mum had something to live for. But her happiness was always contingent on James' mental state and, as we were about to learn, this had all the consistency of a weather vane. We kids were also about to discover that while absolute freedom can be dangerous for 'normal' people, it can be downright lethal to children who have been caged by fear all their young lives.

Todd nearly died at 15 Swinson Street. We'd scored some pink rocks, an especially potent form of heroin, and Mum and James were both in bed when Todd had the privileged first taste. The alarm clock had just gone off on Pink Floyd's 'Dark Side of the Moon'. Suddenly, it was like someone had pulled a plug and all the colours had run out of Todd's body. He was albino white and shivering and sweating at the same time. He kept falling into unconsciousness and we had to smack his face to wake him up. He couldn't focus and his eyes rolled around in his head like the fruit symbols in a poker machine. Pink Floyd was good, but it wasn't *that* good. 'Fuck,' Tony said, 'he's OD'ing. Let's get him in the shower.'

We dragged him down to the bathroom and ripped off his gear. One minute he was a compliant and malleable shop dummy, and the next, a maniacal jack-in-the-box. It was a bit like the villain you'd bet anything is dead in those classic horror movies. You know, the ones where the evil bastard has been shot, stabbed, strangled, incinerated and thrown off a cliff, and when finally it seems certain the innocent schoolgirls will escape with their lives and hymens intact, and you can breathe easy at last, suddenly, way beyond reason, past the parameters of logic, shit-a-brick, great-jumpin'-Jehoshaphat, from out of camera, right out of hell, a bleeding, badly burned, still-smoking hand pounces into frame, grabbing the prettiest virgin by the ankle. Hard.

'I'm cool, man. I'm cool. Fuck off. Just let me get a shower and I'll be okay. Fuck off!'

He was hysterical and baring his teeth and snarling and thrusting out his chest and it wasn't smart to hang about so we left him there. A few minutes later, we heard an almighty crash. He'd done a Titanic in the shower and there was no way in the world we could raise him. We didn't own a phone at 15 Swinson Street, and there was nothing to do but wake up Mum.

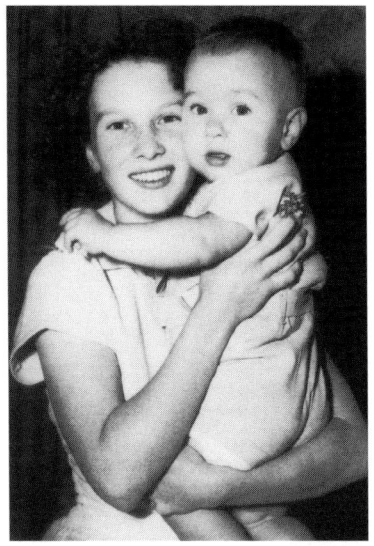

My 17-year-old mum. In 50 years she's never stopped holding me.

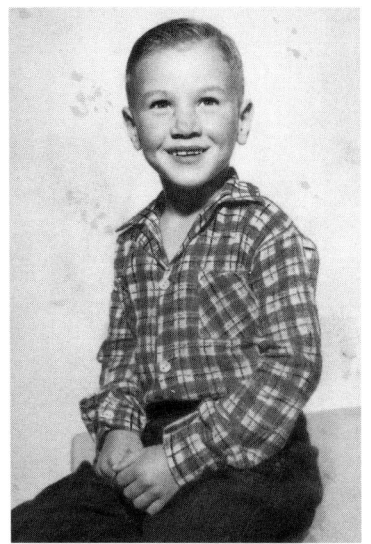

Me at six. The age of innocence. I wish.

Left to right: Richard, the only 'true' Reynard boy, and we never let him forget it; Tony, before terror and despair drove him to drugs; Kelly, when he still knew how to smile; and me, not a sign of the alcoholic or standover man.

*Above:* Mum and her boys. Not much to smile about.

*Right:* From back: Me, Kelly, Tony and Richard. Happy as you can be in hell.

*Below:* Kelly and me during our stay with our real dad in Waratah. As you can see by the piggy faces, it was open slather on the lolly counter.

*Above left:* Me holding my beloved Cha Cha, Richard, Tony, Beth and Sarah.

*Above:* Poor Beth. She was Saul's favourite. No one knew why.

*Left:* Mum on her wedding day. No smile. No hope. No chance.

*Above:* Mum. Fragile as glass. And little wonder.

*Above right:* Mum and me. Putting on a brave face.

*Right:* Me at 16. Grim days.

*Above:* I'm the corporal on the far left who wanted to quit high-school cadets when my bed-wetting secret 'leaked'. Mum insisted I stay on. If the rifle had been loaded, I'd have shot every bastard in sight.

*Left:* Mum and me in our suburban concentration camp.

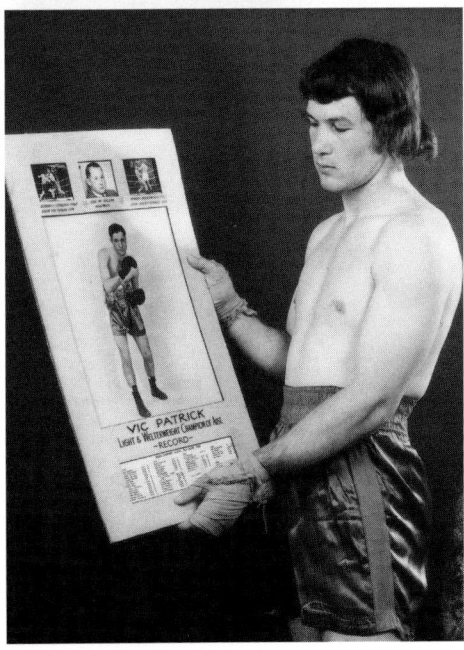

*Left:* I was fighting pro in clubs before I was legally old enough to buy a beer.

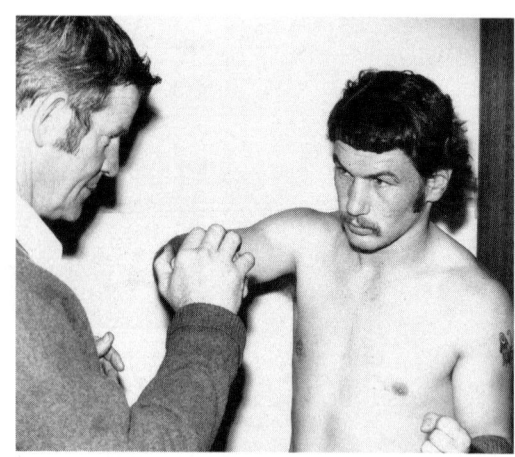

I loved my trainer, Lou, like a father.

Ray Wheatley's gym. That's me in front with the beard.

1996. Drunk, in my dishwasher's uniform, and shooting myself in the head. Again.

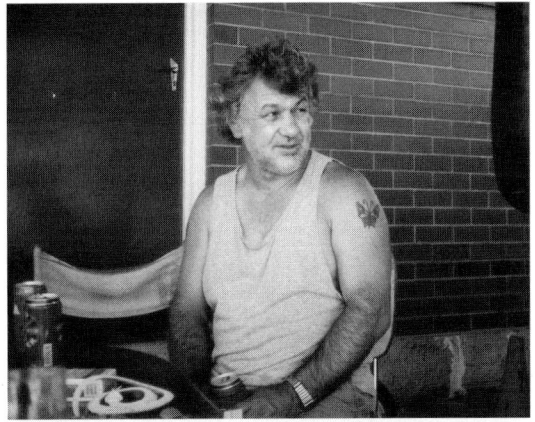

Me. Drunk, fat, 40 and on the slagheap.

Ricky Patterson and I meet more than two decades after our Australian title fight.

Kate and me on our wedding day. A new beginning.

My sister Sarah at my wedding to Kate. We had no idea how short her time was.

My darling Pippa and me.

My gorgeous girls: Olivia, Georgia and Pippa.

She took one look and ran across the road in her nightie to call an ambulance from the house of one of the few neighbours who acknowledged we even lived in the same street. They were Jehovah's Witnesses, and like us in so far as no one gave them the time of day either. Todd was blue and snap frozen in deep sleep when they rushed him off to Blacktown Hospital. They revived him, though, and he scarpered that same night.

I didn't experience the 'kiss of death' at Swinson Street, but I was the hapless recipient of another equally intimate kiss that sure made me wish I were dead. I'm talking about the occasion of my first and only dose of the crabs. And I don't mean the crustaceans you pick up from Sydney Fish Market; I love those bastards. I'm talking the vile translucent mites that nest in your pubes and run around your balls, biting and itching so insanely that you seriously consider tearing off your wedding tackle and flushing it down the toilet.

I was mellowing out on some very nice weed and getting off on the Bee Gees' 'I just gotta get a message to you', when some young thing I'd seen once or twice got her own message to me. She grabbed me directly on the stalk, no warning, no chat, no nothing, just a full-frontal assault on the meatworks. She was a bit on the plump side, but it wasn't every day I got to stick it to a schoolgirl.

With no thought of Charlene, I asked Sarah if I could use her bed, and she said yeah go right ahead but no fucking wet patches or skid marks and I took the girl in there and fucked her so fast and furious that it was all over red rover even before the song finished. 'One more hour and my life will be through.' Well, not quite, but the girl's life was looking pretty precarious when I discovered I had a raging dose of the crabs a few days later.

Out of the blue Richard turned up again and I enlisted his help to move Mum out of Swinson Street and into a Housing Commission flat near Blackett in Mt Druitt. James had been neglecting to take his medication for some time, and had been growing loonier by the day. When he started saying he wanted to take Mum and Beth and Sarah to heaven with him, it was time to take them somewhere safer.

Mum's new flat was a two-storey place, which I know sounds pretty posh, but these were soulless shoeboxes stuck in suburbs where society's exiles went to fight and fuck and forget about ever escaping to the real world again. Richard and I were wrestling a bed up the narrow staircase when I stopped and said, 'For fucksake, hang on, Richard, put it down a second.' He was on the top steps, moving backwards up the staircase. I was following him, but my crotch was alive and I just had to free my hands to sink my fingernails in and do some serious scratching.

Richard looked a little concerned when I screamed out in sheer frustration, ripped my shorts and underwear down and began attacking my cock and balls with a ferocity that would have made the Marquis de Sade wince. He was downright alarmed when, examining the hairy article with 'fine tooth comb' concentration, I yelled, 'Jesus Christ! What the fuck is *this*?' It was like something out of *The Twilight Zone*. My genifuckingtalia had become a life-support system for a teeming population of arachnid aliens.

Richard put down his end of the bed and came closer for a cautious look. 'You got crabs,' he said. 'You fucked someone with crabs.' It didn't take Einstein to work it out.

I went to a doctor who told me to shave off all my pubic hair and gave me some lotion to exterminate the bastards. He told me that this particular STD was highly contagious, and that I should refer anyone I'd had sex with, or who'd even shared the same towels or toiletries, to a doctor. Immediately, I realised I needed to talk to Charlene. I asked the doctor if it was possible to get crabs off a toilet seat.

'Yes, I suppose it is,' he said, 'but you need to be committing an act that's not usually performed on a toilet seat.'

Good onya, doc, I thought on the way out.

I broke the news to Charlene at home. 'Charlene, I gotta ask you something, darlin'.'

She looked at me. She knew something was going down.

'Listen, have you been itchy at all, you know, down there?'

Suddenly she went all sheepish and nodded. I was so strung out on my own guilt that I failed to see that she'd seriously considered the possibility that she had brought the crabs home herself. Too late anyway, I'd already launched my excuse.

'I'm so sorry, darlin'. I was pissed and stoned to the max. She was just a slut. It meant absolutely nothing.'

Mum was disgusted when she heard I'd had my wanton way with some girl. The only one who understood was Todd. We were closer than brothers (which wasn't difficult, considering the degree of dysfunction in my relationship with my siblings, and the fact that Todd was an only child). We did everything together. I was mesmerised by his single-minded savagery. He trusted no one, except me.

Unlike me, Todd had never had the benefit of an education, having left school aged 15. But he was fiercely intelligent and always asking me to share what I was learning at uni. He saw knowledge as another weapon he could deploy.

We had a small-scale dope business that kept us in drugs, paid the rent and gave us some pocket money, and so I said goodbye to uni. Boxing had given us access to some heavy contacts in the St Marys and Granville dope scenes, and we were the preferred dealers for a few of the local 'Mr Bigs'. They liked the way we showed a flagrant disregard for the territorial boundaries that traditionally restricted their business interests. We didn't give a flying fuck where we sold the stuff, as long as the money was there. So sure, we got by, but life certainly wasn't too swish for Charlene and me. And Mum, in particular, was doing it tough.

Our shack in Shannon Road was where the old Mum snuck up and pounced on her. She'd turned up depressed and distressed, wanting to stay 'just a few days, dear, to sort myself out'. Her Aboriginal neighbours in Mt Druitt were giving her a hard time. She'd befriended a girl about eight years old who played in the car park, and who actually looked white. Not that colour was a factor in Mum's hospitality. The child was shoeless, bedraggled and looked hungry. Had she been lime green with yellow spots, this would have been reason enough for Mum to invite her in for a spaghetti dinner.

When the girl turned up, there was a young woman with her. 'Can my auntie have some dinner, too?' asked the girl. Mum had plenty of spag to go round, and readily agreed. Five minutes into the meal, another knock on the door. When Mum answered it, in walked two Aboriginal men drinking beers. 'I wanna talk wif my girlfriend,' one of them said. Despite Mum asking that they leave and wait till the woman returned home, they settled down on the lounge, making themselves comfortable. Before the door was closed, they were joined by six of their drunken friends. Mum sensed trouble and snuck out of her own back door.

She returned a few hours later, when the place seemed quiet. They'd trashed the kitchen. There was spaghetti all over the walls and floors. Worse, two of the men were still in the house. As they forced her up the stairs to the bedroom, Mum saw that the child was still there and pleaded that they send her home. They did. And then one of them raped her while the other watched.

I knew there'd been trouble, but I was unaware of how bad it was. Mum had been too upset to give all the details at the time. Describing what had happened to her would have forced her to relive it. She just wanted to forget. We moved Mum into Talullah's room, where they shared the single bed.

Next morning, Talullah came into our room crying. 'Nana can't talk. Nana can't talk.' When I went to see, Mum was comatose and grey as the sheets. An empty bottle of sleeping tablets lay on the floor. We thought she was dead. Charlene ran over the road in her pyjamas to use the neighbour's phone. She came back to get change. I went ballistic. I was standing over Mum, spewing spit and curses when the ambulance guys walked in.

'You fucking insane bitch. In front of our daughter. You fucking selfish bitch.' Screaming like a banshee, I harangued the ambulance down the drive and up the road until it accelerated away. I know I sound like a heartless bastard, but the truth is, this was how I always reacted when I found myself in a situation over which I had no control. This was the face I showed when I was terrified. It seemed manlier somehow than admitting I was powerless and breaking down in tears. The truth is, I was terrified that Mum had gone too far this time, and that even the doctors wouldn't be able to snatch her back.

But the staff at Blacktown Hospital was well practised at reviving the dead. They pumped out Mum's stomach and a week later they sent her back to her little Housing Commission flat in Mt Druitt. No counselling, no visit from the welfare, no time for silly ladies with a death wish. It was tantamount to putting a bandaid on a cancerous lesion. It won't stop the rot, but it will save people the distress of having to look at it.

Mum was living in a strange set-up. Her own kids were off her hands, yet here she was in Mt Druitt's nightmare nursery, surrounded by single mums with too little money, even less hope and way too much time to think about it. So they drank cheap plonk and schemed and dreamed about the Sir Lancelot who was going to take them away from all this.

My marriage to Charlene was a real-life Punch and Judy Show. I drew the line at physical abuse, but excelled at verbal bashings and public humiliation. I was also an expert at beating up fridges and bashing holes in walls. At the drop of a hat, I'd bring up Charlene's stunted vocabulary. What happened on the fishing trip was typical.

We went out on the Nepean River with Mike, who'd introduced me to Charlene in the first place, and his wife, Josie, one summer's day. The four of us were cramped into a little putt-putt (so named after the sound of the tiny outboard motor). For the whole day, I refused to speak to Charlene's face, instead addressing every word only to her arse. If she stood up to get a drink or just to stretch her legs, I'd look directly at her arse and say things like, 'I'm glad you could make it today, Charlene. You're a real joy to be with.' Mike and Josie thought it was hysterical. For about an hour. Nobody was laughing at the end of a long, hot, fishless day. Charlene said I made her 'feel like nothing'. She always did have a gift for understatement.

But I was by no means Robinson Crusoe when it came to treating women like shit. My brother Tony did quite a useful Saul impersonation himself. His first live-in girlfriend, Julie, was 30 and ten years his senior. A plump girl who'd done the hippie trail and shared Tony's passion for hooch, she wore her blonde hair in a bob, and was training to be a primary school teacher. Poor old Julie always seemed to have a fat lip or a black eye or a bruised arm.

Once, when they were sharing a rented house with Charlene and me, we heard an almighty crash and ran into their bedroom. Tony was screaming at Julie, but she was no longer in the room. He'd pushed her through a plate glass window and she was lying on her back, looking up at him from the ground below. She was lucky. It was a big fall and she was badly shaken, but not cut. She crammed her stuff into a backpack, walked resolutely out the back door and we never saw Julie again.

Isn't it sad and infuriating how the sins of the father are visited upon the children? You'd think that a lifetime of watching your mum being bashed and abused would be enough to turn anyone into a model husband and father. It doesn't work that way. We Weaver boys have all been kitchen commandos to varying degrees. Tony simply expressed himself more strenuously in this medium because, while I had my writing and Kelly had the diversion of another sucker being born every minute, Tony had no other forum in which to assert himself.

As for my sisters, I didn't have much of a relationship with them and it would be some years before I'd register how the sins of the father would affect them.

Mum got a telegram from her brother about a year after her father's visit to 15 Swinson Street. Carey had died of a heart attack. It turned out he'd carked it while sitting on the throne. The young guy he lived with (now *that* got me wondering) found him slumped on the shitter. Good old Carey, even in death he was unable to escape that touch of theatre that had marked him for superstardom in life. Carey who?

Mum and I scraped the money together between the two of us and flew to Brisbane for the funeral. I was selling dope, boxing and selling insurance for Temperance and General (the irony was not lost on me) and I'd managed to wangle an advance on commission.

I got the distinct impression that Mum believed, somewhere deep inside, that the father who had ignored her in life had tucked a little something away for her in death. When I saw where he had lived, a tres ordinaire three-bedroom, brick-veneer cottage in suburbia, I doubted it. The house was the architectural equivalent of 'Poppa' himself, false brick encasing a hollow space.

After the funeral, the half-dozen or so strangers who'd turned up to pay their last respects adjourned to a separate part of the chapel for tea, and ham, tomato and cucumber sandwiches. Mum needed something stiffer. We got a taxi back to the house where a thorough search of the kitchen produced a half-bottle of sherry. It was all her old man had left her.

# ROUND 12

HE LOOKS AT ME WITH assassin's eyes, like he's focusing through the sights on a rifle. Suddenly, I'm directly in range. Whack! His left arm shoots out like a cobra on anabolic steroids and he hits me hard, scoring a bull's eye. And instantly I know why the term 'snotted' is so apt, as my nose weeps a mixture of mucus and blood.

My opponent is Alex Burns. The press had picked up on the connection with the legendary 'Patrick versus Burns' stoush of 1946, saying that it was unlikely our efforts would eclipse those of our namesakes. It was purely academic, of course. And right now, I'm having my own internal academic discourse.

Two hours before stepping into the square ring, I'd been reading about The Third Reich, particularly Hitler's bizarre tastes in interior design. Alex Burns is a living mural; every inch of his epidermis is etched in glorious, four-colour ink. I can't help but think what a magnificent addition he would've made to the Fuhrer's infamous collection of lampshades.

It's a savage, close contest. Although I win on points, Alex leaves the ring with his skin entirely intact, if a little bruised.

During those peace-train, drug-charged years I was also a star on the rise. Six months with Lou Myers had turned me from a punching bag into a mug lair en route to an Australian boxing title. I loved Lou. He was the father I never had. I would have done anything for him. Lou was a Kiwi and, unlike Eddie Raye who'd never laced on a glove, he'd been a rated lightweight in his day.

Lou was your genuine hard man. Paddy and his gang chose to train at Eddie Raye's rather than with Lou because 'The old bastard hits too hard.' But he also had a heart of gold. One of my most cherished memories of Lou is of a night when we were drinking at South's Juniors after Todd had scored a six-round victory. There was a guy who used to turn up to the fights with his bag packed with boxing shorts and bandages. He fought under the name Tommy Thunder, and he was a bit simple. He was such a hopeless fighter that he didn't even have a trainer. If a contestant failed to show, however, the promoter wasn't above throwing Tommy in, whoever the opponent.

This particular night, Tommy had stepped in to a four-rounder at the last minute with a heavier and more experienced opponent. He'd been butchered. He was too proud or too stupid to stay down, though, and he kept dragging himself up off the canvas and going back for more. And more. Before the referee stopped the massacre, even the usual bloodthirsty screams of the crowd had turned to groans of dismay.

Long after the fights had ended, and while we were getting stuck into the grog downstairs, we noticed this lone figure coming down the escalator. It was Tommy. His shoelaces were undone, his hair hadn't been combed and there was a trickle of blood running from a gash over his eye, down his face, and all over his white shirt. Tommy had no idea. He was still in gaga land.

Lou met Tommy at the bottom of the escalator, put his arm around him and escorted him back to where we were sitting. He used cotton wool and vaseline to stop the bleeding, combed Tommy's hair, tucked his shirt in and bought him a beer. That night, Tommy Thunder was one of Lou's boys. I'd never seen Tommy laugh before. I reckon it must have been one of the happiest nights of his life. If you were the sort who judged a book by its cover, you wouldn't suspect that Lou had such a capacity for kindness.

Lou's nose had been broken so many times it looked like a meat patty spread generously over his face. His eyes had been cut so often, the lids hung like half-closed blinds through which you could just see the blue flint of his eyes. His mouth had been split and stitched so he always looked like he was wearing a happy, lopsided smile. This was dangerous. It was impossible to tell if Lou was going to smash you or smooch you. His weakness for a bit of skirt made it advisable to keep a close eye on your girlfriend. In my case, I even thought it smart to look out for Mum. I like to think Todd's granny was safe. As I was about to discover, however, some people weren't even safe from themselves.

The last night we saw Paddy alive he was sitting in the Hood, slumped on a bench, his back to the wall. His eyes were closed and he was dribbling and cooing like a baby and scratching vaguely at his face in the signature slow-mo wave of smackheads. He was dead within the hour. Apparently he'd jumped on his Kwaka 1000 and headed off to the Miller's Hotel about two miles out of town to score more dope. They found what was left of him smeared around a telegraph pole just down the road.

His boxing career had been stopped in the early rounds of his life. Mine was in the ascendancy. Lou had discovered the secret to tapping into my rage and converting it into high-octane fuel that propelled me up the national ratings. His methods were at once unorthodox and ruthlessly effective.

Every second Sunday, Lou led a small, anxious contingent into Parramatta Gaol to box the inmates. I remember jumping into the open-air ring with a leviathan who looked more like Magilla Gorilla than a human being. The reason it sticks in my mind is because I lost two teeth in that encounter. The beast's playfully scarred arms and torso (initials, love hearts and even a game of noughts and crosses) bore testament to a lifetime of gleeful self-mutilation. I was surprised to hear Neanderthal man's buddies urging him on with cries of, 'Stick it up him, Shirley! Atta girl, Shirl!' But I was mortified to see him lock tongues with his proud 'husband' after our stoush. Guys in the boob for anything over ten years had a motto: 'Any hole's a goal.' Chocolate starfish was better than no sweets at all.

And then there were the tent fights. When the annual show passed through Blacktown, the tent fights sprang up alongside the Bearded Lady, the Fattest Man in the Universe and Cyclops the One-eyed Giant. Lou would sign up Todd and me to travel with the troupe for a month or so. 'There's no weight divisions, no rules and no doctor,' he'd chuckle. 'You'll get tough or you'll fuckin' get eaten alive.'

Invariably, the other fighters on Bobby Tute's Boxing Troupe were all Kooris. I met Kevin Mundine, brother of the mercurial Tony Mundine, Australian middleweight, light-heavy and heavyweight champion, on one of our stints. Todd and I were the token whites.

The troupe travelled to the country towns, taking on all-comers. The boxers stood on a raised plank in front of the tent in our shiny shorts, arms crossed, looking as tough as possible while the rats of fear were feeding on our guts, eating us from the inside out. Bobby was a master spruiker and brilliant at getting the local boys to have a go. 'Step right up, step right up. Pick a punchie, go three one-minute rounds and take home a quid. Come on, muscles,' he'd say, pointing to someone close to the stage. 'Show your sweetheart what you're made of. Be the first to put a punchie in the hearse!'

A big, fat, baby-faced boong, so black he was almost purple, beat a huge side-drum to attract the crowd. Boom, boom, boom. His jowls shuddered and his tits wobbled with every whack. And you could bet the bank on there always being a smart arse who'd yell, 'Give me the drummer boy.' And then it was a case of bloody blue murder. Over three one-minute rounds, the gargantuan jellyfish was a relentless thrashing machine with explosives in both fists. He was unstoppable. He felt no pain. And he loved cutting the white boys to pieces. Especially in front of their smug-faced girlfriends.

The boongs slept in the boxing tent. Todd and I crashed in our sleeping bags under the stars. The irony wasn't wasted on me. We fronted up for breakfast with our black brothers on our first morning. The boys were sitting around sucking on flagons. They were just about to cook up a feast of fried eggs over a campfire blazing under the big top. The fat in the pan was studded with plump, green-bellied blowflies. They either didn't notice or were grateful for the extra protein. We declined their invitation to eat, but shared a drink before making the long trek into town.

Between drinks and drugs I learned a thing or two about smashing a man into submission. Under Lou's guidance, I never lost a fight at 11 stone. Ray Mitchell, who refereed most of my fights, said my style was reminiscent of Vic Patrick, the great Australian welterweight. I was a bulldog. I never took a backward step, and took whatever my opponent dished out. I beat all the top contenders in my division, and drew with one. Lou gave me a great tip that really held me in good stead. He said, 'Shane, you're a short arse, that's your best asset. Don't punch up to the bastards. Make 'em work to find you. Make yourself even smaller.'

Except for the half-dozen or so fights I had before I met her, Charlene attended every bout I had. She loved the fights. It was an excuse to put on her glad rags, and the pugs, trainers, promoters, journos, photographers and entourage of hangers-on were as close as we ever got to 'high society'. The first time I met her parents was the night I fought Johnny Huvvoch in my first six-rounder at South Sydney Juniors. Lou picked me up outside Sydney Uni on his way to the city and I met Charlene and her mum and dad at the club. I won on points and Scott, Charlene's father, said it was the best fight he'd seen.

I was young and fit then, and the piss and drugs were more about recreation than devastation. Charlene was my first love, and I loved her truly, deeply, madly. I couldn't get enough of her. In my bed, in my head, and in every way imaginable, she was my all-consuming, combustible, ball-busting passion. But while we were unable to live apart, nor could we live together, and my pot-fuelled frustration triggered my fury, fanning it into an inferno that destroyed us both, incinerating our relationship and scorching everyone close to us.

Only one bloke ever sat me down, and that was Terry Fox, the South Australian light heavyweight champion. Sure, he could thump, but I should never have been in the ring with him in the first place. The promoter falsified my weight on the card and put me in as a middleweight. He subtracted a few kilos from Fox and, voila, we were on. Lou made one of his rare miscalculations and gave the go ahead.

The next thing, it was round two and I was on my arse, looking the ringside punters directly in the eyes. I was up on my feet like a jack-in-the-box. Ray Mitchell, the referee, put a standing-eight count on me. When we hopped back into it, Fox floored me again with his very next punch. I didn't even see it coming and to this day I don't know what he whacked me with, only that it felt like a plank of four by two, and my brain throbbed for a week. Once again I was up in a flash, but Ray stopped the fight. I protested loudly, because it's sort of expected, but Ray was on the ball. My mouth was moving, but I didn't have the foggiest what I was saying or even who I was. I took a self-imposed six-month break after Fox, hitting the piss and the pot with single-minded dedication.

While I was out of the ring, Sarah had a real fight on her hands. She was barely 16 when she became pregnant to her first serious boyfriend. I don't know what happened when Sarah announced she was pregnant. I don't remember her carrying the baby, or the birth. But I'll never forget the funeral. Sarah had a girl, Stephanie. Regrettably, the baby only lived for a few minutes.

In those days, burying an unbaptised baby born out of wedlock was like trying to get the Pope to perform an abortion. Mum and I knocked on the door of every church in the district before we found a Lutheran minister willing to conduct the funeral and put the dead baby to rest in hallowed ground.

Mum, me, Charlene, Sarah and the dead baby's father, Peter, were the only people who knew or cared about the birth and death of little Stephanie. Even then, I had come to support Mum and my sister; I had not come to cry. When I saw Sarah, only a child herself, cradling a cardboard coffin no bigger than a shoebox, I wasn't so strong. And when Peter, his face streaked with tears, kneeled and pressed a homemade cross into the earth to mark the place where his baby daughter had to stay while we went home, I lost it.

I drank a lot of beers, lamenting the premature death of my first niece. The obscene thing, of course, is that if I hadn't had the funeral of a baby as an excuse, I'd have found another. There would always be a reason, and the result would always be the same.

My weight ballooned. I was almost 13 stone, hungover, and sucking on the dregs of a joint when the chance of a lifetime landed in my ample lap. The Water Board truck pulled up. Lou caught me in the front yard, checking the letterbox for my dole cheque. I was gob-smacked when he told me I'd earned a shot at the Australian light middleweight title. In three months. My overnight elevation to number two contender had come via a unique set of circumstances. Charkey Ramon, the reigning Aussie champ and number one contender for Koichi Wajima's world title, had smashed his shoulder in a horrific surfing accident. He would never fight again. The obvious contender for the vacant title was a Darwinian Aborigine named Ricky Patterson, a southpaw who'd knocked out every rated opponent with a single, lethal rip to the stomach. Except for me. He'd slaughtered me at North Sydney Leagues Club, but I'd managed somehow to stay upright. When the bell rang, I slumped to the canvas and crawled back to my corner on all fours. I couldn't breathe normally for half an hour. Nevertheless, I'd gone the distance, so I was it.

Lou knocked the joint out of my mouth, bundled me into the Water Board truck, and we headed for the trotting track. I was running for the next 90 days. He dragged me along to every gym in Sydney that boasted a southpaw of any note. One day I was in with world-rated junior lightweight Billy Moeller, the next with a rated light-heavy contender. Patterson was an awesome body puncher. I remember seeing him almost disembowel ex Aussie welterweight champ, Billy O'Donnell, with a sickening left rip to the guts. Billy sank to one knee. I was sitting ringside, and I could see in his eyes that he desperately wanted to get up, but Patterson had literally knocked the wind out of his sails. Lou set out to make my stomach Patterson-proof. During spars he ordered me to raise my arms to cover my face, leaving my lower half entirely exposed so my sparring partners could pound away at will. Come fight night, my guts was harder than Mike Tyson's dick at a beauty pageant.

Behind the scenes, the promoter, Frankie Hobbs, was doing everything he could to have my fight with Patterson stopped. Frankie was one of the real personalities of local boxing. He had thick, wavy hair, the colour and consistency of steel wool, and he was famous for taking street kids and turning them into skilled gladiators. He'd re-make them into whatever image he thought appropriate. He'd even change their names. Charkey, though no street kid, was actually an asthmatic named Dave Ballard. He was the epitome of Frankie's ideal boxer, dropping his hands low and delivering murderous left hooks from the floor.

Legend had it that Frankie sent the Chark to ballet lessons, believing that if a fight were close, the 'prettiest' fighter would get the nod. The Chark's brother was re-born Bricky Squire and, under Frankie's tutelage, he went on to become a rated lightweight. Limbo Nicky was missing a finger, and Bronco Hourigan was a tireless workhorse. There was a six-foot welterweight who lived in the gym and looked like he'd never seen the sun. He rattled into the ring as Rigor Mortice. When the master of ceremonies announced him over the microphone, he separated the words into two distinct entities, rolling the last 'r' on 'Rigor,' and clipping 'Mortice' short. I liked the fact that very few in the audience knew that Rigorrrr Mortice was a reference to the fighter's pasty pallor. It made me feel smarter than the rest of them. So sure, Frankie had a funny side, but he was a formidable opponent.

Frankie contacted the Australian Boxing Federation screaming 'mismatch'. He reckoned Patterson would knock me into a coma. The fact that I was the only Aussie to have lasted the distance with him, and that I'd beaten everyone else in the division, suggested that Frankie, like most trainer–promoters, had another agenda. Almost all my fights had been at South Sydney Leagues, where Frankie was the promoter. Lou, however, had arranged the title fight for Blacktown RSL. A strong home crowd was a guarantee of big takings at the gate. It must have really pissed Frankie off to miss the cream for a fight where your own boxer had been the champion, and where the number one contender had been nurtured at your own club.

By now it was September 1975, I was 22 years old, and I'd been fighting professionally on and off for five years. Despite Frankie doing his damnedest, the Australian Light Middleweight Title Fight was scheduled at a venue close to my heart: Blacktown RSL Club, official home of the returned soldiers. Whenever I walked into an RSL I couldn't help but think of Anzac Days with Saul.

Anzac Day had always been something of a dichotomy at Edward Street. It was a national holiday, when the old diggers paid respect to their fallen comrades. They squeezed into yesteryear's uniforms and army boots. They dusted off their ribbons and Akubras and buffed up their medals with brasso.

The day began with Dawn Service at the local RSL. Breakfast was a gutful of grog before boarding buses to Sydney for the big televised march. It was more of a shabby shuffle – the walking, wheeling, wheezing wounded on parade. Limping amputees, leftovers in wheelchairs, forgotten, forgetful, bitter old men who would be heroes, just for one day. We always knew that when Saul wobbled off for the Dawn Service, World War Three would erupt on his return. Anzac Day is 25 April. God help me, Anzac Day is also my birthday.

On fight night, I was preparing for my own war. I sat in the dressing room, reading and re-living every glorious Charkey Ramon victory. Old copies of *Fighter* magazine littered the floor. The Chark was my inspiration and reports of his demolition of champions the calibre of Aussie champ Paul Lovi, and Commonwealth title-holder Pat Dwyer, fuelled my resolve.

When I stepped into the ring that night and looked out over the crowd, I saw myself in every face. The drunken braggart, the bully, the greedy punter, the nervous young man, the dispassionate observer, the guy on the take, and the woman on the make. And fuck, I hated them all. I wanted to smash them all. Nor was I surprised to see Saul sitting at ringside. After all, he'd 'fed the Weaver bastard' for almost 20 years, and if there was any free piss or reflected glory to be had, he was entitled, eh. I had a fleeting image of my real father. It registered like a tiny stab to the heart, and I wondered if he'd ever know how far his first son had come.

Then the bell rang and the beast was unleashed. Ricky Patterson wasn't facing a man that night. He was in there with two decades of gale-force ferocity. This was my one and only chance to make a difference in my life, and I knew it. The whipping boy was about to snatch the whip handle and shove it right up the arse of every fucking bastard who'd ever given him grief. It was payback time.

Patterson didn't have a clue what hit him. The 'easy-beat', as I was called by nearly all pre-fight publicity which touted Patterson, took everything he threw and just kept on punching. In the third round, I floored Patterson with a cruel left hook. On the count of eight, he got up, grinning. But he wasn't happy. It was more a grim acknowledgement that he was in for more of a fight than he'd dared to expect.

In the fifth round he split my left eye like a peach. It was a bad cut and I had trouble seeing as blood streamed into my eye. Fight doctors home in like sharks when they smell blood. Sure enough, when the round was over, Dr Johns was in my corner, flapping about like an old sheila.

'Mmm. Not good,' he said. 'I'm sorry, but I may have to stop the fight.'

Lou was doing what he could to stem the flow, pinching the flaps of flesh together with his fingers and liberally applying vaseline as a coagulant. Through a veil of red, I looked the good doctor directly in the eye and I said calmly and deliberately, 'Doctor, you stop this fight and I promise you wholeheartedly and unreservedly that I will find out where you live, and I will fucking torture and kill you.'

The fight continued.

Fifteen three-minute rounds, two badly gashed eyes, a missing tooth and one smashed nose later (all mine) Jimmy Carruthers – a former Australian world bantamweight champion – raised my hand in victory.

Mum had given me a card before I climbed into the ring, with strict instructions not to read it till the fight was over. Even though my hands were shaking and I was bleeding like a stuck pig, I tore the envelope open the minute I got back to the dressing room. The card said, 'My dear son, Shane, I have never been so proud of you as I am at this moment.' Mum had given me this, even before the result was known; that meant more to me than all the other accolades to come.

The doctor stitched up my eyebrows without anaesthetic. 'You're high on adrenaline. You won't feel a thing,' he promised. He was right. Then we set off en masse for the Doonside Hotel. This was Lou's watering hole, and they'd sponsored me for the title fight – meaning they'd provided me with a faux satin gown emblazoned with their name, and agreed to open up after hours and put on free piss and nibbles if I wore it and won.

What a night. Blacktown had its first-ever Australian boxing champion and everyone wanted a piece. Over 100 people crammed into the front bar – the mob from Eddie Raye's gym, 'Sugar' Ray Wheatley, Todd, my school mates, neighbours, Mum, Jimmy, Charlene, her parents, a few of my teachers, the guys from the gym and plenty of people I never knew from a bar of soap. I even spotted Saul there, chewing the fat with some RSL mates and saying how he always knew I had it in me. I let him stay. Somehow it was important to me that he saw my victory celebrated. I was still starving for the bastard's approval. Ricky and his entourage declined our offer to join us. I understood.

At one stage the cops crashed the party to see what the after-hours trading was all about. After a quick huddle with Lou and the publican, followed by a phone call, another paddy wagon pulled up and all the boys in blue stayed on drinking piss into the wee hours. The party raged all night. Most people didn't stop drinking until well after the sun came up the next day. Shit, I was still getting stuck in three decades later.

I was going to make a fortune out of boxing. I was going to fight for the Commonwealth title. I was going to be the champion of the world. Yeah, in my dreams. Instead, I stopped training and the celebration raged, day in, day out, until I no longer even remembered what the party was for.

I left my job selling insurance at Temperance & General and was unemployed until need forced me to get a job in a factory. Charlene and I got by on fight money, drug money, dole money, and any money I was able to rip off from anywhere at all. Every day I woke up pissed to the eyeballs and every night I fell asleep pissed to the eyeballs.

I was drunk so often that I'd developed the ability to fall asleep on my feet, and even though I was non compos mentis, I continued to walk and talk in the world of the awake and aware. People would regale me with horrifying accounts of creatures I'd thumped or humped and it was always news to me. Bleeding knuckles, empty pockets, gore-spattered clothing, love bites in the weirdest places and the occasional chafed dick gave credence to their claims.

Even by my standards, I was especially crazy at this time. My favourite word was 'misanthrope', and it summed me up to a T. I hated people, both as a species and on a personal level. I had this little game I played in my head for my own amusement. I particularly liked applying it to crowds. When I saw people pouring out of the railway station en masse, or queuing for the footy or the pictures looking so respectable and civilised, I'd imagine a colossal boulder of shit moulded from the collective skid marks scraped from their underwear.

Years later, watching *Raiders of the Lost Ark*, I couldn't help but smile at that memorable scene where the hero is running from a monumental marble of granite that's thundering after him. In a flashback, I could see all humanity crushed under a gargantuan bowling ball built from its own excrement.

# ROUND 13

IF FEDERATION AND GOTHIC Architecture had banged and had a baby, it would have been the Robin Hood Hotel. It squatted like it was about to take a dump in the main street over the road from Blacktown Railway Station. It was a brick-red gargoyle on steroids, smack-bang in the dead heart of town. The stench of stale beer and the cloying disinfectant stink of industrial cleaners combined to set off the gag reflex from 100 yards away. In this regard, the Hood was probably the most honest establishment in Blacktown.

At one end, the brain-dead and dying gathered in the Saloon Bar, where memories and middies were the order of the day. At the other, the wasted generation met in the Public Bar, sculling schooners and spilling over onto the steps. On really hot days, when the place was packed, we overflowed like boiling lava out onto the footpath. The bottle shop sat like an uneasy truce in the middle. The Lounge Bar (a misnomer) cowered around the back of the pub and was only accessible via the alley. The pool tables and dartboards were there.

This was where you went to hear Tom 'of the hairy chest and tight, dick-focused daks' Jones crooning 'The Green, Green Grass of Home' on the jukebox, over and over, ad nauseam. Or if you fancied a meat pie, mash and peas counter lunch. Or a suck on the bean off a toothless pensioner who'd swallow happily for a half-bourbon. Not my cup of tea, but I knew a few blokes who reckoned that the only difference between Samantha Stephens' mouth and that of any hag from the lounge was the head that surrounded it. 'Close your eyes and it's the sheila from *Bewitched*, man.'

Decent local women knew better than to even walk past the Hood. They crossed the road or took a detour. 'Blow-ins' walked by only once. The boys knew how to treat a lady. 'Pervin Mervin', for example, had perfected a line of patter including such gems as, 'Hey, gorgeous, I could suck ya shit to a point and stab meself to deff wiff it.' But Jacko really took the cake. His favourite party trick was sitting on the steps of the Hood with his knees parted and his body angled so passersby could see him front-on from about 50 yards off. He carefully removed the family jewels from his footy shorts, arranging the gear so it was fully exposed. And then he sat back, sipping his beer, seemingly oblivious to the hairy escapee.

But he knew what he was doing all right. He was tickled pink at the shocked double takes. Thrilled when mothers shielded their children's eyes and broke into a trot. The most excited I ever saw him, though, was when he told me about a 'hot, middle-aged slut' who pretended not to notice, but who cruised by five times. He reckoned he actually saw a wet patch form around the crotch of her jeans. 'Talk about wet, man, her pussy was droolin'. If you'd sat her down and dragged her round on her bum, she'd have left a snail trail, eh.'

And when the action outside was slow, then there was always the indoor entertainment. Like Guy Smith, or 'Smithy' to his mates. He was the personification of western suburbs charm. His old man ran a small farm out near Penrith, and he'd regale us with 'filfy fun on the farm' stories. 'All ridgy-didge, eh. No shit.' Here were two of his favourites.

'Ya look about for a poddy calf, eh. Now, poddy calves always 'ave snotty noses, eh. What ya do, eh, is ya stick ya frobbing dick up its leff nostril, eh, grab the bugger by the ears, and skull-fuck the fing. Hard. But the trick, eh, the trick is to have honey all round ya balls, coz then its tongue's coming out, eh, licking ya goolies while ya pumping.' And he thrust out his tongue and did a demented Gene Simmons on speed.

Or there was Smithy's legendary chook saga. I felt like chucking when I first heard it. 'You need a mate for this one, but it's worf it, eh. Ya get hold of a fair-sized chook. Ya grab it by its legs and ya work ya frobber right up into its arse, eh.' And he had an imaginary chook's leg in each hand, and he was humping the air and rotating his hips so you'd get the picture. 'But here's the best bit, eh. When ya just about to blow ya bolt, ya get ya mate to chop its 'ead off, eh. Coz in its def agony, its arse goes . . .' And as he spoke the punch line, Smithy repeatedly clenched his fist, showing you the tightening and relaxing of the hole where his thumb and pointer finger came together like a sphincter in extremis. And he cackled like a hen house gone crazy.

I had arrived. I was one of the boys. A party to the piss-ups, gang bangs and dope deals. Another fixture in the Hood. And I was about as happy as a puppy in the RSPCA when the little girl turns her back and focuses her attention and her laughter on the doggy in the next cage. It was all so shallow. No matter how stoned or pissed I got, when the effect wore off, I still had to confront 'me' and who I was, and I fucking loathed what I'd become.

Even my meteoric rise up the boxing ratings was tempered by reality. I was in the Hood one night, fairly well lubricated, when a skeletal, bald guy who looked as dangerous as a terminal cancer patient on last legs chemo bumped into me, spilling my beer. Normally I'd have snotted him on the spot, but this guy was such a dweeb I was prepared to let it pass. What I didn't expect was his reaction.

'Hey, you clumsy cunt,' he spat, 'lick that slop up or outside. Now!'

I was taken aback, but I wasn't even mildly angry as I gestured to the door and led the way to the car park. It was bad timing. Being around ten o'clock on a Monday night, it was dark, and none of my mates was around. I walked through the cars and over to the fence and turned to look at my antagonist, who was shaping up and swaying like a very silly cobra. I hit him with a fast left hook and he went down like a bag of shit. I wasn't interested in putting the boot in, and was actually in the process of helping him to his feet when the first one smacked me in the head. Looking up, I was surrounded by five fit bastards who weren't there by accident. Obviously, the skinny one had been the bait.

'So you thought you'd give our little mate a serve, did ya?' Whack. Another king hit. And before I could move, each of them was taking it in turns to land bombs on my head. No body shots. These guys wanted me out cold on the ground. I leaned back against the fence and they went hell for leather until their arms were so tired they couldn't throw another punch. Fighting back was a lost cause. I simply focused on staying on my feet. I knew if I hit the deck, they'd kick the living shit out of me.

'Fuck, let's get out of here, Boo Boo,' one of them said, and suddenly they were gone. My head was on fire and I leaned against that fence for what seemed like hours till I managed to make my way to the cab stand and get a taxi home. Blacktown cabbies were accustomed to taking passengers who looked like they'd be more comfortable in an ambulance. The next morning, my head was a swollen purple melon. I had a main event lined up in two weeks, but when Lou saw the damage, he cancelled. So the bastards had cost me money.

All I had to go on was the name I heard one of them use: 'Boo Boo'. A few weeks later, after my head was in better shape, and with Todd as my backup, I started to search for him. As it turned out, he was a house painter and he drank in the lounge of the Hood or the Stockade Hotel in Seven Hills. We found him in the Hood on a Thursday night, playing pool. He denied any knowledge of the incident, but his scabby knuckles gave the game away. That and the fact that there was only one dude in that part of the known universe nicknamed Boo Boo. I told him what was going to happen.

'My name is Shane Patrick. I'm a pro fighter. You and your mates fucked up my paycheque when you fucked up my face. This is Todd. He has only one job here – to make sure it's just you and me. Now, we're going outside and I'm going to smash you until you give me the names of your four mates, and 25 dollars cash. That's your part of the dough I would've earned fighting.'

We escorted him outside. His knees buckled and we had to sort of sling him along. It was like leading a condemned man to the gallows. It felt good. Todd kept an eye on the crowd that followed. And I commenced delivering series after series of vicious combinations to Boo Boo's body and head. Whenever he hit the dirt, I grabbed his hair and yanked him up again. He was no hero without his mates. The third time I got him to his feet, he was holding his wallet. He gave up the 25 bucks and the names of his mates so fast I felt obliged to splatter his nose with a final big punch, just on principle.

Over the next two weeks we tracked down three of Boo Boo's mates and broke a few teeth, collecting 75 bucks on the way. The last bloke had apparently left town and was untraceable. I went back to Boo Boo, explaining why I figured it was fair that he pay the outstanding share and cop his mate's serve on his behalf. He agreed.

The *Blacktown Advocate* got wind of what happened (I think Lou had leaked the story) and ran an article called 'Patrick's revenge'. It was the usual local rag bullshit. A superficial, sanitised, sugar-coated travesty of the truth. There was a coy reference to me 'convincing' my attackers to 'compensate' me for the money their assault had cost me. There was no mention that the retribution had been as cold-blooded and merciless as the crime. It all contributed to my grossly distorted perception of myself. I was seeing the masked avenger, when in reality I was a thug with all the scruples of a shithouse rat.

I bought my first car with savings from my fight money. It was a light green, second-hand VW. It cost a few hundred bucks. I was into drink driving and road rage long before they were fashionable. Once, I was flying down Doonside Road, literally blind drunk, when some fool in a Holden made me brake by forcing the right of way. Sure, I let the prick go, because I had to, but I put my foot to the floor and rode his arse for a mile, until he did something completely unexpected — he slammed on the brakes. My heart leapt into my throat and I went into emergency-stop mode, flooring the brake and racing down the gears, screeching to a halt a bee's dick from the bastard's bumper. I sat there in shock for maybe 30 seconds. Then I got out of the car and walked slowly round to the driver's side.

The window was open and there was a middle-aged bloke sitting behind the wheel with what was probably his missus beside him. He looked like he was pissed, and she was a mousy little thing who looked like she'd probably die on the spot if you said 'Boo!' too loudly. 'Do you drive?' I asked the woman. She nodded yes. And I smacked the bloke in the head so hard it sounded like a watermelon squishing. I could still hear his woman screaming as I drove off.

Another time, my mate Jacko 'the Robin Hood flasher' and I were crawling down the main drag in Parramatta on his Norton 850. It was peak hour and some boofhead in a car had given us the finger because he believed we'd breached a rule of road etiquette. (Fuck, when you're in the saddle of a Norton 850, *you* make the rules.) His bravado was fired by the fact that his lane was moving and ours wasn't. He didn't expect to see me again. A red light put a stop to that theory. I jumped from the bike and he saw me coming in the rear-vision mirror. What he did next put the final nail in his coffin. He grinned at me like a cheeky monkey, clicked the locks on the doors and gave me the finger again.

I exploded. Tearing off my helmet and wielding it like a battering ram, I started smashing in the front windscreen of his vehicle. When he jumped out, one punch put him away. Everything else I did to his face was entirely gratuitous. Jacko yelled out for me to scarper, pointing to the other side of the shopping centre. A few well-intentioned citizens tried to detain me, but common sense and an instinct for self-preservation tempered their vigilante efforts, and I disappeared into the crowd with minimum interference.

My rage was taking over my life. It was terrifying that, at the slightest provocation, I could be engulfed in a blinding white heat where I would say and do things over which I had absolutely no control. Where once smoking grass used to calm me down, now it was just making me paranoid. Heroin was the only drug that dulled my temper and slowed my rage. I was spending more and more time smacked out of it.

I measured a hit by whether or not it made me spew. If I chucked, it was shit-hot shit! The preferred place to do the business was in someone's car round the back of the Hood. The cops had to turn off the main road and drive up the alley to get access, giving our lookouts plenty of time to sound the alert.

I got Todd or Jason or whoever was holding to do the honours because I couldn't cop the idea of whacking myself with a needle. If we didn't have a pick, we told the chemist next door to the pub that we needed a syringe to inject our greyhounds with vitamins. Greyhounds were called 'the poor man's racehorses', and hundreds of local families put their destinies on the backs of these skinny beasts. The chemist never asked questions, but the price of needles tripled overnight. To cut costs, we shared picks for weeks until they got so blunt it was like trying to stick a knitting needle into your vein. Between hits, we hid the needle in a tree or in a hole in the ground.

One Thursday night, I found a blood-spattered Jason in the Robin Hood car park, looking like he'd just finished a day's work at Riverstone Meatworks. He hadn't been able to find a vein and the needle was blunt as a fork. He was standing there with blood all over his shirt, his mouth was open and he was sobbing his heart out. Not from pain but from sheer frustration. His craving was killing him, and he was so close but so far away.

My sister Sarah's life was going the same way. Not from drugs, but from another craving just as strong – a craving for some sort of normalcy. God knows why, you'd think her own childhood would've taught her differently, but she seemed to equate happiness with a man and a family. There was a new man in her life and, like the father of her dead baby, Stephanie, his name was also Peter. Except that Peter number two was old enough to be her father. Instead, he fathered Sarah's second baby girl who she called Billie.

And I was even more surprised that, for the first few years of her life, Billie's home was 63 Edward Street, Blacktown. Sarah and the second Peter lived in a caravan in Saul's backyard. Why did she go back? Maybe the rent was cheap and they couldn't afford anything else. Maybe it was because Saul hadn't objected to her growing a few dope plants in among the tomatoes. Maybe this in itself was another 'up yours' act of defiance by a young girl who was committed to doing the last thing anyone would ever expect. She wasn't alone. I was about to do something unexpected myself.

# ROUND 14

ONE WAY OR ANOTHER, MOVIES have played a dramatic role in my life. My parents had seen the Western, *Shane*, starring Alan Ladd, in 1953, the year I was born. (It could have been worse. Had I come along 12 months later, I might've been Godzilla.)

The next big cinematic impact came in 1975, when I saw *One Flew Over the Cuckoo's Nest*, starring Jack Nicholson. It was about a lunatic asylum where chemical and physical restraints were poor substitutes for care and counselling. The stiff, white-uniformed Nurse Ratched personified the institution's dehumanisation of the inmates. I identified with these poor bastards like they were family. Indeed, in a way, they were. Mum had done her time in the cotton wool world of the institutions, and in the early days James was in as much as he was out. Shit, if I hadn't walked out of the whacko bin in Cairns, I might still be starting every day with 20 push-ups!

Apart from a natural empathy with society's exiles, I knew it was make or break time for me personally. My drunkenness and drug abuse were costing me more than money. The blackouts were becoming more common. My life was spiralling out of control and I thought focusing on helping others might help me snap out of it.

Finally, in 1980, five years after having seen the movie, I decided to become a nut-house nurse. Unlike Jack Nicholson's character, whose unhappy incarceration compelled him to try to buck the system from a position of weakness, I opted to save the loonies by working from the inside. Armed with the uniform and the magic keys, I would teach society's 'retreads' (as they were affectionately known by the nursing community) how to fly.

Ironically, or perhaps appropriately, my application for the job of nurse entailed an episode of self-mutilation. I was working as a machinist in a factory called Rondo Building Services at St Marys, and needed time off to apply for a position at Rydalmere Hospital. Worker's compo seemed the most convenient and cost-effective solution. My job involved feeding giant rolls of sheet metal into a machine that shaped them into gutters for houses. These monster-sized rolls could only be moved with a forklift. I 'accidentally-on-purpose' dropped one on my hand. I'd made my mind up earlier, and when the time was right, I went into what I call 'meat mode' – it's like suspended animation, where the body and the mind are disconnected and pain becomes so peripheral it barely registers. At least that's the theory.

The scream that followed wasn't staged. The thing literally weighed a ton and pulverised three fingers on my left hand like sausage rolls in a press. Two burly blokes struggled to lift the weight enough for me to slide my hand out, and I was rushed to Nepean Hospital. Three-and-a-half hours, an x-ray and one officially fucked hand later, I was at the Hood killing the pain with copious amounts of piss and laughing with the boys.

I did my interview at Rydalmere Hospital the next day. My stint at uni and my pugilistic past made me an ideal candidate. The required balance of brains and brawn. I got the job and began my internship as a nurse at Rydalmere Psychiatric Hospital. The hospital was split into two camps, one for the psychiatric patients, and the other for the mentally retarded, who were also, of course, disturbed. I was allotted the responsibility of tending to the needs of the latter group. Fast hands and a broken nose pre-qualified me for long stints in the locked or 'violent' wards, where two nurses were often left with up to 40 off-the-wall, head-rotating Linda Blair clones (we were encouraged to call them 'residents').

New interns were expected to hit the ground running. Training was comprised of on-the-job experience, with three-week study blocks and exams four times a year. What you learned in the classroom was not remotely related to life in the wards. For example, there were no lessons on flossing for faeces. And let me assure you, cleaning the teeth of people who eat their own shit is not an inspiring start to the day. The attrition rate among interns in the first few months was alarming.

I stayed three years. My substance abuse soared to dizzy new heights, and by now I had a second child, David, named after the baby Saul ripped away from Mum that night he thumped her in the kitchen. I was stoned so often, David's existence barely registered. I had once thought Blacktown was the drug university of the world. It was kindergarten. It wasn't uncommon for treatment nurses to pocket the residents' medication. Of course, no one gave much credence to a loony's claims that he'd been short-changed of his dose. That's in the unlikely event, of course, that a resident would be lucid enough to even notice, let alone get it together to file an official complaint. The nurses either used the medication themselves, or exchanged it on the black market for their drug of choice. Heroin abuse was as common as caffeine addiction, and just as easily appeased. While I had dabbled in smack before playing nurse, now I was a regular user. And my drinking topped up from deadly serious to downright suicidal.

My second daughter, Anna, was born in November 1981. I was 28. I barely noticed. I'd flitted back to 1972. Lou Reed's 'Take a walk on the wild side' had become my personal anthem, and I'd started wearing eye shadow and lipstick to the pubs. God help anyone who looked twice. Once, at the urinal, the guy next to me sneaked a sideways glance. I stopped midstream, knocked him out cold and finished my piss all over his face. There were a few other wannabees in the bog. No one said fucking boo.

I wasn't an overt cat (Blacktown-speak for gay), but there was a definite ambivalence to my sexuality that both excited and scared the fuck out of me. Wearing make-up was my concession to it; smashing anyone who stopped for a closer look was my rejection of any suggestion of a feminine side. Maybe I protested too much. Whatever, I was seriously fucked in the head. The unrelenting pace at Rydalmere Hospital fed the madness.

We worked rostered day and night shifts, seven nights straight from six until six. Although night duty was supposed to be followed by seven days off, the real money was in doing overtime. The place was always under-resourced and there was plenty to go round. Accordingly, nurses were never fully rested and everyone was strung out like trip wires and ticking like time bombs.

The odd working hours alienated us from the rest of the community; it's difficult meeting 'normal' people when you're at the human zoo every waking moment. Nor did our cynical perception of the human race, influenced, as it was, by the people in our supposed care, endear us to others. Most of us, of course, were sick puppies, seeking treatment vicariously. We worked together and we played together. 'Play' equated to baiting the retreads or 'getting out of it'. There was no joy for me in making the residents' lives more miserable, but I did find consolation in the other distractions.

Monday mornings after night duty, a noose of nurses would circle the bar at Dorrie's early-opener, a grubby little boozer opposite Parramatta Railway Station, several stops from Blacktown on the Western line. Ironically, it was also the establishment favoured by many of the out-patients we counselled. Nurses, easily identified by their white shirts (blue for interns) and prodigious thirst, would congregate down one end, and the honest misfits down the other.

Around noon, blinking like a bat in the sunlight, I'd lurch out of Dorrie's, dare-devil across the road and pour myself into a Blacktown-bound train for the 20-minute ride home. Invariably, I'd awake several hours later. I'd have blacked out and travelled to the end of the line at Penrith and all the way back to Central, over and over. It was terrifying, my consciousness crawling out of a coma, wondering who and where the fuck I was. Usually, I'd have pissed myself. My fellow passengers would either pretend I wasn't there, or regard me as one would a fresh dog's turd on the seat. At Blacktown station, I'd career over to the Hood and join the boys on the dole. Later, I'd go home to Charlene and the kids and when I'd open my mouth, Saul would speak and the long night would begin.

I'd started at Rydalmere with the best of intentions. I really wanted to make a difference. I was driven in my studies, diligent in my duties. I did the dirty jobs with gusto. For instance, most nurses treated the residents' morning shower as a fast-track production line. One nurse washed and the other wiped. I often saw garden hoses (meant for cleaning the bathroom, not the patients) turned full force on shivering residents, naked and huddling like beasts in wild-eyed terror. My heart would break for them. And to my shame, when I was a junior-junior nurse, I did nothing. I wasn't able to speak out. I felt my intestines screw up into a tight, hard knot, and I heard Saul calling me a fucking gutless wonder. Even so, I tried to do what was right in my own way. As I attained a more senior status within what was a very hierarchical institution, I developed my own code of honour. I broke it only once, and on that day I resigned.

Before then, however, there were many memorable occasions. Like the day we never went to Taronga Park Zoo. I was working in Ward 30, the Medical Ward (even mad people get sick). The Sister gave my partner and I the keys to a hospital vehicle, three patients and orders to 'Take the guys to the zoo'. The pub was a more attractive proposition. I drove west, Hoodward bound.

Our crazy cargo comprised Sally Tibbs: senile dementia; Carolyn Watson: paranoid schizophrenia; and

Don Rickards: autism. They sat drugged and relatively docile in the back, but every now and then their lunacy broke through like a shard of sunshine crashing through the clouds. Ripples of inappropriate laughter, playing with themselves, or picking their noses and eating it with all the joyous self-abandon of five-year-olds.

To cover our arses, we devised an ingenious plan. Every time we saw a dog or a cat, we pointed excitedly out the window, screaming, 'Oooh, a lion', or 'Wow, an elephant'. We made noises mimicking beasts of the jungle. It was a hoot. Our passengers were passionate disciples of the school of echolalia, and they repeated every sound. Before long, we'd whipped them up into a crescendo of dribbling anticipation. Then we pulled up at the Robin Hood car park.

While our clueless cargo sat in the vehicle with the windows up and the doors locked (there was no way they'd be able to work out how to escape), we hit the Hood and hopped into the piss big time. We charged our mates a schooner each to wander out to the car park and ogle the squawking, screeching, hissing crew in the back seat of the car.

I know such cavalier behaviour seems callous, but the truth is, it wasn't always grounded in barbarism. Often, it was more a defence mechanism. We were so badly trained and so inadequately staffed that we couldn't afford to care with all our hearts – because nothing breaks your heart more than becoming emotionally embroiled in a cause that cannot be won. This doesn't exonerate us, of course, but is cowardice not more palatable than cruelty?

A skinful, four hours and two packets of breath fresheners later, we pulled up back at the hospital. On the way, we repeated our animal antics to ensure the three musketeers were primed for a command performance. Members of senior staff were suitably impressed when they alighted from the vehicle, hooting and ululating like a menagerie. But life in the slow lane was not always so joyous ...

Discovering Pamela Smith's peculiar talent will stay with me forever. One night, an insistent mechanical squeaking led me, torch in hand, to one of the wards in the women's section. The stench stopped me like a brick wall at the door. Switching on the light, I saw Pamela sitting bolt upright in her bed, rocking rhythmically backwards and forwards. Her slack, slow mouth was dripping green shit. Her fingers and hands were putrid with blood and shit. Dollops of brownish green, blood-streaked shit were blobbed over the floor. The senior nurse later explained the phenomenon of 'manual evacuation' to me.

Apparently, Pamela was so repulsive that no one with half a brain would touch her. For that matter, even the other patients avoided her. She was starved for human contact. To her mind, even a punch in the head was better than nothing at all. It was as though pain validated her existence. Experience had taught her that soiling her clothes was a guaranteed attention-getter. But what if she felt like relating, and was unable to move her bowels. No problemo. Pamela simply inserted her hand into her anus and worked it up into her bowel, dragging out shit and smearing it everywhere. I had to clean up my own vomit before I got round to Pamela's mess.

Sunset proclaimed The Night of the Nurse. There was one senior supervisor for the entire hospital, and the nurses knew exactly where he or she was at any given moment. A ward-to-ward telephone relay monitored every step of their rounds. The night supervisor never arrived without everyone knowing well in advance. Mostly, night shift was spent getting stoned and pissed and watching TV or listening to music. Neglect was epidemic. Sometimes, however, the agenda was more sinister.

John Martin had Korsakoff's Psychosis. This is probably the worst fate that can befall an alcoholic. It's certainly more serious than death. Knowing I had a problem with the piss, I became something of an expert on Mr Martin's condition. Three symptoms clinched the diagnosis: peripheral neuritis ('pins and needles' in the extremities), short-term memory loss and confabulation (telling grandiose lies to make up for the memory loss: 'Last night? Why, I was helping the Prime Minister balance the budget'). Most alkies suffer from one or two of these. All three places them in Korsakoff's bin. The disease is dogged and degenerative.

Mr Martin had been reduced to little more than a breathing beanbag, immobile save for restricted movement in his left leg. When he was desperate to have a lighted cigarette stuck in his mouth, or distressed because he'd pissed or shat himself, he raised his left leg in protest and thumped it up and down repeatedly on the wooden floor. This was accompanied by an unnerving wail akin to that of a baby seal being bludgeoned with a club. It put your teeth on edge and it went on and on and on until Mr Martin's needs were met. Or other measures were taken.

Nurse Walker had a solution. Every night duty, he picked up Mr Martin and carried him like a withered old baby into the ward, tossing him onto his bed. Next, he divested Mr Martin of his pyjamas, before methodically sponging every inch of his pale, pathetic body with cold water. Then, the coup de grace. He threw open the windows to the icy wind of a Sydney winter. The last sound before the slamming door was the paper-thin screaming of a tortured seal. A few months after I left Rydalmere, I got a letter from a friend. She wrote that all was well and by the way, Mr Martin had passed away. The death certificate cited pneumonia.

A hospital is a microcosm of the world, and even in the midst of death, new beginnings were being made. At first, I wasn't sure whether it was love or lust, but whichever it was, it had cast a spell over Donald Smythe so powerful that he would literally put his body on the line. The first time I became aware of his nocturnal trysts, it was 2 a.m. I was at the night duty station, which comprised a chair and a desk situated strategically in the hall between the male and female wards. My nose was buried deep in the old record books. I was fascinated by the true-life stories of how these people came to be discarded and devoured by the system, forgotten and forsaken by the outside world.

Often, it was so unfair. For example, in the 1950s, some people with Down Syndrome, although not afflicted with any psychiatric disorder, ended up in the nut house simply because their parents had died or had grown too old to care for them. There was just nowhere else for them to go. If they weren't mad when they arrived, they certainly were after a few years. Often, their families visited in the early days, but even the most conscientious relatives dropped off after a year or two.

Engrossed in my reading, I didn't hear a sound, but I knew he was there. His hunger and his fear were so intense you could smell them, and I felt the searchlights of his eyes trained on me. As I looked up from my book, he was slinking past me, clinging fast like a shadow to the wall, stealing softly and fleet-footed in his slippers along the corridor. He'd already passed me when I'd noticed him, but his neck was twisted right round so one frantic eye kept me in focus. I sat still, watching him as he stopped short of the female ward and turned instead into the last male ward. I waited a few minutes, and then I followed him.

Throwing on the light switch, I saw that his pyjamas were lying on the floor by the bed of one of the more 'neuronally challenged' residents, Mr Jacobs. He was pressed up against his friend tighter than a limpet on a rock. Mr Jacobs had an IQ below 50, and he was oblivious to my presence and uncaring of the consequences of his situation. He was cooing like a baby and dribbling with joy.

Mr Smythe was much smarter. For him, there was no bliss in ignorance. Quite the opposite. Every night he took a calculated risk. If the night nurse happened to hate poofters, whether in the name of Jesus or just good old-fashioned homophobia, Mr Smythe had a good chance of getting a fat lip or even a full-on bashing (after which an Accident Report would be completed, designating another patient as the assailant).

As he hugged his purring partner, I couldn't help feeling that his arms were clasped around Mr Jacobs in an embrace of protection and devotion. It was more a longing for closeness and warmth than a consummation of lust. And the awful light in his unblinking eyes seemed to scream, 'Kill me if you want, but please, please don't hurt my best friend.' I was humbled by the ferocity and the purity of such love, and ashamed at my intrusion. I turned off the light and softly closed the door. I never followed Mr Smythe again. I never looked up from my reading as he stole past. But the terrible uncertainty of his sad ritual didn't allow him to take any kindness for granted, and I always knew he was watching me.

On the morning of my metamorphosis into Nurse Ratched, we lined up the residents of Ward 14 outside the bathroom. Their pyjamas were thrown in heaps on the floor. Their naked bodies were so desensitised to callous scrutiny that they'd forgotten the meaning of embarrassment, if ever they knew it. In single file they followed, one after the other, in an Auschwitz shuffle to the showers. Typically, this entailed a perfunctory cold-water spray with the hose and a cursory wipe with a towel. Depending on who was on duty, it sometimes meant fun and games with the garden hoses.

When you're dealing with bodies that have never been touched by toilet paper, nor observed any of the niceties of personal hygiene, either option is hardly an adequate response. Contrary to the custom, I waded in, paying particular attention to those nooks and crannies that demanded a more robust reception. The washers were hospital-white and, burrowing in (imagine an excremental version of Lady Macbeth), I scrubbed until the brown water ran white.

The night shift crew had obviously been shit-faced. You could always tell. The dirty linen bags, yellow for shit and blood, white for piss and garden-variety grubby, were empty. This meant none of the beds had been changed and we found the residents wallowing in their filth. The other dead giveaway was the residents' clothing room, which was a huge walk-in wardrobe. It was in immaculate order. Every item was folded and aligned in perfect piles under the respective owners' names. A sure sign of obsessive-compulsive, speed-induced behaviour. And then there was the 'silly shorts' incident.

Tony Tarantino was six feet tall with an IQ around 25. He was also cursed with elephantiasis of the penis, a sorry purple appendage that swung like a hairy saddlebag between his legs. One of the night nurses (a female, incidentally) had left a pair of tiny shorts out on the end of his bed. It would have taken major surgery for these to entrap the engorged genitalia of Mr Tarantino. Yet, God only knows how, my partner (another female) had somehow managed to squeeze him into them. He had to walk sideways, though, and he resembled a giant hirsute Sicilian crab, moving around the outdoor cage that we euphemistically called 'the yard'. I felt sorry for the poor bastard, and I made a mental note to dress him properly first chance I got.

A few residents stood out. Terry Smothers sat in a corner, hypnotised by the flight of his flapping fingers, open-mouthed, head turning like one of those ping-pong-gulping clowns at the fair. Roger Davies prowled the yard like a hyena, falling on cigarette butts, hapless ants, small stones and anything he could put in his mouth. He suffered from pica, a disease where sufferers eat inedible objects. We had a joke: Roger swallows! Periodically, his guts would balloon in protest, and they'd have to open him up and clean him out like a fish. We put boxing gloves on him so he couldn't rip out the stitches and disembowel himself before they healed.

It was hard to like Mr Davies. He'd been inside for two decades and he behaved more like a beast than a man. I once put my hand out to pat him, thinking I may be able to comfort him. But he reeled back in terror as though I was going to smash his face. Whenever anyone had ever reached out to him, it had been to thump him or snatch something from him before he could cram it into his mouth. It was soul-destroying being unable to offer hope because, no matter what you did, everything would turn to shit, literally, the minute you knocked off. Eventually, you move from fury to despair and then, God help us, to nothing. Because 'nothing' is the one place where you can't be hurt by the nagging reminder of your inadequacy.

The day I threw in the towel at Rydalmere started unspectacularly. Johnny Chinchwade was shuffling aimlessly around the yard. His shorts were pulled up way too high. I saw that his legs were wet and brown, as though he'd been wading in a river of mud, except the banks had obviously burst at the estuary of his arse. The flies were holding a corroboree on his shorts and hairy legs. As I frog-marched him to the bathroom, I swear I hadn't the slightest intention of harming him.

Chinch was a full-force, off-his-face, moon-howling, pop-eyed psychotic. His madness manifested itself in a particularly bizarre and ritualistic behaviour. He would suddenly become agitated and point at an apparition on the floor, shaking his body and head so vigorously his jowls wobbled, proclaiming in a deep and horrified baritone, 'There it is, a dead horse. There it is, a rotten apple.' I once asked a senior nurse why he said that and she looked at me like it was the most inane question she'd ever heard. 'Because he sees a horse's head and a rotten apple, Weaver. Why else?'

I kneeled and began gingerly peeling off his filthy shorts. And at that precise moment as I was crouched in front of him, trying to get him to step out of them, Chinch went into his 'horse's head' routine. As he did so, his shirt, soaked in filth, flicked around and splashed a dribble of shit across my face. I didn't think. It was pure reflex. I rose from the floor, winding up a giant uppercut on the way. It landed like a grenade on his head. Chinch lifted and crashed backwards, lying on his back, a trickle of blood coming from his nose, mouth and one ear. He didn't so much as twitch. I panicked and went to find the treatment nurse. An Asian male, who I didn't know personally, took one look at the crumpled Mr Chinchwade and suggested I take an early lunch.

I was sitting under a tree on the sports field toking on a calming joint when two nurses came to say I was required in Sister Schultz's office – 'Immediately'. The Sister knew me well. I'd been slaving in Ward 14 for eight months straight, which was about three times longer than the usual stint in the 'bad behaviour' wards. 'Did you . . . ?' I was going to deny smacking Chinch, claiming that he must have slipped on the wet tiles. But I didn't. I admitted that I'd 'lost it'.

'No you didn't,' said the good Sister. 'Mr Chinchwade was assaulted by Mr Tarantino, and an accident report will be completed to that effect.' She did the paperwork. Chinch survived. I resigned.

All the time I was at Rydalmere Hospital, the smell of shit stayed with me. Despite the most thorough purging with Hibiclens, hospital-strength liquid soap, I was never able to expunge the stench from my hands and it malingered, subtle but distinct, like faecal fragrance. It is with me still. Today, I am gripped by a Howard Hughes obsession when it comes to washing my hands. A TV program I saw around a decade ago exacerbated this. A team of medical students took swabs from everyday surfaces like lift buttons and door handles and seats on public transport. The cultures they grew from these harboured every disease short of the Bubonic Plague.

You can tell very quickly if someone has worked with me – my passion for cleanliness is virulent, and colleagues press the buttons on lifts with their knuckles or with a newspaper, ensuring that the ingestion of lunch will be as germ-free as possible in this dirty, dirty world. Back then, however, I was unable to see the filth that lurked much closer to home.

Like many drunks, I looked everywhere but in the mirror for the reason my life had turned to shit. I blamed Saul, I blamed Charlene and I blamed Blacktown. I even blamed God. But He was about to have a word with me in a most surprising way, in a most unexpected place.

# ROUND 15

I MET JESUS IN THE TOILET at the Beaconsfield Tavern in Western Australia. I was down on my knees, barfing a confession into the bowl and dribbling, God help me, down the front of my T-shirt. When I staggered out, I must have looked like death warmed up. The barmaid declined to serve me another drink and I schlurred a pointed suggestion about what she could do with a shhhcooner glassh. The manager suggested I leave. I disagreed and he had me escorted outside. Getting up, the first thing I saw was the blue light in the doctor's surgery directly over the road. It was a beacon for a ship leaving a sinking rat. A visit to that doctor the next day would save my life.

Western Australia is a bloody long way from Blacktown. That was the attraction. As well as the fact that, if I'd stayed, a consortium of smackheads had threatened to blow my brains out. I'd developed a habit of standing over their dealers and confiscating their dope. It was easy. I'd ask them if they were holding. We'd disappear into the pub shithouse or the car park to do the business and they'd hand over a sachet for me to inspect. I'd take out my wallet for reassurance, saying I wanted six or seven. I'd always smile. When they produced them, I'd simply pocket the lot, thanking my benefactors and announcing that this shit now had a new owner.

Being a fair man, I'd then give them the option of either fighting me, or taking a bag back for themselves. I was never angry. I never once raised my voice. They could tell that I honestly didn't give a fuck one way or the other. I'd explain that they could always pocket a bag and tell their boss that Shane Patrick had ripped off the lot. These guys were hard-core users, smacked-out-of-their-head space cadets and incapable of fighting their way out of a wet paper bag. Invariably, they'd choose option 'B'. Once, however, a skinny doper with a misplaced sense of integrity surprised me by getting me in a headlock. I picked him up and smashed him face-first into the asphalt before kicking the living shit out of him. Around this time, informed rumour suggested I should leave town. Fast.

My last night in Blacktown was a fitting conclusion to my last 30 years there. I invited a melee of mates over for a barbie and a piss-up. Word had spread, and over and beyond the official invitees, there was a squalid squall of blow-ins. It was raucous, but my mad-dog reputation and the presence of a big boxing contingent kept the lid on any serious trouble. Still, an undercurrent of hostility crackled like electricity.

It was winter and bitterly cold. When the firewood ran out, we began dismantling furniture from inside the house. Kitchen table and chairs. Kids' toys. Even the vinyl lounge went up in a black, stinking pall. Rockhead, a drinking buddy from the Hood, did his nickname proud by head-butting wooden palings off the fence and feeding them to the flames. Bulldog and Smithy and a few semi-naked sheilas danced around the fire, whooping like red Indians. David Bowie wailed, 'Who'll love Aladdin Sane?' The neighbours never made a peep, and the cops, as usual, had better things to do. The fire raged and the dope-distorted night crept like a bad memory into the empty remorse of morning.

The fence was a toothless grin encircling the backyard. The fire smouldered and smoked like resentment that's spent but still unfulfilled. Bodies lay huddled and shivering under filthy washing that had been ripped from the clothesline. The neighbour's cocker spaniel was licking frozen spew from beside the beautiful face of Smithy's wasted girlfriend. Broken bottles, discarded cans and used needles were scattered around like landmines. I left the mess, the missus, and three tin lids aged seven, four and 18 months and headed off with my brother Kelly to a new beginning in Western Australia.

Given the history of mutual loathing between Kelly and myself, it's fair enough to wonder how I came to make this epiphanic journey in his company. It was expedient. Kelly had left New South Wales for the West a few years earlier and just happened to be in town on business at the same time it was prudent for me to be leaving. My new status as former boxing champion and local stand-over man had changed our relationship. There was no love lost, but maybe he could see how I might be useful in the future. As for me, the fastest way out was all that mattered.

There were four of us in his Mazda that morning: Kelly and his mate Jake; Kelly's woman, a tall, gangly, thin-lipped creature with all the personal charm of a praying mantis; and me. The day's *Sydney Morning Herald* featured the story of a gang of Blacktown youths who had stabbed a taxi driver to death and jumped all over the body 'to watch the blood spurt out'. This was typical of the mindless mayhem that marked time and motion in Blacktown.

On one hand, it was sheer relief to be leaving. But at the same time, it felt like emotional amputation to be leaving Charlene and the kids. Sure, Charlene and I had had our differences, to put it mildly, but I loved her and I adored my kids. Why didn't I ever show it? The pathetically inadequate truth is because I just didn't know how. The notion of a father kissing one of his children, for example, was alien to me. There were times I ached to put my arms around them and say, 'Hey, you know what, I love you,' but the gap between the thought and the action was too far for me to leap.

As the car screamed down the main street, I honestly believed the downward spiral of my life was ending. I had visions of a job and a home and a happy place where drink and drugs were superfluous. I genuinely believed that if I could just get away from Blacktown, everything would be okay. I was right, but first, I had further to fall. Much further.

Three thousand-odd kilometres and four days later, we pulled up at Kelly and Olive's modest rented home in suburban Victoria Park. Jake jumped into his car, which was parked in the driveway, and headed for his own home. After three days of living in each other's pockets, sharing farts and even the grumbling of our stomachs, no one said goodbye. I followed Kelly and Olive into the house.

It was like living in the jaws of a mousetrap. Olive disappeared to her government job in Perth every day, and Kelly spent his time locked indoors with the blinds drawn, pacing the house like he was waiting to walk the last mile. At the sound of every passing car, he peered through the blinds, his face pinched and ghastly, like a voyeur at a traffic accident.

He refused to be drawn on what was going down or who he was expecting. I had a fair idea, however. I didn't fancy staying for the conclusion. And yet, as I was to discover, sometimes conclusions have a way of imposing themselves on you.

It was one of the rare days when Kelly was out and I was in the house alone. There was a knock at the door. Upon answering it, I was confronted by an extremely agitated young man who promptly stuck a handgun in my face. I felt my knees buckle. He smashed the side of my head with the gun and he turned and left. It had all happened in less than 30 seconds. I stood transfixed for what seemed like ages, bleeding all over myself, before I had the presence of mind to close the door. My plans to find new digs took on a renewed sense of urgency.

Small world that it is, Charlene had a long-lost brother who lived in Beaconsfield, near Fremantle. Dave had been in a Boys' Home for 'uncontrollable' kids in England when his parents migrated to Australia. When he got out, he saved some money and followed his tribe over to Blackett, near Mt Druitt, about 15 minutes from Blacktown by car (doing 20 miles an hour over the speed limit). New South Wales didn't work out as he'd hoped, and Durable Dave hitched over to West Oz. The only family member he bothered to keep in touch with was his sister, Charlene.

I phoned Dave and he said he was in the process of moving from his place above a Salvation Army second-hand clothing shop. He'd found somewhere that wasn't alive with cockroaches and didn't leak. If I moved quickly, I could take over the lease. It was cheap, and the landlord didn't give a shit if the occupants were working, only that they paid their rent on time. It was handy to Fremantle dole office and, happy days, the Beaconsfield Tavern was right over the road. I was in hog heaven, and trotted in within the week.

It wasn't difficult to get on the dole in West Oz. I just turned up at Freo social security office and said I'd made the move from Sydney in a desperate attempt to find work. It was simply a matter of transferring my fortnightly application; my payments never missed a beat. The plan was that Charlene would bludge the dough from her old man and join me with the kids in a month or so.

It took just over six months. They were the loneliest and most agonising days of my life. I worried about how they were getting on. Could they pay the rent? Were they eating enough? And I was haunted by nightmares of Charlene hopping into bed with my mates. I had nightmares of her replacing me. She never had the phone on so I was unable to call her. I virtually leapt on the postman every day, sweating on a letter. They were few and far between. I am either blessed or cursed, depending on the context, with a vivid imagination. To block the porno movie playing in my head of my woman sucking and fucking everyone I'd ever worked with or been to school with or played footy against or boxed or even nodded at in the street, I killed the cognitive process with copious amounts of grog. I couldn't afford beer, and had taken to buying flagons of cheap wine. Luckily, while I used heroin I was never an addict, so not having the money to score didn't bother me.

Charlene, Talullah, David and Anna finally made the marathon journey on a Greyhound bus. By then, I was a dead man walking. I felt strangely disembodied, almost as though I were watching someone else's actions when in fact it was I who was going through the motions. My body (so the doctor had told me later) was unable to synthesise vitamin B, and my mouth had erupted in weeping sores. I was shitting through the eye of a needle and spewing blood. Eating wasn't on the menu and I had taken to begging in the streets to get drink money. I shook like palsy, my paranoia raged and I wanted to lie down and die.

When Charlene and the kids turned up, they had only the clothes on their backs. Thankfully, the Salvos' clothing bin outside was a continuous and free source of what we dubbed 'footpath fashion' – that is until the night of my most humiliating bust. I'd taken a wire coat hanger and twisted it into an instrument for hooking out clothes. Because the bin was relatively empty, and I'm relatively short, I had to jump up and insert my head and shoulders inside. My feet weren't touching the ground. I felt an aggressive tapping on my arse. I was legless, as usual, and when I finally extricated myself, I was holding an outsize pair of woman's knickers.

'Fremantle detectives, son. What exactly are you doing?'

'Er, I'm putting closthes in for the Shalvos, shir.'

'Oh yeah,' barked the biggest detective, baring his yellow teeth and pointing at the bent coat hanger. He stuck his head right in my face, so close I could taste the garlic on his breath. 'And what's *that* for? Poking 'em right in are ya, so no *cunt* can steal 'em?'

I told him about the missus and kids upstairs. He said they'd come up and check it out, and if I wasn't telling a porky, they wouldn't bust me. There was no furniture. A few boxes served as chairs and we were all sleeping on nests made from rags on the floor. We never even had a fridge and literally lived day to day.

'Jesus, son, we've got welfare places for people like you,' he said, shaking his head.

They left, but I knew he'd run a warrant check on me as soon as he got back to the station. I had warrants out in New South Wales for assault, thieving and skipping bail. A few days later, when they came back for me, I wasn't home. I was drying out.

Old Doc Nathan's prognosis was unequivocal. 'Stop drinking or you'll be dead within six months.' He told me about a place with a significantly higher than average success rate for rehabilitating 'last chance' alcoholics. He prescribed a minimum three months' stay. The next day, I sat drunk as a skunk on a bus bound for Bedfordale and a converted army barracks by the sea called Home of Peace.

Talk about misnomers. Home of Peace reeked of Rydalmere Hospital. Days at the Home were rigidly structured. Everyone had a job. I started out in the kitchen, peeling spuds for a month, before graduating to raking leaves and hosing the gardens. After a two-week probationary period during which you had to keep a waterproof on your bed and weren't allowed outside the front gate, you were permitted to walk into Bedfordale three times a week to top up your supplies of fags and Coke (as in cola!). These excursions were limited to one hour. On your return you could be randomly breathalysed or relieved of a urine sample. Any trace of dope or booze, and you were out on your ear. No questions asked. No how-do-you-do's. Ta-tah.

The residents at the Home were not as neuronally challenged as the crew at Rydalmere Psychiatric Hospital, but whatever intelligence they had was focused on self-destruction. Alf, however, was a few sandwiches short of a picnic. He hadn't been born that way, but sick of drinking himself to death, he'd opted for a faster exit. One plonk-drenched night he lay down on his back in the middle of a major highway and, staring up at the cold, unblinking stars, waited patiently for a truck to run over him. A big Mack obliged but failed to finish him off, instead breaking nearly every bone in his body. Now he moved like he was walking on eggshells and slobbered and gibbered about the steel plate that held his head together. 'Lithsen,' he'd scream, rapping his head like he was knocking on a door. Poor bastard, no one was home. 'Wanna feel it?' There were no takers at the Home. We all had our own sore points.

Brian was 30 years old and a music teacher at a high school in Beverley. He didn't look like he had a problem with the booze. Good job, loving wife, two beautiful kids and an inexplicable urge to nuke the lot. The sly drunk, he played the piano at home with one hand, so his naïve wife thought he was practising, while he sculled piss with the other. Or he stretched out on his belly on the lawn, apparently sunbaking, but he was sucking Scotch up through a straw from a bottle of whisky buried in the ground. It took his wife ages to work out why, the more sunburned he got, the more off-his-face he became.

Ray had the face of a choirboy. He was 30, but he didn't look a day over 20. Thick, shoulder-length, sandy hair, and peaches and cream complexion. Ray's party trick was stealing his mother's wedding ring when she was taking a shower. The poor woman had spent a fortune redeeming it from hock shops. He was in the Home after being found guilty of smashing the window of a bridal shop while out of his skull on the piss. He told the judge that the mannequin had offered him a root in exchange for busting her out. He was given the option of returning to gaol, or doing his time at the Home. Ray's chocolate starfish still quivered and clenched tight whenever he recalled his last stint in boob; he chose the Home.

Reggie was on his fifth stay at the Home. He was around 35, six feet tall, fifteen-and-a-half stone, tattooed to the whites of his eyes, and while he didn't exactly drag his knuckles along the ground, he remains the most convincing argument I've ever seen for Darwin's theory of evolution. For Reggie, the Home was another place he scarpered to when the cops were closing in, or his wife was hunting him for maintenance, or he couldn't pay his rent, or he owed money to dope dealers or bookies. He went there to get his ducks in a row, pump weights and prepare for his next assault on the world. I only ever heard Reggie share his story once. I'll never forget it.

He stood awkwardly at the front of the group. 'Ah, my name's Reg,' he faltered, 'and I'm an alcoholic.' He looked straight ahead, but he didn't meet anyone's gaze. It was like he was talking to someone at the back of the room who no one else could see. It was painful watching the search for the right words start as a tremble at his lips and travel like a cloud all around his face before he opened his mouth. He spoke slowly and the sounds broke like odd-shaped objects thawing from ice. He said his father had made him take it up the arse when he was a kid. Sometimes, to make him buck harder, his father stubbed out fags on his back while he was doing him.

He couldn't tell his mum because she was drunk all the time. His giant shoulders heaved as he spoke, but he somehow kept the storm inside. No one so much as coughed (amazing in an AA meeting, where fags and coffee are the currency of conversation). Suddenly, big Reggie didn't look so mean.

Luke was my best mate at the Home. Thirty years older than me, he had spent most of his life working like a beast in the mines. He was currently a chef at a city hotel, but more of the cooking wine was going down his throat than into the stew, and his bosses had suggested he take a few months off to dry out. Luke was well read and had a teacher's spirit. He taught me how 'stinkin' thinkin' leads to drinkin' '. He had a soft, Welsh, sing-song lilt to his voice and it wasn't easy to fish the meaning out of his thick accent. He spent hours with me. He taught me that willpower is alcohol soluble. In retrospect, Saint Luke, as I called him, was the original bumper sticker philosopher, but at that stage of my life's journey, I figure I was blessed to be riding his tail-lights.

AA meetings at the Home were compulsory. And they were sobering. On one hand, it was like attending an autopsy – an insight into the bloated underbelly of lives gone rotten. The old-timers knew that 'new boys', like me, might hear the stories and be tempted to think, 'Geez, I'm not so bad after all. At least I haven't done *that*.' They'd look at you reproachfully and say, 'Yeah, kid, you haven't done that. *Yet.*' In their lexicon, 'yet' was an acronym for, '*You're Eligible Too*'.

On the other hand, it was empowering to see how some people had managed to crawl out of the shit. 'The only difference between a rut and a grave is the depth,' Luke said. We were all born again, but not necessarily in the hallelujah Christian sense. Sure, the AA program was unashamedly spiritual in so far as disciples had to acknowledge a 'Higher Power'. There was, however, flexibility. Ted, for example, took as his Higher Power a suburban bus, 'Because it can go past a pub while I can't.'

I needed more than public transport to take me to the Promised Land. I found a copy of the Gideon's Bible in my bedside bureau and started reading. It struck me that my presence at the Home was not accidental. Luke had told me that nothing happens by accident. He said FATE was best understood as an acronym for 'From All Thoughts Everywhere'. I realised that Jesus had heard my cry that night in the Beaconsfield Tavern and had delivered me to this converted army barracks. Luke explained what I was feeling by saying that inside every man was a God-shaped vacuum. I was about to get drunk on the Holy Spirit.

Hand in hand with my Bible study, I embarked on the 12 steps of recovery that underpin the AA program. For me, the Fifth Step was cathartic. It is described in the manual *Twelve Steps and Twelve Traditions* as 'Admitting to God, to ourselves, and to another human being the exact nature of our wrongs'. I ascended the Fifth Step in the Home's modest library. My confessor was an ordained minister of the Methodist Church. It was not mandatory to have a 'man of the cloth' – a garbage man would do the trick. But given my unequivocal choice of the Christian God as my 'Higher Power', the minister seemed more appropriate.

The hour I spent with him felt like something between an exorcism and an emetic. I left the room merged, purged and forgiven. Hallelujah Jesus! One month later I was reunited with my family on top of the Salvation Army second-hand shop, on top of my drinking problem, on top of Charlene, and on top of the world. And God 'Who helps those who help themselves' went to work for me.

The first day out, I bought a copy of *The West Australian* newspaper and began job hunting. I was happy to do anything. One ad leapt out, grabbed me by the throat, and shook me until I rattled. 'Wanted. Dog's body, 19 years or younger, desperate to become a copywriter.' I stayed up all night, handwriting this letter.

*In reference to your advertisement for an apprentice copywriter (*The West Australian, 9.6.84*), which of these gentlemen would you employ?*

*a) 'Canna Sinee Draf' \*. Fish lips slimy with the mucous muck of too many White Ox cigarettes regurgitate the words sloppily. A scud of spittle, anchored to the gunk on his mouth bridges the gap between his parted lips and creates the illusion of preventing the unshaved jaw dropping to the bar room floor.*

\* *A can of Sydney Draught, if you please, thank you, bartender.*

*He has the dishevelled appearance of a discarded
marionette, exhumed from some ancient vaudeville
trunk, imbued with supernatural power, and
operating gawkily without the strings. Glazed eyes
focus on an alien reality. In the vague, blowfly buzz
of his cerebral cortex, a thousand resentments fester
and putrefy. The seething acrimony of his psyche is
not apparent in the blank of his bloodless face.
A hand, as though disembodied, jerks towards the
can, knuckles whiten, hinting at the nightmare this
kitchen commando's family will endure when he
reels home at last.*

*In the cold twilight of early morning a baby
screams, startled from slumber by violent argument.
There is no asylum in sleep for his wife, only the
waking sleep of the combat soldier, the clammy-sweat
sleep of the condemned. The dread deep in her guts
has wriggled up into her throat like a fleshy gourd.
The grotesque parody of a person does not hear her
dry retching above the obscene torrent of his abuse.*

*b) 'Christ! I reckon he's got muscles in his shit.'*

*The southpaw had just launched another
portside torpedo to his opponent's midriff. After ten
rounds of fierce body punches, an angry contusion
bloomed on Patrick's belly. The audience grimaced
and winced in vicarious pain as he absorbed the
blows. Absorbed them and retaliated with
mounting ferocity.*

*It had been anticipated that Shane Patrick would
put up a gallant display, but all the money was on
the southpaw sensation who habitually dispatched*

*opponents with a fusillade of crippling belts to the breadbasket.*

*The fight crowd was a wild beast whose sentiments had run the range from disbelief to dismay and, finally, to a grudging respect for the underdog's tenacity.*

*Patrick was oblivious to the cries of the beast, unmindful of the claret that trickled from a gash over his left eyebrow, impairing his vision. He had trained like a Spartan for six months, running seven miles every day, travelling anywhere to engage suitable sparring partners. He had read somewhere that Cassius Clay had abstained from sexual intercourse before a bout. If it was good enough for Clay ...*

*The referee, Jimmy Carruthers, had told him 'If you don't do anything silly, you've got it!' Five more rounds between him and an Australian title. Pain was a luxury he could not afford. Compassion a frill no boxer could wear. He was a robot, greased with liniment and programmed to destroy.*

*When the final bell sounded the end of hostilities, Patrick knew he'd won even before the referee raised his arm. He saw the anguish of defeat screaming in his opponent's eyes.*

*His head throbbed, an insistent tom-tom in the echo chamber of his skull. His hands ached as though he'd just done a 'Rocky' on a full side of beef (except it was human beef he'd pummelled).*

*The tears in Patrick's eyes were more than just a mixture of pain and exhilaration. In a flash of cognisance as disquieting as revelation, he realised that nobody had won.*

*c) I feel more like a gaoler with this great bunch of keys on my belt. They can hear me coming from a hundred yards away. A curried egg sandwich for lunch and I wish I hadn't as I cop a whiff of the day-room.*

*You can intellectualise the situation when you're away from them. You can say things like, 'I don't understand how our civilised society can maintain human life at this level. It's immoral.' But when you're with them, it's difficult to maintain the defence mechanisms. You want to cry or puke, comfort or kick. Sometimes you laugh, but too often, it's a bitter laugh.*

*Julie Wilson has on a daffodil-yellow dress. She's staring at her reflection in the window pane, lamenting the death of the little girl trapped within those big bovine eyes. Mesmerised by the funeral in the mirror.*

*'Why does the window pane haunt me, nurse?'*

*The daffodil screams. Blood knuckles smash the naughty little girl in the window pane. Poor Julie.*

*Terry Smothers is fascinated by his flapping fingers and his blind gaze follows their frantic flight. Terry has chronic rhinitis and as he giggles a green snake of snot disappears and reemerges from his nostril. Informed rumour designates him as a carrier of Hepatitis B. I pretend I don't even see him to avoid cleaning him up.*

*Henry Tonkin bounces around the ward. He is a manic, human pogo stick. The piercing scream accompanying this exercise grates your teeth on edge. If any of the male nurses were in this room alone with him, I reckon an Accident Form would need to be filled out. Maybe even one of the sheilas would thump him if he wasn't so volatile.*

*Jenny Hunter is an obscene Buddha squatting on the floor, waiting stoically for that excremental process which will present her with afternoon tea. 'Down Syndrome' patients squat because they often have congenital respiratory defects, and this posture facilitates breathing. Jenny just figures she may as well eat while she's there.*

*Ultimately, I think a reasonable person adopts a philosophical attitude, almost of sufferance. He decides that, right or wrong, these people are here, and it is his responsibility to keep them comfortable. After all, it is the system that dehumanises them. No toilet paper in the bathrooms, colour uncoordinated and tasteless clothing, inadequate staffing.*

*Yeah, but there are limits. I mean, could you really expect anyone to give mouth-to-mouth to Jenny if she choked on her afternoon tea?*

*Dear Sir, it is unlikely that any of these 'gentlemen' fulfil the criteria for the advertised position. Who would employ a slovenly drunk? The boxer has probably lost more neurons than he has left, and a mental retardation nurse is a glorified shit-sweeper.*

*No one in their right mind would employ any one of them. A perceptive personnel officer, representing the best interests of an advertising agency, however, would smack his lips at an articulate composite of all three.*

*A copywriter must empathise with the people to whom he is directing his ideas. The more people he is able to relate to, the broader his capacity for communication.*

*It is not casually, sir, that I confess to being each of the people depicted. Are we not still stuck with a drunk, an ex pug and a shit-sweeper?*

*Were this the case, I would not waste your time.*

*Yes. I am each of these people. I am, and yet I am none of them. Each represents a facet of my development, an evolutionary phase.*

*I am an alcoholic, but I am not drunk this day. Nor have I imbibed since the full import of this disease, and a solution, became known to me. My alcoholism was a symptom of a more insidious disease: the malaise of my personality. Alcohol stripped away the tenuous veneer of civility and the character defects glared like beacons.*

*I am no longer spiritually impoverished. God is with me. My family has remained loyal despite the trauma of the past.*

*'The past is another country, they do things differently there.'*

*While my canonisation is not imminent, I am a better person.*

*The boxer wasn't a bad bloke. He was a battler, really. To supplement a Teachers' Scholarship, he donned the gloves around the clubs at night. Accidentally, he became the light middleweight champion of Australia.*

*The battler was unprepared for success – I handled it immaturely. One spot on the* Won Casey *show and I was a celebrity. Everyone wanted to buy the champ a drink. The champ was a chump who couldn't say 'No'.*

*The mental retardation nurse was a victim as much as the patients. I'd seen* One Flew Over the Cuckoo's Nest *and, incensed by the brutality, I elected to 'crack a job in a nut house and stop this shit'.*

*Three years taught me how immutable the system is (I suppose it's because people still maintain a strong link with their primeval ancestry. The savagery is just below the surface).*

*Let us not omit perhaps the most salient consideration, sir. The drunk, the nurse and the boxer could all write. Each was endowed with a certain sensitivity. To be sure, it extended from morbidity to the sublime, but it was always a creative sensitivity.*

*Words are the most common currency we use. I weigh each one before I spend it. It is the habit of a lifetime. It is not a belaboured process.*

*Lately, sir, something has been happening which, in all fairness to myself, I must mention. Complete strangers will accost me in the street with cries of, 'Hey, dog's body!'*

*Now, I'm not particularly hirsute, sir. Nor do I physically resemble, as far as I am aware, any of the canine species. I do have this aura about me, however, this psychic emanation, which seems to suggest a dog's body.*

*In the light of the wording employed in your advertisement, sir, I find this quite remarkable. So significant, in fact, that it must surely mitigate the matter of my age. I am 31 years old.*

*The last decade has been spent gleaning the experience and honing the skills to qualify me for the very position advertised. The insight of the rehabilitated alcoholic, the fierce tenacity of the pugilist, the sad knowledge of the nurse – each of these qualities married in eloquence to a creative sensitivity.*

*I will compound my presumption, sir, and say, unequivocally, we need each other. In anticipation of your reply, I remain,*

*Yours faithfully,
S Weaver*

I was standing outside Fremantle post office when it opened the next morning. It was critical that the recipient know my letter had been penned overnight. They needed to see how quickly I responded under pressure. They had to be able to measure the magnitude of my hunger. Then I waited. Patiently, because I already knew the reply was preordained.

Sure enough, the telegram arrived four days later. We had no phone, and this was the fastest way to reach me. It was from the Creative Director of an international ad agency called McCann-Erickson. It was from a bloke named Gordon Dawson.

After talking with him for nearly two hours, he said he wanted to hire me. But he added a caveat. 'You scare the shit out of me,' he said. 'I want you to meet our key people. I want them to tell me I should hire you. That way, if you fuck up, I won't have to take the rap.'

After running a gauntlet of interviews, I got the job.

Shortly after I joined the agency, the senior writer at McCanns was promoted to Creative Director at the Adelaide office. He needed someone to rent his executive home in Gosnells. Four bedrooms, plush carpet, telephones times two – and a swimming pool! An in-ground swimming pool with a shallow end and a deep end for fucksake!

When we moved in, I discovered that not only was my landlord a Christian, but our next door neighbours were 'singing in the coliseum' zealots. A reformed alcoholic who was engaged in a personal relationship with Jesus must have seemed like a Godsend.

Faster than a death-row conversion, I became a regular at Kelmscott Church of Christ and eventually Charlene did too. I was living proof that God could snatch back from Satan even the most leprous example of paganism. Of course, being a Christian brings certain responsibilities – marriage for Charlene and me was no longer optional – it was mandatory.

# ROUND 16

'YOU DON'T SOUND LIKE MY Shane, dear. There's lots of cults out there. You do know that the devil sometimes comes as an angel of light, don't you, dear? I'm coming over to check that church out.'

Mum was mortified to hear that I'd been 'born again' and was marrying Charlene in the Kelmscott Church of Christ in a month's time. I'm not sure, however, whether it was my choice of the Bride of Christ or the Bride of Blackett that concerned her most. I sent the fare and she flew in a week before the wedding.

We met her at Perth International Airport. Mum looked smaller than her five feet. She strode towards us straight and pointed as a question, filled with the determination and sense of sanctimonious surety, which are the hallmarks of the cult-buster. 'Are you all right, dear?' she quizzed.

When I assured her I was fine, she reached out and touched me, running her fingers over my skin like she was reading an unspoken message in braille – some arcane meaning that my lips would not betray.

My mind shot back to a time in the Edward Street days when Mum was the resident white witch. She visited the homes of ladies who paid her in butter or milk or sometimes sausages or mince to discern their past, present and future in the bottoms of teacups. Swirling the residue around, she peered intently past the leafy detritus into the empty cups of their lives. 'I see a lot of pain,' she spoke softly, and they nodded sadly at this confirmation of everything that was already writ large in the lines on their faces as they reached for another fag. 'Oh my God,' she said, 'do you know someone with blonde hair? Not necessarily a natural blonde, mind you.' And in this, the era of Marilyn worship and dumbness by peroxide, Mum invariably struck a chord and the stage was set for vicarious scandals and virtual romances and sometimes a short, sexually explosive affair. Well worth a bottle of milk or some fatty mince.

'Come on, Mum, the car's this way,' I said, proud that we didn't need to take a bus or taxi. I wanted Mum to see how God had provided for us. Charlene and I had left the cockroaches above the Salvation Army far behind. Or so I thought.

As it turned out, we'd made a mistake of biblical proportions: we'd brought an old lounge we'd managed to rip off from the second-hand shop downstairs. (Our specialty was getting stuff that had been dumped outside on the footpath overnight, long before the ladies who kept shop began their morning's work.) Over the first few weeks, we noticed the odd cockroach or two, scuttling around our new home. We didn't really think that much about it. After all, it was nothing compared to the company of cockroaches we had kept in our Freo dump.

But as the weather warmed, the incidence of sightings escalated. And there was an alarming number of ebony 'babies'. When it got to the point that we couldn't walk around at night without scrunching the bastards, we alerted our neighbours. Fortuitously, Peter, the man of the house, was not a 'fisher of men' but a fisher of creepy-crawlies. He was a part-time pest exterminator.

He offered to fumigate our place for free. No one was prepared for what happened next. Using a machine that worked like a vacuum cleaner in reverse, he blasted a stream of noxious gases into the lounge room and we stood back and watched. Within seconds, a black plague of tiny, medium and monstrous cockroaches came gushing out of every crevice in our old lounge. The floodgates had opened and they literally poured forth in a tidal wave of filth. We fled outside in their wake, shocked at the magnitude of this cockroach calamity.

Apparently, we had transported the pests from Freo and our lounge had served as an incubator for a million eggs. As summer turned up the heat, the insects hatched and made themselves at home. When the gas had settled, we ventured back inside. The fawn carpet in the lounge was a twitching black blanket of dead and dying roaches. This dramatic purging was a prelude to the personal purification that was coming soon.

The Church of Christ preached baptism by total immersion, and I was duly plunged into the watery grave in a mini-pool in full view of a psalm-singing, hand-clapping congregation to arise resplendent in my bathers, cleansed and forgiven and born-again. I set out across the soul-bleached suburbs, eyes blazing like burning bushes, telling the story of my deliverance and imploring sinners to turn their backs on the father of lies and to turn to Jesus. My favourite hymn was 'Majesty' and I worshipped His Majesty daily and passionately without question or qualm.

The big day was set for 13 March 1985. It was a small wedding. Luke, my saint at the Home of Peace, was the best man. Ruth, our neighbour, was the bridesmaid. My colleague and landlord flew in from South Australia. Mum was a witness. Our three children, Talullah, David and Anna, were present. There were a few people from work, along with some close friends from Bible study. Pastor John Bond did the honours, and after the ceremony, we went to Gosnells Park for photos.

Someone knew someone who knew someone who was 'nearly professional', and they videotaped the *Charlene & Shane Show* for posterity. Ruth had tied a doll in a wedding dress onto the bonnet of the white Holden that served as our wedding car. When we went to get in after the ceremony, we saw that the wind had blown Barbie's dress up over her head and spread-eagled her legs. At the time I thought it was a cosmic reference to our wedding night.

We'd abstained from sex for months as a token of respect for God. Our union that evening was an exquisite embrace between trepidation and tenderness. As I eased myself into her, Charlene seemed so much tighter than before and I felt the coy grip of resistance before pushing through to the wet release of a warm welcome. I thought another miracle had restored her virginity. She told me later that one of the ladies at the Church had taught her some 'pelvic floor exercises'. Hallelujah! Praise the Lord!

Along with Richard, Beth and Sarah, who had come over to Western Australia in dribs and drabs, my brother, Tony, had also made the lemming-like march to Western Australia. Although we were a dysfunctional bunch and in a way all disconnected, we were also trapped in the web of our shared experience. I was determined to break free.

McCann-Erickson Advertising, even in the forgotten back pocket (some would say 'arsehole') of Perth, was a real eye-opener for a boy from Blacktown. The moment I stepped out of the lift, I felt like a five-year-old in Disneyland. There were wide-screen, colour TV sets embedded into the walls of the plush reception, and the agency's award-winning Coca-Cola commercials played over and over. There was a grand boardroom with a giant, polished wooden table where our most valued (and valuable) clients were feted and corporate destinies were decided over glasses of vintage wine ('Orange juice for me, please').

And the place was populated with gifted but decidedly strange people. Star Childe, for example, was born bat-shit boring Warren Wilson, but he had fallen under the spell of the Orange People and made the pilgrimage to India where the Bhagwan gave him a new moniker and mission in life. He chanted and burned incense in his office cubicle and floated around the agency, smiling like he could see something that was vaguely funny and invisible to everyone else. Later, when symptom substitution kicked in and I swapped thoughts of piss for pipes of pot, Star and I floated around, grinning in perfect harmony. While he was stoned on spiritual awareness, however, my nirvana came at $30 an ounce.

My career at McCann's lasted for 12 months. Once again, it didn't matter how far or how fast I ran, my drinking caught up with me.

It started again on the occasion of the McCann's Xmas do. It was a pool party and the Creative Director, Gordon, threw his home open to us. I don't know how I rationalised it to myself; most likely I figured I'd earned it, so I had a few cans. And then a few more, followed by . . . well, you know how it goes: 'The man took a drink, the drink took a drink, and then the drink took the man.'

When I saw Gordon at work the next week, he pulled me to one side. He wasn't a happy man. He said, 'I've met the monster.' Apparently I'd, metaphorically speaking, thank goodness, pissed on their pool party. I'd yanked the bikini top off one of the sheilas in the creative department, and grabbed her on the tit. When Gordon had suggested I desist, I threatened to 'Fuck his face up'.

When McCann's hired me, the deal had been that I would be paid the equivalent of the dole until I proved myself, after which time my wage would be reviewed. After a year, I approached Gordon and suggested the time had come. He referred me to the decision maker, an intellectual leprechaun, who, after the party, was unable to see any reason to change the status quo. I resigned on the spot amidst absolutely no protest whatsoever.

I started ringing around the same day. Demand for an unproven 30-plus junior copywriter with a puny portfolio, smashed nose and a history of alcoholism was scant. I began to re-evaluate my position. Maybe I'd acted hastily. This was no time for pride. I had mouths to feed. My second son, Bradley, had been born during my time at the agency. I phoned Gordon from a phone box in West

Perth and asked for my job back, but he'd already filled the gap. I'd understood no one was indispensable, but fuck, they'd managed to replace me in less than three hours!

It was getting late. I was tired, depressed and terrified that I might be en route back to the same rock I'd crawled out from under. Then I remembered a shingle I'd seen just around the corner proclaiming Woods Advertising. I'd never heard of them, but heck, they wouldn't have heard of me either. I figured I might as well have a go. I went in and the receptionist said that the Creative Director, John Woods, would see me.

I had a handful of what, in retrospect, were pretty pedestrian ads. He gave them a cursory once-over and asked if there was anything else. 'Only my original application to McCann's,' I said. He nodded. 'Read it to me.' I did. He listened without interruption, smiling and nodding occasionally. 'Start tomorrow at 8.30,' he said. 'We've got lots on.'

And they did. Letters. Lots of letters. I was churning out sometimes up to six direct-mail packs a day – communications sent out by banks, frequent-flyer programs, retail outlets and the like. I met a former accountant turned Account Director there named Greg Wallace. He introduced me to a book by Herschell Gordon Lewis, the man I consider the world's foremost direct-mail copywriter. His book, *The Art of Writing Copy*, became my bible. I learned the principles of my craft, as expounded by Herschell, verbatim. I copied his style until I developed my own. And, by all accounts, I became a handy direct-response copywriter in my own right.

John Woods, as it turned out, was one of the pioneers of direct marketing in Western Australia. Direct marketing was focused on results. It was accountable. At the end of the day, you were able to add up the coupons or the phone calls or the money in the till. And the practitioners of this no-nonsense style of marketing were less up-your-nose-with-a-rubber-hose than their 'Above-the-Line' counterparts. Words without wank. It was a philosophy that suited me right down to the ground. I was at home.

At least, I was at home when I was at work. The marital home was another story altogether. I was back on the piss and the pot and my paranoia was raging and soon the cracks in my relationship with Charlene turned into earthquakes and our world opened up and all of us, the kids and me and her, were swallowed up.

Ironically, a multinational ad agency named Ogilvy & Mather had seen some of my direct mail and offered me a senior writer's job, and my career was moving in the right direction at the same time I was moving out of the marital home. I set myself up in a poky, one-room flat in South Perth. It was so close to Perth Zoo, you could hear the cacophony of animals fucking, fighting and screaming and dreaming late into the night. I went through the motions, rolling into work half-cut every day and doodling death heads and skeletons in coitus on a sketch pad until I took an early lunch, heading into Freo, trawling the bars for strays and drugs and a drunken ear to drown in.

This was where I discovered Peter Capp's poetry readings. Peter was Fremantle's unofficial Poet Laureate, and the Pied Piper for the manic, the medicated and the morose. Every Wednesday night, we staggered into the West End Hotel like the zombies in *The Night of the Living Dead*. A few of us could actually write. Most of us just bled or ejaculated or vomited on paper. I started drinking at the Federal in the early afternoon and followed my misery to the West End in the evening, where I regaled the punters with hate-felt renditions of poetry snatched from the squalid cellar of my interior world. 'Double Bed' was a real crowd pleaser:

> *You gave me your Judas kiss*
> *Light and dry*
> *Saving your juices for the other guy*
> *But fuck, I don't hate you*
> *No, I need you instead*
> *Like a man needs a hole*
> *In his big double bed.*

I was a latter day Johnny Rotten. Iggy Pop with a beer belly. Cappy (as I came to know the MC) introduced me as 'The Vicar of Vitriol'. I spat my rancid rhymes into the audience. I spewed them out. I roared until my voice croaked. I punched my head for emphasis. The holocaust of my hate was so close you could feel its hot breath on your face. I attracted a faithful following of sickos. I wallowed in self-pity and piss and the applause of idiots and losers. And it was taking a toll. My liver was screaming. Sometimes the pain was so acute it dropped me in the street, clutching my side as though I'd been harpooned in the guts.

But with Charlene and me, love and hate had historically been cyclical phenomena. After six months, the blizzard thawed and we caught up on the occasional weekend. Sometimes, she'd even let me sleep with her. And whenever she did, I'd be worried sick that my dick failed to fuck with sufficient cavalier creativity to impress her.

Or that I came too early or too late. My clit consciousness was so intense that every hump became a frantic quest for the Holy Gristle. Ogilvy let me go the same week Charlene told me she was pregnant – hardly surprising given that I was spending more time at the pub than I was at work anyway, and even when I was at work I was wishing I was at the pub. My fifth and last child from my first marriage, Kimberley, was on the way.

And so we got back together again 'for the sake of the kids', but this time we were actually buying a home in Gosnells with what I'd managed to save. It was a historic occasion: I was the first ever Weaver boy to be buying his own home. It didn't last long. Soon after Kimberley was born, Charlene left me for a labourer she'd met through our neighbours. At her behest, I sold the house and gave her half the loot. I rented another apartment. At the same time, I was paying the rent for a house Charlene and the kids could call home. I know I sound like a madman. Well, I was. Mad enough to think we'd still get back together again. But I was about to fall in love with someone strong enough to stare down my madness.

# ROUND 17

I HAD MET KATE AT Ogilvy & Mather Advertising in Perth in 1990. She was the new girl who'd smiled at me whenever I stormed past her workstation. I've always been an 'eyes' man, and she had the most incredible aqua green eyes. They sparkled like sunshine dancing on the ocean and I got the distinct impression that there was a lot going on in there. It was like you could plunge right into them and swim to an underwater world of her thoughts. By the time I found out they were contact lenses, without which she was blind as a fruit bat, it was too late; I was already in too deep.

She told me about the first time she saw me. She had been scoffing her habitual sausage roll with sauce for breakfast in the cafe downstairs from our office when she spotted me walking by. Kate said that from that moment, she knew we would be together. She said that she could see I was 'a good man'. This was in flagrant contradiction to every murderous thought running through my mind at that time. She said she saw an 'indomitable strength' in me. Again, I was puzzled. I had felt raw and exposed like an open vein.

My own motives were more about dependency than devotion. I was separated from Charlene and living in the house we'd once rented together, sans furniture and kids. By now she'd moved in to her boyfriend's place, far too close by for comfort. I needed someone to get mindlessly drunk with, and Kate was there. I needed someone to slag off Charlene to, and Kate was there. I needed someone who cared enough to clean up my house when I was so shit-faced or depressed that even taking a shower was out of the question. I needed someone to lie out on the back lawn with me at night when I was brain-fucked and spinning and overwhelmed by how tiny my misery was against the backdrop of the Milky Way and the Southern Cross and the Great Bear and the vast, glittering conspiracy of infinity. I needed someone to lie with, period. It was all about me, me, me, and, God help me, so much of my life has been like that.

Kate didn't know what hit her. Sometimes I called her Charlene. Not because I was being a smart arse, but because I was so out of it she *was* Charlene. Once I bit her face like an animal and laughed while she screamed. (This was an alarming development; I'd never laid a hand on Charlene.) More than a few times, she woke up soaked because I'd pissed the bed. More often than I care to remember, I ordered her to get the fuck out of my life. And she steadfastly went nowhere. Kate loved me unconditionally and unreservedly at a time when there was no other way in the world anyone could possibly have loved me.

'You need me and I'm staying,' she said. 'Better get used to it.'

She had landed in Australia from England about six weeks before she started work at Ogilvy's. She was, it turned out, escaping a few ghosts of her own. She'd been embroiled in a relationship with a bloke who'd earned her parents' disapproval, and the situation was so tense that leaving for the other side of the world was a viable option. Kate didn't just get me on the rebound, I found her the same way; we were both boomerangs circling for an outstretched hand, although we'd begun our flights from vastly different places.

In the early days, Kate seemed as far removed from the centre of my experience as Buckingham Palace is from the Robin Hood Hotel. And yet, she stuck with me every gruesome step of the way. Almost every weekend, she left her flat in Mosman Park and drove out to my husk of a home in Gosnells. Kate would clean and cook and wash my clothes and drink and sleep with me, before leaving for her own place on Sunday evening.

Finally, it seemed like even the house – literally – had had a gutful of what was happening. When the toilet and sinks and just about every orifice began spewing shit and it seemed nothing would stem the tide, I sent an SOS out to my brother Richard. He came around and diagnosed a full to bursting septic tank that would cost around $350 to have emptied. By then, the yard was a brown-bomb minefield and the turds on the carpet had crawled as far up the hall as the lounge room. I upped stakes and scarpered to Kate's flat, owing two weeks' rent.

I was amazed at how compatible Kate and I were. Sometimes we had the same thoughts at the same time, everything from snatches of songs to shared feelings about people to what pub we'd go to for lunch. Which brings me to something else we had in common – a prodigious capacity for alcohol. To this day, Kate remains the only woman who could ever drink one-for-one with me. A dubious distinction indeed. The difference was that Kate knew when enough was enough, and simply went to bed and to sleep; I continued pouring grog down my throat until I blacked out. I woke up, dry retching, dehydrated, and racked with remorse, every jangled nerve screaming for a hair of the dog.

Living with Kate opened my eyes to how tough she is. Her flat was ten minutes' walk from the railway station in the nasty part of Mosman Park. Someone who'd been brought up as a cotton wool kid would have been eaten alive; this was barbed wire territory. In fact, the street she lived in had been called 'Battle Street', but the council changed the name because it was becoming a self-fulfilling prophecy.

The flats were populated with a mixed bag of tenants, from pot-smoking uni students, to hard-core smack freaks, part-time prostitutes, petty thieves, 'serious offenders' and even one or two respectable, if understandably low-profile, owner-residents. A few teenaged girls had disappeared from the neighbourhood around the time we were living there. One of them was discovered by a backhoe during excavations for a shop upgrade just down the road.

Kate hadn't chosen the place as much as it had chosen her. It was cheap. What Ogilvy & Mather paid her was barely enough to feed a budgie. Her staple diet was curried chicken and 'spag bog'. She had three changes of clothes, one pair of shoes and she had to hand wash her underwear every night for the next day. The only reason she had a car was because her old man had sent her the money. And if the truth were known, the only reason she asked for it was because of me. Public transport from Mosman Park to my place in Gosnells, or to whatever pub I was pissed in and required extricating from, was virtually non-existent. She couldn't afford cabs; she either drove herself or she didn't go.

I didn't think Kate and I would stay together for long, and did nothing to encourage the idea. Quite the contrary, I did all I could to convince Kate that ours was a short-term liaison. I thought Charlene and I would get back together. After all, that had been the pattern of our lives over 15 years. Our last carnal encounter, which took place when I was seeing Kate, typified the extreme ambivalence that underscored our relationship.

Charlene was living with the labourer. I called her and said I wanted to sleep with her one last time. I said I now understood that it was all over between us. I said I respected her decision, but explained that I wanted to say goodbye in the same way we'd said hello two decades earlier. And she agreed, and we did. But I knew I would betray her.

I began phoning that night. I called, she answered, and I asked to speak to her boyfriend. She was horrified. 'What do you want with him?' she asked.

'I have something very important I need to tell him.' I smiled into the receiver. I felt the electric current of her terror vibrate along the telephone line.

'Well, he's not here,' she whispered. 'Don't call back.'

I called back every 15 minutes for hours. Finally, he answered.

'Yeah, what?'

'Wanna know something about your woman and me?' I offered.

'I dowanna hear nuffin' you've got to say. Fuck off,' he snarled.

But he stayed on the line. So I told him. And I hung up.

I knew at that point I'd done my dash with Charlene. I knew for certain that we'd never be together again. What I didn't know, of course, was that this was the best thing that could ever have happened to me.

I was seeing more and more of Kate. She stuck by me, although she was disgusted when I told her about my clandestine meeting with Charlene. And she was there again when my sister Beth had to relive the horror of her own childhood.

I'd always suspected that Beth had married beneath her. Her husband earned our contempt the day Beth found the note from their eldest daughter, then not quite 12. Scrawled in a young girl's hand was a damning reference to her father's demands. A trip to the doctor showed that she had a venereal disease.

A police investigation showed that the three younger kids, two girls and a boy, had also been subjected to varying degrees of molestation. Their father said in his defence that the kids had 'led him on'. The judge smiled when she sentenced him to five years. It seemed to take a lot longer before my nieces and nephew could smile again.

For Beth, it was hell. I went to the trial with her while Kate looked after the kids. Until then, I hadn't known that Saul touched my sister. I didn't know he robbed her of her innocence and dirtied her babyhood with his stinking mouth and vile fingers and the glasses he wore to magnify her misery and augment his lust. I watched Beth's own past flicker before her eyes like a filthy movie. I watched her curse herself for not being able to see what was happening to her children, right under her nose, right under her own roof. I watched her suffer the terror and loneliness and betrayal they must have felt. I watched her hate so much there was no room left for anything else. And then I watched her be transformed.

Born-again was how we described it. Saved. For Beth, the choice was clear-cut. Be eaten alive by an all-consuming hate, or throw herself into the blinding light of a love so intense it cast out all fear and imbued her world with perfect peace. When Beth arose from the waters of baptism, her arms clasped across her chest, her life began again.

The sky was the colour of dead tuna. For better or for worse Kate and I tied the knot on Monument Hill in Fremantle on 3 March 1992. It was drizzling rain, but we refused to submit to brollies and carried on like it was a bright summer's day. I knew deep in my being that this was the woman I would be with 'till death do us part'. I knew it because Kate had already been with me through 'death'. She'd seen the living corpse, unthinking and unfeeling, and yet she loved me still.

There were about 20 guests. Kate's parents had flown in and were the official witnesses. Bill, her father, was a self-made man who put himself through night school, cutting a swathe through the ranks to become an international trouble-shooter with Price Waterhouse. He looked like an accountant out of a Dilbert comic. Balding, bespectacled and with a calculator for a mind.

Kate's mother was a genteel and strikingly beautiful woman from South Africa, possessed of a somewhat ethereal air. She didn't walk; she sort of wafted. And she didn't actually speak so much as she whispered in a way more in tune with emphysema than with elocution. You could easily have written her off as 'dippy', but you'd be wrong. She graduated aged 18 with a degree in Politics and History. Behind the sometimes dithering, distracted masquerade, Lyn was exclamation-mark smart.

Wayne Saxton, my colleague and mate for over a decade, was there with his wife Jacqui. Peter Lawless, an Account Director from the McCann era, accepted our invitation. Ken Jones, a colleague and good mate from my Woods Advertising days, acted as the official photographer. My son David, now 13, registered his disapproval with his absence. My daughter Talullah and I were still on speaking terms, and she turned up with her boyfriend. Anna, Bradley and Kimberley came, too.

Tony was there with his third serious lady friend (they've never married). He met Maria while he was in a psychiatric hospital undergoing shock therapy for acute depression. She has a flat a five-minute walk from Tony's, and they meet up for coffee or coitus and to talk about how she just lost all her food money at the casino, or how the fucking government has spies watching his apartment. Maria's fierce work ethic is stronger than her gambling addiction and she works hard as a cleaner. To my knowledge, Tony's only thumped her a few times, maybe because they don't actually live together. But more probably because he doesn't love her with the same wild fanaticism he did his other ladies.

Mum couldn't afford to come and no one could afford to fund her but she rang us on the day and wished us all the best.

My brother Richard was the best man, but he was lucky to make it. We'd met at the Nash the previous evening for a two-man stag night. After I'd gone home, he got busted for 'drunk and disorderly' and possession of grass. He swore blind the pot was a plant, excuse the pun.

Richard and I had become good friends now that my Richard-baiting had stopped. He has a big heart and could forgive even that which he couldn't forget. We didn't discuss the past.

When the ceremony was over, we sent Anna, Bradley and Kimberley home in a cab. The rest of us assembled at Sails Seafood Restaurant on Fishing Boat Harbour for the wedding feast. Kate and I both got legless and the cleaners had to sweep us out.

After the wedding reception (we declined wedding gifts and asked everyone to buy their own dinner and drinks instead), we retired to the honeymoon suite at the nearby Esplanade Hotel. My sister Sarah had some blonde hash and I invited her and a few mates up to our room where we got utterly wasted. Except for the liquid kind, Kate was never into drugs. She was spectacularly unimpressed and passed the evening with her head under the blankets.

Mum and James visited us in Western Australia a few months after our wedding. They had got back together again because Mum could no longer bear to be separated from him. They now lived in Merrylands, which I always thought must have been someone's idea of a joke, in Sydney's west. Anyway, Mum loved the area, probably for all the same reasons others thought it a bit down market – the ethnicity, the flea markets, the 'real' bread shops and fresh fish shops and the joie de vivre that seems to be the birthright of those unencumbered by issues like the sort of car you drive or the label on your jacket. She wrote often, and sometimes we spoke on the phone. Once, when I was topped up, I thrust the phone into Kate's hand and insisted that she talk. Later Mum said she got 'completely the wrong impression' from that call. 'I thought she was a snooty old cow,' she said. 'Just goes to show you can't pick a person by their accent, love.'

I was expecting Mum's visit. I knew she'd want a much closer look at Kate than the photos I'd sent had afforded her. She and James came for two weeks, one of which they spent with my sister Sarah and her daughter, Billie. The last week was spent with Kate and me in the house we were renting in Fremantle. Over the first few days, we learned that she and James had been having some problems. Apparently he hadn't been taking his medication (the perennial problem with people afflicted with manic depression) and he'd become fixated on the age difference between them. He was only eight years older than I was, after all. He said he wanted 'a younger chick'.

Before they left for the return journey to Sydney, Mum said to me, 'I don't know how much more of this I can take, dear. You know how much I love James, but the strain's too much for me on my own. Now that you're all over here, I have no support. His family won't even talk to me.'

James' family thought he should have married a nice Yugoslav girl, not a twice married and much older woman with six kids. When we drove them to the airport, no one spoke except James, who was singing a rendition of the Cat's 'Give Me a Hard-headed Woman'. It was delivered with an abandon that startled me not as much for its musical discordance as for its demonstration of how out of tune he was with Mum's feelings.

Over the next few months, James' condition deteriorated rapidly. Mum seemed to take him to hospital every other day. His attitude to her had changed from one of ambivalence to overt hostility. He belittled her, constantly harping on about her weight and the lines and sunspots on her face. 'But you have to remember, love, it's not James talking, not our dear James. It's his sickness,' she said.

So Mum's phone call was not entirely out of the blue. 'I'm sorry to have to ask you, love, but there's no one else, and I need a favour. I have to get out of the house. I've had to have James put away in hospital. His behaviour was becoming quite bizarre. I can't tell you the things he was doing, love, but I know I can't be here when he gets out. I need to get away while he sorts himself out. It will only be for a month or so at the most.'

She spoke softly, almost dispassionately, like this was a decision based not on emotion, but on cold, hard, practical common sense. It wasn't about hysteria; it was about survival. 'I was wondering if you kids could lend me the money for my fare. There's nowhere else to go, no one else to ask.'

All the kids, except for Scrooge McKelly, chipped in for Mum to fly over to Western Australia. The plan was that she'd stay with each of us in turn, and she moved in with Sarah for what was to be the first few weeks. It soon became obvious that Mum intended staying at Sarah's for some time.

Sarah had been barely able to cope as it was, consoling

herself with the knowledge that it wasn't forever. Having Mum there cramped her style. Sarah grew her own dope and she was a prolific smoker. She loved her music and she played it loud. She liked a bourbon or 50. Sometimes, she had male friends over. When three weeks passed and it became obvious that Mum was entrenched, the shit really hit the fan. Accusations flew like hatchets. Some found their mark and stuck.

'You knew what Saul was doing, you bitch. Don't say you didn't, you knew damn well. And you did nothing.'

I wasn't convinced that Mum knew what was going on. I'd seen her literally throw herself between Saul and us kids so many times it was hard to imagine her turning a blind eye to something as heinous as that.

There was a respectful lull in hostilities after Mum got the phone call. James was dead. A mate had found him on his bed. The autopsy showed he hadn't overdosed, and there were no suspicious circumstances. Mum said sadly that he'd just 'worn out'. There's probably some truth in that. Manic-depressives expend a lot of energy, whether they're on the move or nailed to a black mood. Walking or worrying, laughing or crying, they all take a toll when done to an extreme. Personally, however, I think James died of a broken heart. He absolutely adored Mum, regardless of his short-lived second adolescence. And make no bones about it, Mum loved James more dearly than any man she'd ever met.

After much agonising, she decided not to return for the funeral. She said James' parents would only ignore her, and she didn't want to say goodbye in an atmosphere that was tense and bitter. 'Our James deserved more than that, love,' she said.

Reports of the funeral filtered back from her friends in Sydney. She heard that James' parents had refused to let him die as James Deacon, the name he'd adopted in a desperate attempt to quell his ethnicity and win acceptance in a country that wasn't kind to 'wogs'. He chose this name after seeing James Dean in *Rebel Without a Cause*. Nevertheless, his tombstone was inscribed Marko Knezevic. Passersby would never know that it was our James lying there in the Garden of Memories at Pine Grove Cemetery, humming 'Sad Lisa' in his head, hopefully oblivious to the stranger's name that marked his short time with us. Mum was disgusted. 'The bastards,' she said, 'even in death they couldn't let him have his way.'

There was no reason now for Mum to return east. She applied to Homeswest for an apartment, citing the fact that all her children lived in WA, her husband was dead and that she'd be alone and isolated if she moved back to Sydney. Her application was duly approved and she moved into a brand-spanking-new apartment in an old people's village about a ten-minute walk from Sarah's. It was a walk she didn't take very often. It was hard enough battling with old age let alone battling Sarah too.

Meanwhile, Sarah was ensconced in a relationship with man number three. Sarah was 32 and bringing up a child on her Pat Malone. Ron was fifty. The first time he met her, Sarah said it cost him $150 for an hour. He would then ask for her by name whenever he called the agency. From there it developed just like it does in those trashy novels. 'I love you, baby. You deserve more. Let me take you away from all this.' It seemed uncharacteristic to me, but Sarah let him. Maybe she loved him. Maybe she saw him as an ally in her love–hate war with Mum.

Ron was a psychopathic liar. He disappeared on 'work trips' for weeks at a time, saying his job as an engineer meant he had to stay on-site. Sarah smelled a rat. She followed him one day and discovered that Ron was leading a double life. His wife and kids were welcoming him home shortly after Sarah had waved him goodbye. She destroyed his computer, burned his clothes and smashed all his CDs. Then she forgave him and took him back.

I met Ron many times, but I never knew him. Getting him to talk was harder than prising open a rock oyster with your fingers. He wasn't a big fan of our family anyway, especially Mum, and he was rapt when he managed to persuade Sarah to pack up and move with Billie thousands of miles away to Wyndham in the remote north of Western Australia. The day before they left, Sarah drove round to our house in Freo and presented me with three big garbage bags stuffed full of pot she'd pulled up from her garden. I got stoned on Sarah for about six months.

She wrote occasionally. She had an office job in a government department, which was a big step up for a girl with no education. But Sarah was smart and ambitious, and I wasn't surprised. In fact, Sarah had always worked and worked bloody hard. It was a point of personal honour that she didn't need a man to pay her way. More than that, she could do just about any job a man could do. Over the years she'd worked as a labourer, factory worker, handyman and fruit picker. Sarah was what we called a classic 'gofor'. Give her even the vaguest whiff of an opportunity, and she'd go for it.

But despite Sarah's tenacity, her flagrant disdain for the rules worried me. Every fibre of her being screamed 'Fuck you!' It was as though bucking the system validated her as a person. Her choice of Ron as a partner was symptomatic of a more serious disease. Even though I couldn't put my finger on it, I knew there was something odd about him and I worried about her.

My first daughter with Kate was born on 26 February 1993. One of my favourite albums back in the Charlene era had been *Silk Degrees* by Boz Scaggs, and the song 'Georgia' was one we particularly liked. Rather than relinquish the tune, I shifted its focus. I named our daughter Georgia. She was the archetypal little girl, sugar and spice and all things nice. 'Georgie Porgie, pumpkin and pie, kiss the boys and make them cry.'

Georgia's arrival had been planned, but it was strange being a dad again at 40. I was a bit pissed off when the nurse at the hospital smiled expansively and said, 'Go right in. Grandparents are always welcome.' And Kate was a bit pissed off when I staggered in, dribbling drunk, stinking like a brewery and raving about how I wasn't going to make the same mistakes this time. But of course I was making some doozies, professionally as well as personally.

Perth is a small town and the advertising industry is incestuous and vain. The creative gene pool is relatively small, and the talent seems to swim round and round from agency to agency. Clients, too, are stuck in the same goldfish bowl. Same old ad people, same old clients, same old, same old.

Piss pots are okay, as long as they have an award pedigree, drink in the right company and don't get so out of it that they forget their own lies. Piss pots with a penchant for violence and Norman Bates' sense of humour don't get much agency work.

If I wanted to survive in the ad world, I'd have to do it my way. Kate and I started our own company called WordWeaver. I wrote my own direct-mail letters, Kate typed them out, and together we walked around stuffing them in the letterboxes of retail outlets and factories around Fremantle. I offered a free analysis of their current advertising and a written report. When I was able to convert respondents into paying jobs, and when clients paid up on time, we ate. Other times we did it tough. On a few occasions, Kate had to call her folks and ask for a few hundred bucks. They always helped us out.

Eventually, I registered for the dole so we'd have food and rent money when the work dried up. Rather than accept how dire our circumstances had become, I opted to drown the reality in glasses of beer. The problem was that reality didn't die; it just swam underwater for as long as possible before breaking through the surface again, a considerable distance from where it had started out. After sucking in a huge lungful of air, it was set to remind me again of what a hopeless, helpless dipshit I'd become.

I'd developed the habit of borrowing money from the publican till dole day, and instead of shopping properly, we paid my pub debts. On those rare days when I wasn't too drunk or hung-over to see beyond my own selfish regrets, I saw that Kate wore sorrow and despair like a heavy garment. It wrapped around her and stooped her shoulders and slowed her steps. The buoyant optimism that marked her personality when we met had been stifled. Our next baby, my seventh child, was also planned, but probably not well timed.

Olivia made a dramatic entrance on 1 June 1994. It was 6 a.m. and raining heavily. I drove Kate to Fremantle's Woodside Hospital and took her into reception before heading off again to pick up Georgia. We'd left her sound asleep in her cot and the plan was that I'd drop her with friends and hurry back to share the birth of our second child. Although I'd made the round trip in half an hour, I'd missed the show. Kate hadn't even made it to the labour room. Olivia had inserted herself, red-faced and shrieking, into the world ten minutes after I'd gone.

Talullah, David and Anna had been profoundly affected by my remarriage and return to fatherhood. They felt they'd been replaced. Talullah had simply cut me off and I think it was curiosity that got her to our wedding. I'd heard about her open resentment of me and rather than talk with her about it, I'd chosen to bury my head in the sand.

David's love for me was so fierce that he wasn't able to find it in his heart to condemn me. Instead he blamed his mother and had difficulty concealing his antagonism towards Kate and his mother's new man, both of whom he saw as usurpers.

Anna's heart was broken when my marriage to her mother disintegrated. She hadn't accepted that it was over finally and forever until Charlene and I had both remarried and I had other kids. After all, her entire life had been a series of dramatic separations and tearful reunions. She'd lived with the drugs and the drink and the rage for so long, she believed this was how every family lived. She preferred the insanity of the status quo to the insanity of the unknown. And she knew, whatever was happening, that both her mother and I loved her. I think this made it harder for Anna in many ways. It's easier to watch people walk out of your life, at least from that place they'd once occupied there, when you don't like them and know they feel the same way about you. Love is the salt in the wound.

It's difficult to know how Bradley felt. He's so non-judgemental. Rather than say anything negative about anyone he'll just say nothing. The problem, of course, is that you never know for sure the pain the silence might conceal.

Kimberley was so young when we divorced that she was spared the pain of bereavement. Charlene presented her new man to all the kids as their 'new dad', and Kimberley was best placed to accept it. For her, the transition was seamless.

To say that I was the 'father' of seven children isn't strictly accurate. Actually, I was more of a sperm donor. I wasn't prepared to be accountable for their confusion and pain. I knew that if I looked too closely at their suffering, I'd have to confront the terrible enormity of my failure. And I knew this would tear me to pieces. I preferred to see their world through the bottom of a beer glass, where the facts were dulled and distorted, and my own responsibilities were always out of focus. But even looking through the cirrus of my glass telescope, I was about to see the consequences of my wanton, wasted life with a clarity that would shock me to the core.

# ROUND 18

IT WAS JANUARY 1996. It was not a happy new year. The doctor said I had Hepatitis C, most probably from using dirty needles in my youth. His tone was matter-of-fact and professional, not unlike a weather report: 'It's going to rain shit.' On top of the chronic liver disease and alcoholism it would, he assured me, kill me. I asked him the obvious question, but he couldn't put a time on it. 'We're all different,' he said. 'Your liver's shot. It could be as little as a year. Maybe as many as ten. But, unless you get run over by a bus, liver failure will kill you.'

He explained there was a relatively new treatment that was proving highly effective. It was called Interferon and, although hideously expensive, it was available free to people who couldn't afford it. While I qualified on the poverty scale, being both jobless and destitute, he doubted that the drug company would consider me because I was a practising alcoholic. I remember thinking that this made it sound like I was a devotee of an age-old religion, lending a sort of nobility to my ritual tipple. But it was just a passing thought. The good doctor's grim reaper demeanour put an end to any romantic notions about my predicament.

I begged. There's no other word for it. I shamelessly, unreservedly and demonstratively begged. I insisted that I hadn't had a drink in two weeks. (It was true. I'd been feeling crook and couldn't keep a drink, or much else, down – which was why I'd been referred to him in the first place.) I told him I had seven kids and that I couldn't afford to check out early (this was true, too, although my absence wouldn't have made a whit of difference to my kids' quality of life). I swore blind my drinking days were over (I believed this was true). I explained how my premature death would devastate my old, pensioner Mum (absolutely true). I invoked the holy name of God. I wept. And at last the doctor relented and agreed to apply to the drug company on my behalf. But he wouldn't conceal my alcoholic history, and he couldn't make any promises.

I left Fremantle Hospital feeling as drained as a schooner glass on Anzac Day. My first thought was how badly I needed a drink, and I set out on automatic towards the National Hotel. That's when the SuperShane Effect came back to me – my saviour in my youth. And I knew. I knew I didn't need a drink. I knew the drug company would give me the Interferon. And I knew I'd get a job and that my life was going to change. Again. I'd just received a death sentence and a reprieve at the same time. I didn't wait for the bus. I flew home. And I sat down at the kitchen table and wrote two letters. One to a local Swedish restaurant and one to a popular Italian place. Neither had advertised a position vacant. I just knew that this was what I had to do.

The letter introduced 'an amazing robot that made kitchen hands obsolete'. That robot was yours truly. I positioned myself as an automaton that combined the relentless efficiency of a machine with the best human attributes of loyalty and taking pride in a job well done. And applying my direct-response know-how, I made an offer that if they acted now the government would subsidise my wages because I was on the dole.

Two weeks later, the Head Chef at Miss Maud's phoned and asked me to come in for an interview. We sat at an empty table in the restaurant and as we talked, I saw the staff going about their duties, clearing dishes and serving. I was old enough to be their father, and my immediate concern was that this was exactly what the Head Chef was thinking. I opted to cut him off at the pass.

'Hey,' I said, 'I might have grey hair and, sure, there's a few miles on the clock, but I gotta tell you, I'm stronger and more committed than any kid you have working here.'

Maybe I spoke with a conviction that swayed him. Maybe my candour or desperation embarrassed him. Maybe I reminded him of his old man. Whatever, I got the job. The accoutrements of office were a pair of blue overalls and an official plastic ID Card. I started work as a kitchen hand on 1/2/96. I'm looking at that card now. The photo shows me lit up like a happy beacon, which was perhaps a little incongruous since I was a 43-year-old, self-confessed dish-washing machine with a hard-core dependency on drugs, two chins, long, thinning white hair, and I'd just been diagnosed with a killer disease on par with AIDS.

But I've never shirked work. Any time I've been unemployed, it hasn't been through lack of trying. Over the last 30 years I've been a pro boxer, pub bouncer, nuthouse nurse and factory worker. I've swept shit and hosed down blood at the abattoirs. I've been a debt collector for bookies and an insurance salesman. I've worked as a brickie's labourer and a kitchen hand. Usually the last thing a drunk loses is his job. First his sense of responsibility goes, then his self-respect, followed by his family. His job is the only real guarantee of another drink, and in his mind, that is the most important priority.

Kate and I were so broke when I started at Miss Maud's that Kate had to hock our typewriter to eat and pay the rent until my first salary. She was actually on a first name basis with the crew at Freo Cash Converters. (I was too proud – Kate says, 'ashamed' – to go into a hock-shop.)

Why had I even applied for a job as a kitchen hand? Simple. Because my piss-head reputation had cost me any credibility as an advertising copywriter, and I wasn't qualified to do anything else. Except maybe 'bounce boof-heads' in a pub, and my plan was to keep well away from those places. I'd considered applying for the relatively up-market post of waiter, but didn't want to risk being exposed to the public in case any of my drinking buddies, or more excruciating still, former clients, saw me. As a kitchen hand, I was very much behind the scenes.

I worked like a dog. My days comprised mainly tenhour shifts starting at 5 a.m. or 5 p.m. I scraped plates, washed dishes, mopped floors, diced vegetables and lugged bags and boxes of supplies up two flights of stairs from the cold or dry store to the kitchen, at the chef's command. My old boxing injuries screamed in protest, and often I worked in pain.

They paid peanuts and the prospects for advancement were limited There wasn't, for example, a Director of Kitchen Hands. But it was honest work. Somewhere to go. And it kept me off the streets and off the piss, although I confess there were a few nights when I lobbed home with a slab and drank myself back to Blacktown. It was on one such night that I picked up the phone and called a ghost.

Kate and I were living in a rented house in Beaconsfield (yes, I'd come full circle). I'd developed the very expensive habit of using people from my past as phone fodder; stoned and dribbling drunk, I'd call them up wherever they were, whatever the time. On this occasion I rang Saul.

I can't tell you what I said because the next morning all memory of our conversation had evaporated, but a puzzled Richard called me and said that Saul had rung him, announcing that I'd suggested we 'let bygones be bygones', and that he was welcome to come to West Aussie and stay at our place. He was on his way. Kate was livid. She'd heard about Saul's track record and vowed that he wouldn't be getting anywhere near her kids, except over her dead body.

Although Richard said his old man could stay with him, he lived way out in the sticks and Saul was dead keen on catching up with his daughters. Sarah was living in Wyndham with her new man, so she was out of reach. Beth was fair game though. When Beth and Mum found out, they were spitting chips. To them, I may as well have invited Jeffrey Dahmer home for Christmas dinner. (And let him do the cooking.)

Richard had arranged for Saul to stay at the Norfolk Hotel in Freo. I was to meet him at the National Hotel just a stroll down the road at one o'clock the day he arrived. It was a Friday, and my rostered day off at the restaurant.

My commitment to staying off the piss wasn't even a vague consideration in the context of Saul's visit. Beer was the only language we both spoke fluently. I hit the Nash as the doors were opening at ten on the knocker. I needed to get a skinful into me before he lobbed. Sure, I was a big boy now, but Saul and I went back a long way and he still held the devil's place in my nightmares. It was dole cheque day, and by one o'clock the place was buzzing. I had my eye on the doors. I hadn't seen Saul for around ten years, and I wasn't quite sure what to expect. What happened next was certainly unexpected.

My first thought was how small he looked. The door opened and he literally fell into the pub. As I was looking that way, our eyes collided. He didn't recognise me, and anyway, our meeting was the last thing on his mind. He had more pressing issues. He was obviously busting for a piss. Indeed, he'd already started.

'Mate, I need the shithouse.' He was pointing to the darkening stain growing on his grey trousers and his voice reeked of the 'It isn't fair. Why me?' whining of a school kid who feels everyone is picking on him. I pointed and watched him wobble off to the loo. I felt the gooseflesh rise on the back of my neck as his lopsided gait took me back two-and-a-half decades. He bumped a few of the boys on the way, and I saw one of the regulars make a mental note to smack him later.

When he finally emerged, he was scanning the bar for the stepson he hadn't seen in a decade. I waved him over. He didn't remember that we'd spoken just a few minutes earlier. He'd dried his pants as best he could on the hand drier. It seemed that this was an established modus operandi. I asked him if he wanted a beer and he belched, 'You betcha.' He'd obviously had a gutful already, but he grabbed that grog with a desperation that made me feel crook.

I got over it. We talked and sucked piss for the rest of the day. We never once mentioned 63 Edward Street. I told him how I was a successful, self-employed advertising man and forced a WordWeaver business card into his claw hand. I avoided any reference to my kitchen-hand duties just down the road. Even now, I had something to prove. After all these years, I still needed to hear him say, 'Well done, son, you've done a man's job.'

Saul had other priorities. He wanted to know where Beth and Sarah lived so he could drop by and 'surprise my little girls, eh'. I told him Sarah was living way up north with her new man, and that I'd need to check first with Beth before giving him her address. He looked at me, and although his eyes were magnified through his glasses, I wasn't able to see even a glimmer of what he was thinking. He had lizard's eyes – cold and watery windows to a world I never wanted to return to.

Mum and Beth were interested in catching up with him all right. A few days later they formed a two-lady posse and, starting at the Nash, scoured the bars in search of the man who'd introduced them to misery on such intimate terms. They never did find Saul. It's just as well.

A few weeks later, however, I found someone. Someone completely unexpected. Or rather, he found me. I didn't have a clue who I was talking to when I answered the phone.

'Yep,' I answered. 'Who is it?'

'It's me, 'n' I got some unfinished business wiff you from firty years ago.'

'Oh yeah. And who the fuck is "me" when he's at 'ome?' I demanded.

'Me. Ricky Patterson. We fought for the title. Tom, a mate of yours, gave me ya phone number and said to look y'up if ever I was in town like. Well I'm 'ere. Fort you might wanna say g'day.'

Bloody hell, this really was a thunderbolt right out of the blue. Tom was a good mate of mine, a pot-smoking-hippie-beatnik-journo-gypsy-tiler-teacher-whatever-it-took-to-make-a-quid six-feet-something skinny guy with a nose like a raptor's beak. Apparently, he'd been up in the Northern Territory and had managed to sniff out my old adversary.

I went into panic mode. The last thing I needed was a drunken has-been around my house. What would the neighbours think? Shit, if I let him in, would I ever be able to get the bastard out again? And what if he was serious about wanting a reprise at the title, albeit 30 years later? And what if he had half his whole fucking tribe with him?

It was my rostered day off and I arranged to meet him at the Nash. I called a mate to accompany me in case I needed backup, and to take a few snaps of this historic occasion, whatever happened. I knew him the moment I walked into the bar. Not just because he was an Aborigine – the portside bars attracted many indigenous patrons. It was the combination of his skin and the way he moved that identified him. He reminded me of a big cat, a panther maybe. His movements were fluid and relaxed, yet deliberate and precise at the same time. I recognised the powerful shoulders and long arms, and, like a true southpaw, he was holding his glass in his left hand.

Our eyes met and an affable smile broke at his lips and rippled across his face, creasing the corners of his eyes. We embraced like buddies who'd battled side by side in the war. It reminded me of the one thing I loved about boxing: when the final bell rang, there was never any residual hostility. After you've thumped the living daylights out of someone for 15 rounds, your hatred is spent and is replaced by a bond of mateship. Not like rugby league, where players take grudges into the next match and tackles turn into paybacks.

Over the next few hours, the only thing louder than my voice was my hypocrisy. I was knocking back schooners like I was putting out a bushfire in my throat. I justified it to myself by saying that this was a once-in-a-lifetime occasion that shouldn't be allowed to pass without a celebratory drink. On the other hand, Ricky had been off the grog for six months, and was sipping lemon squash. He was softly spoken and a genuinely nice bloke. He had a natural humility. I was possessed by a braggadocio so immense that, once or twice, it even embarrassed me. I knew that if Ricky had won the title all those years ago he would have used it not just for his personal advancement, but to promote hope and pride among the Aboriginal people.

Around three hours later, Ricky, over-brimming with schooners of lemon squash, announced he had to go. 'Got a long way to drive,' he smiled. I scribbled down his address in the Northern Territory, and he shook my hand. I promised to send him copies of the photos my mate had taken. I stayed on in the pub for hours, toasting my title win all those years ago, and re-living every moment of the big fight with every poor bastard within earshot. I lost Rick's address, but I've kept his photos. Maybe we'll catch up again one day.

Meanwhile, another photo opportunity was about to manifest itself. Our last and final attempt at a boy arrived on 5 May 1997. Philippa is the only child I ever visited sober in hospital. I never believed in good-luck charms but I came to believe in good-luck babies.

Call it dumb luck, fate or destiny. Call it the fighter who never dogged a round. But me, I prefer to think it was the dynamic duo of SuperShane and my Higher Power – the little boy who dreamed he could fly and the God I found as an adult. When Anne Humphries called, it set off a chain of events that signalled another dramatic change in my life. My dish-washing days were coming to an end.

Anne was my contact at Australia Post. On and off for around a decade, I'd been doing seminars on direct mail for her. It was good for Oz Post because the more businesses that leveraged direct mail, the more money they made in postage, delivery and associated services. And it was good for me because it added to WordWeaver's profile, earned me a grand and invariably resulted in two or three new projects.

I hadn't heard a peep out of Anne in the last nine months, but I knew why. It was all due to our last conversation. As usual, she'd rung me the day before I was due to do a seminar to check that everything was okay. It was bad timing. I was drunk and in the middle of a screaming match with Charlene about getting access to the kids. I told Anne where she could shove her seminar. As well as being downright rude, it was commercially senseless, as Anne had always been a staunch WordWeaver ally.

Anyway, Anne was a genuinely nice person, and she'd decided to give me another chance. She wanted me to strut my stuff at the Esplanade Hotel in Fremantle. Naturally, I agreed. And this particular seminar was especially kind to me.

The seminar room at the Esplanade Hotel in Freo was abuzz with businesspeople. My wife, Kate, came along to give me moral support. We stood in the middle of the room and I breathed in the energy and excitement from the crowd. All my Oz Post seminars began with a sense of theatre. As I trotted towards the podium, the theme from *Rocky* played. The effect was always the same: it stirred the emotions of the crowd, alerting them to the fact that this wasn't going to be a dry discourse by some tired professional.

When Anne introduced me to the audience as a multi-award-winning direct-mail practitioner and former Australian boxing champion, I exploded into action, throwing combinations into the air, challenging all the old direct-mail conventions, showing 'out of the box' examples and preaching the power of direct-mail to stand out and deliver outstanding results. I felt invincible. Bullets would have bounced off me. Everyone was 'entertained, informed and inspired'. Just like it promised in the brochure. 'Or your money back.'

Sitting in the audience was John Cooke, the newly appointed marketing manager for Solahart, which sells hot water heaters throughout Asia Pacific. His mandate from management was to use direct marketing to get new business and maximise the value of their current customers. He believed direct mail was the way, and he liked my gung-ho marketing philosophy of 'You get noticed or you get nothing!' He commissioned me to do the first of what would be several big-scale direct-mail projects. And I swore to myself that I wouldn't screw up.

I gave the mandatory week's notice at Maudy's the next day. Tim, the Head Chef, said I was one of the best kitchen hands they'd ever had, and I was welcome back any time. I liked Tim very much, and he whipped up a terrific Spaghetti Carbonara, but the next time I see him in a kitchen will be too soon.

I'd been pretty well off the grog and on the Interferon for a month. This entailed me injecting some sort of animal protein directly into my stomach three times a day, three days a week. My gut resembled an angry pincushion, but I was feeling stronger and the pain and nausea had dropped right off. These injections were scheduled for three months, and the doctor checked for the presence of Hep C monthly.

The first month, the virus persisted. He was doubtful about my chances and warned me not to get my hopes up. But I knew otherwise. And I was right. All traces of Hepatitis C disappeared the next month, and I've been clean ever since. Another miracle in my life – not that I've ever done anything to deserve it.

My involvement with Solahart was a launching pad for WordWeaver. Two wildly successful local direct-mail campaigns saw me doing work that ran Australia-wide from my modest bedroom office in Beaconsfield. At the same time, a new agency in town had adopted me as their direct marketing specialist.

Core Marketing ran on a different paradigm to traditional agencies. They out-sourced all creative work. The MD was a strong-willed, savvy lady with integrity and class. Yvonne Renshaw liked me and she liked my work. Ditto.

Courtesy of Core, I was on a few steady earners with clients like the Homestead Hardware Group and the Western Australian Greyhound Racing Association. As well, Australia Post continued offering seminar opportunities. Within two years, WordWeaver had gone from being a card I flashed when I was pissed as a newt and big-noting myself, to a respectable business raking in around $120,000 a year.

But even while things were going well, drink and drugs continued to dog me. It was like I was terrified of succeeding and sought to sabotage myself at every turn. Although God was a force in my life, even He wasn't always able to save me from my most dangerous adversary: myself.

The weekend of the Homestead Hardware Symposium was almost catastrophic. The venue was a posh country club, and I was the keynote speaker, charged with talking about how the power of one-to-one marketing would give Homestead the edge over their bigger-spending competitors. I was to be paid a fee and my accommodation and expenses were included. Kate and I set out in our ancient Volvo warhorse on Friday afternoon. My talk was on the Sunday morning.

I fell at the first hurdle. Our chalet had a bar fridge and I started with one cold beer, followed by several more, after which I called room service and ordered a slab. At dinner we were at liberty to either join the Homesteaders at their welcome barbecue or dine in the restaurant. I explained to Kate that, as I was the 'big gun' at this event, it was better if I resisted unleashing my personality on the group until my actual presentation.

What I really meant was that it was smarter if they didn't see the raging piss pot who supposedly had the panacea for their eroding market share. And so, after champagne and more champagne followed by a few more champagnes, the condemned man ate a hearty, and obscenely expensive, lobster meal. I was loud enough to earn the disgust of the other diners and the attention of the staff, but not quite so raucous that anyone could actually nail me. Yet. As it turned out, my execution was to be stayed until the next evening.

I awoke in a fog on the Saturday and promptly had a bong to clear my head. I spent the day in our chalet, sucking cones and drinking the bar fridge dry. Kate went for a walk, preferring to check out the five-star facilities to watching me get wasted. At one stage, Paul McCrae, the Homestead Account Director at Core, dropped by to see if I'd arrived and if the arrangements were to my satisfaction. I offered him a cone, which he politely declined. 'See you tomorrow at 8.30. You're on at nine,' he said, backing out of the room. I could have sworn I saw an expression somewhere between incredulity and dismay sweep across his face. He must have been clairvoyant.

By the time Kate returned it was early evening. I was maggoty drunk and mindlessly stoned. 'Come on, let's get some fucking dinner into us then,' I said in my most belligerent, Saul-like voice.

'Can we eat in tonight, Shane?' she asked. 'Let's order room service.'

'What, you're fucking ashamed of me, are ya? I'm the fucking keynote fucking shpeaker, and I'm still not good enough for you, eh?'

She didn't like it, but she accompanied me to the restaurant. The Homesteaders were cutting costs and enjoying another 'let's get to know each other better' barbecue. Kate and I avoided them and sat in the posh restaurant where I ordered more champagne. That's when I spotted this bloke in a mechanised wheelchair.

It seemed that the only things he could move were his eyelids, and even that looked painful. He was reduced to drinking his Scotch through a long straw. What really made him conspicuous, however, was the drop-dead gorgeous sheila with him. Much to Kate's absolute horror, I picked up our bottle of champagne, grabbed her by the elbow and steered her over to their table.

'G'day,' I said, 'I'm the keynote shpeaker at a big shymposium here tomorrow. My name's Shane, and this 'ere's Kate, me wife, eh.'

And I offered my hand to the guy in the wheelchair. Given that he was patently unable to even scratch himself, it was an insensitive gesture to say the least. As I was about to discover, however, while my new friend's body was a captive, his mind was most agile.

'Somewhat presumptuous, I'd venture,' he said, referring to the hand suspended rather awkwardly in the space between us.

That's when the pin-up girl made her move, taking my hand firmly and looking me directly in the eye.

'Hello, Shane,' she smiled expansively. 'My name's Kym, and you've already met my husband, Peter.'

'Husmand?' I replied, clearly taken aback.

'And why is that so surprising,' Peter interjected. Then, reading my mind, he set the tone for the rest of the evening. 'I assure you, Shane, I can do with my tongue anything you might be able to achieve with your penis.'

'Perhaps even more,' Kym purred.

In retrospect, I can see that this topic of conversation probably presented the dynamic, if somewhat defective, duo with its own form of entertainment. They were accustomed to being looked at and inspiring whispered conversations and inaudible asides. Here I was, a clown who was happy to move the focus. And I assumed the role of bawdy buffoon with gusto, quizzing them on exactly how they managed the 'act'.

It was fascinating. The trouble is, like most drunks, the more pissed I got, the louder I spoke, and the entire restaurant was privy to my perverse line of questioning.

'How long can you stick it up her? Can you make her come just with your tongue?'

Poor Kate, relatively sober and entirely sane, could see the storm clouds gathering.

'Shane, I think we should go now. Come on. Please, can we please go now?'

'Hey, fuck you, we'll go when I'm good and ready. I'm talkin' to my besht frenz, eh.'

When the manager approached our table and asked me to leave, I was more than a little indignant.

'Who the fuck do you think you are, kitshen nazi? Do you have any fucking idea who you're talkin' to? I'm the keynote shpeaker at the Homeshtead Shimposshum. Now fuck off.'

'Sir, if you don't leave now, right now, I'll call the police.'

I'm not sure how, but Kate managed to get me out, and she drove me back to the chalet. I'd never been so inshulted. I drank all night and shouted at her until I finally ran out of gas and passed out on the bed. Two hours later, she woke me. I'd pissed myself. It was eight o'clock. I had to meet Paul in half an hour, and I was addressing the Homesteaders at nine. I barely had time to grab a quick shower and get changed. When I arrived at the venue, my eyes were still stuck together and my mouth was so dry my lips were sealed with stuff that looked like cockroach guts. Paul nailed me before I even managed to get a foot out of the car.

'Jesus, what happened to you last night? Management came and told us they wanted you off the resort. The CEO of Homestead doesn't want you to speak. He just wants you to go.'

'Bullshit,' I said, 'I'm here to speak and speak I will.'

As I was talking, the CEO himself approached us.

'Just leave,' he said. 'You're in no state to talk with my team.' He was holding my bill from the restaurant.

'No one could operate after drinking this much in one night,' he said, waving the itemised account in my face. 'Go home.'

'No, please, I'm fine,' I protested. 'Honestly, I just need a drink and I'll be fine.'

This sent him into a state of apoplexy. 'A drink. A drink. Paul, you heard that, he needs a drink. For crying out loud, get him out of my sight. Now.'

'No,' I croaked, 'Not alcohol, water. My mouth's as dry as a nun's cunt. I just need water and I'll be okay.' It felt like I was talking with my gob stuffed with cotton wool. Paul passed me a glass of water and I gulped it down like a camel. The CEO looked at me with pure, undisguised contempt. I begged him to let me do my presentation. I promised I'd have his team more energised and inspired than he'd ever seen them. What did he have to lose, I asked. Finally, and with Paul's grudging endorsement, he agreed.

And I pulled it off. At the end of a one-hour presentation, all 80 Homesteaders rose as one to give me a standing ovation. My talk had been on 'Sex, Drugs, Rock 'n' Roll and Marketing,' and it blew them away. The CEO shook my hand, Paul was grinning ear to ear, as much from relief as anything else, and WordWeaver would live to fight another day. Kate and I drove home in silence.

We had no idea, of course, but the biggest opportunity of my life was about to land in my lap.

# ROUND 19

TO THIS DAY, I HAVE no idea how the headhunter got my name.

'I have a job going in Singapore for a direct marketing copywriter. Are you interested?'

Does a bear shit in the woods? I thought. A week later, I was sitting opposite the baby-faced Managing Director of a Singapore-based ad agency in Perth. Matthew Atkinson had just turned 30. He typified the new breed of wunderkind who was powering agencies into the 21st century on the glimpse of a vision and the gasoline of sheer guts and adrenaline. He knew his stuff, but every time I looked at him it felt like I was being interviewed by my son. He apologised that there was a conference on in Perth and that this three-star hotel was the only one he could get. Fuck, had he agreed to meet me in a cubicle in the shithouse at the zoo I would've been grateful.

I presented my work to Matthew with all the passion and purpose I could summon. I performed with the desperation of an old gladiator who knows that a thumbs-up from the Emperor means the difference between lobster and baked beans. I showed him letters of testimonial from delighted clients. I told him about my boxing background and refusal to take a backward step in my quest to be the best direct-response copywriter on earth. I told him that whether he hired me or not, I was going to set the world on fire with direct mail that leapt out of the letterbox, grabbed the addressee by the throat, turned him upside down and shook him until the money rained from his pockets. The only issue was whether I'd be doing it in Singapore or in Perth.

I didn't mention my marathon battle with the bottle or the death sentence the doctor had dealt me. He didn't ask. Two weeks later, I got the call. The job was mine. Three weeks after that, I was happily ensconced in Le Meridien Hotel in Singapore.

The name of the advertising agency was Tequila. There I was, a die-hard piss pot, working as a senior writer for a company whose namesake was a Mexican drink. Caramba! Actually, the name Tequila is an anagram of the French word 'Qualité', and has nothing whatsoever to do with alcohol.

Our biggest client was Rothmans, and I spent most of my working life at Tequila devising ways to push fags to peasants in third-world countries who had much more meaningful things to do with their money. And I was good at it. After a year, management decided I'd make a more effective Creative Director than the incumbent. I accepted the post and a pay hike to $20,000 a month.

I sent another plea for approval off to my real father care of my grandparents' address in Queensland. I enclosed a copy of my contract and some business cards. I wanted him to know that the suicidal loser he knew in Cairns had been replaced. He was impressed that I was now a successful executive living a life you only read about in novels. But the Blacktown tentacles were about to reach out and drag me back to where it all began.

Sarah's suicide didn't seem real. It was a sad epilogue to a drama that had begun almost exactly a year before. We'd been staggered by the news that her man Ron was dead. He'd killed himself. He'd channelled the exhaust fumes back into the car and left the motor running. I always suspected that Ron had a few problems, but I must admit, I hadn't seen that one coming. Typically, Sarah decided to tough it out and stay on in Wyndham until Billie had finished high school. A year later, the day before her daughter's 17th birthday and almost to the day Ron sped past the final checkered flag, Mum called our home in Singapore.

Kate phoned me at the office. It was about 11 o'clock on a Friday morning. She said she was sorry, but she had bad news and I'd better sit down. Sarah was dead. She'd driven off to the same place as Ron, in the same car. She was 35. Someone at work was playing the CD of a band called Live and the lead singer was screaming, 'The angel opens her eyes, her pale blue coloured eyes.' Whenever I hear that song, I think of my little sister's blue eyes and her steadfast focus on the end.

I wondered what had gone through her mind as she sat in the car that night, speeding to nowhere, waiting for the lights to turn red. We found out later that she was pissed and stoned out of her brain. Knowing Sarah, it wouldn't have been to numb the dying, but to amplify it. I wondered how she felt in the last-gasp moments, when it was all slipping away and too late to claw it back, even if her life depended on it, with the radio screaming and the gases swirling and death starting to kick in. Did Ron sit beside her and hold her hand, telling her to take deep breaths, whispering everything's gonna be okay now, sweetheart? Or was the only sound she heard the long, heartfelt sigh of a young woman who's terminally weary of the waiting? Was she angry? Frightened? Did she think of Billie? Did she taste revenge or regret or just the tart metallic intoxication of the fumes on her tongue?

I didn't fly home for Sarah's funeral. I was halfway through a big campaign, and anyway, my absence would have made no difference to Sarah. Kelly obviously found it more prudent to stay in Queensland – 'Beautiful one day, perfect the next.' While the rest of the family was saying goodbye to Sarah, I said a prayer for the living and remembered the day a girl carried a coffin the size of a shoebox to a hole in the ground so tiny it was unbearable. And I shut the door to my office and I bawled like a baby.

One year and seven international advertising awards later, a call came from another headhunter. Ogilvy & Mather, the biggest brand name in the world of advertising was in the market for a Creative Director for both OgilvyOne and OgilvyInteractive. I felt like justice had been served as this was the same O&M that had dispensed with my services all those years ago. The job would make me OgilvyOne Worlwide's first and only Creative Director of both the online and offline direct marketing divisions – some would say 'guinea pig'.

I met the Chairman, Paul Davies, and Executive Creative Director, Andy Greenaway, on the night of the Tequila Christmas party. I liked Paul and Andy right away. They seemed like 'what you see is what you get' type people in an industry of impostors and prima donnas sporting carefully cultivated five o'clock shadows and ponytails. (QUESTION: What do you invariably find under a ponytail? ANSWER: An arsehole.) They had a clear vision of what it would take to make OgilvyOne the leading agency in Asia Pacific and I wanted to be part of it. I went to the Tequila Christmas party that night feeling like Mr Iscariot. In my mind, I'd already resigned. I made it official the first week after Christmas.

My career has given me opportunities I never dreamed of just six years ago when I was scraping plates and washing dishes. I've been all over Asia and to Europe. My last European trip was to present a campaign to a group of 150 German journalists. I've built a reputation as a passionate presenter, and some have kindly said that we've won business as a direct result of my ability to sell the vision behind our work.

However the 'ice man' I'm not, and there are times when I find the idea of 'tap dancing' (an industry euphemism for presenting creative work) in front of a marketing-savvy CEO of a multinational company somewhat daunting. But I've developed a fail-safe mechanism for coping. I look across the table and I ask myself, 'What can they actually do to me?' I compare the prospect of tangling with them to that of stepping into the ring with Patterson on the night of the title fight. Or I take myself back to the day in West Aussie when I answered a knock at my brother's door, only to have an angry young man stick a gun in my face. Sometimes I even think about Saul and shudder. It helps me get things in perspective.

# ROUND 20

IF I'VE GIVEN YOU THE impression that I've escaped unscathed from a life that has been somewhat less than temperate, let me address that now. I've been impotent for around ten years. The three children born in the interim are more the result of ferociously committed (if few and far between) sperm than nights of unbridled passion. Like most men with this affliction, I fear and avoid the closeness of my wife because affection is invariably a prelude to the consummation of my inadequacy.

When I first consulted doctors in Western Australia they did tests that indicated an extremely low hormone count. Apparently this is another unhappy by-product of a lifetime of alcohol and drug abuse. They recommended needles. It was bloody excruciating – psychologically as well as physiologically. Before I could hope to deliver a meat injection, I had to first whack myself in the dick with a needle that looked like it was designed for putting down elephants. It worked okay but it hurt like crazy and, I hope you'll forgive me, Kate, it just wasn't worth it.

One of the first things I did when I came to Singapore was to take my impotency to a doctor. He ran more extensive, and ludicrously expensive, tests. And fittingly, his diagnosis was more alarming. Haemochromatosis. Also alcohol induced. Apparently my body is unable to excrete iron, which is building up in poisonous proportions and attacking the major organs in my body. The effects are cumulative and can be fatal. It's called 'the silent killer'. He recommended a modern bloodletting ritual a few times a week. I declined but asked about Viagra. Liver damage made me ineligible, and so he gave me some testosterone patches instead.

I was sitting on a bus on my way to the office at Tequila one morning, and imagining how pathetic it would be if I died in a traffic accident. I could just imagine the look of consternation on the pretty young morgue attendant's face (she's never an old frump in these reflective moments, is she?) when it came time to wash the goolies and she peeled the sad little patch from my damp citrus-skin scrotum. Sort of like the cliched 'make sure you wear clean underwear' line, but with a lemon twist.

Anyway, I didn't find the 'bandaid on the ball bag' routine terribly effective. I went to another doctor a few months ago and pretty well demanded Viagra. After filling out a few forms and scrupulously avoiding any reference whatsoever to liver disease, he handed me the panacea for a floppy flamingo. Kate and I went on holiday to Indonesia shortly after, and I gave them a test(osterone) drive. Not bad at all, even if I do say so myself. Trouble is, there are all these reports of blokes having heart attacks while on the nest, and with the toll the iron overload's taking on my ticker, I'm a bit wary of pushing my luck. Still, I believe in living dangerously every now and then. It seems to be part of my nature.

The nosebleeds are a nuisance. It's another of the symptoms of chronic liver disease. Without warning my nose (which, as I've explained, is an organ of generous proportions) will suddenly begin to bleed. Not a sniffle. Not a dribble. Not a drip. I'm talking about a serious gusher. It's okay when it happens at home. Kate and the kids are used to seeing me walking around the house with half a toilet roll stuffed up my nostrils. I find that around 30 minutes of this 'seal and soak' tactic usually does the trick.

It's not quite so easy when the blood gates open at work, however. A while ago I was giving a presentation to the OgilvyOne staff in Manila when my nose went through its 'that time of the month' routine. I explained to my startled audience that I'd hit my head earlier and carried on with a hankie clamped to the old snout. But do you know what the real piss off was? They were videotaping the presentation. My nose didn't merely bleed for half an hour, thanks to technology it'll be bleeding in the Philippines forever.

There were other more serious problems, however, that couldn't be fixed with a pill or a strategically placed tissue. For many years Talullah, my eldest daughter, had refused to talk with me. From all accounts she loathed me and never missed an opportunity to put the boot in. In Talullah's eyes, I was still the obnoxious drunk. I saw this as a positive sign. I've always believed that indifference is the real death knell for any relationship, and that hatred says you still care.

Nevertheless, it took me a selfish, stubborn decade to finally face the fact that I was the parent, and that the onus was on me to try to bridge the chasm. A year ago, when I was visiting Mum in Perth, I asked my son David for Talullah's phone number and I bit the bullet and rang. I got the answering machine. 'You've called Sean, Talullah and Robbie. We're not here to take your call, but if you leave a message after the tone, one of us will get back to you as soon as we can.'

I stopped for a heartbeat. It sounded just like her mother's voice.

'Hello, Talullah. This is your dad. Not the one you remember though. I'm someone else today. I'm different. The only thing that hasn't changed is that I love you very much. If you'd like to call . . .' And I left my number and I waited.

Later that evening, the phone rang and Kate answered it. She said, 'It's for you. It's Talullah.' The conversation was stilted, but I was encouraged that it was happening at all. I suggested Kate and I meet her and Sean for dinner that evening, if they could make it, as I was returning to Singapore the next day.

She agreed, and we met Talullah and her husband outside Sails Seafood Restaurant at Fishing Boat Harbour in Fremantle (the same place Kate and I had our wedding reception). Taking our cues from the venue, our conversation barely skimmed across the surface. Even when it dipped and plunged precariously close to the nets of the past, we scuttled sideways like cliches across ocean floors. We exchanged pleasantries and platitudes and must have looked like any normal family. Safer and more civilised, we tacitly agreed, to take our fish and chips without the vinegar of recrimination.

'And how old is your son now? Two. What a delightful age! Do you enjoy living in Maddington? And what do you do for work, Sean? I believe you're a promising soccer player?'

When we left the restaurant that night, I gave my eldest child a hug and a kiss and felt the aching distance echo in our embrace. I have a lot of catching up to do.

It was the next morning, nearly five o'clock when, summoned by some sense of urgency more powerful than sleep, I found myself at the computer, waiting for thoughts to solidify into words. In the grey ghost caress of dawn, memories dripped, dripped, dripped like cold water from a tap I couldn't turn off . . .

I stagger into the kitchen in our hovel above the Salvation Army shop in Beaconsfield, Western Australia. I'm pissed as a newt. Charlene and the kids are sleeping, or pretending to. On the packing case we use as a kitchen table, I see a young girl's school essay. Talullah is about eight, I think. She's left it there for me to read. A drunk's hand takes a red pen. He doesn't see his daughter's desperate attempt to be a bit like her dad, deft of pen and quick with the apt word.

In the morning, the child sees every grammatical error, every slip in syntax, every spelling mistake and every sloppy expression ravaged in red, a bleeding testimony to her father's insensitivity and mindlessness.

When Charlene tells me how Talullah cried, I break down. I thought I was helping. I honestly meant no harm.

The first casualty of divorce is the kids. I'm ashamed I can't recall more details of their childhood. My life has been laced with so many chemical intruders, I don't have memories so much as I have flashbacks. All my kids from my first marriage are wounded in their own way. Once I thought I was entirely to blame. We were probably both at fault. Talullah certainly blamed the two of us for a long time. She's forgiven me, but has blacklisted her mother from her life. I can understand. Nonetheless, I've told Talullah that life's too short, and I pray she can forgive her mother as she seems to have forgiven me. If death is a thief in the night then the most precious thing it can steal from us is the last chance to release those we love from the chains of our vindictiveness. Because when they leave us, as they must, drained of living and all its shallow encumbrances, it is those who are left behind who are shackled still by the bonds of our bitterness.

I learned this lesson when my real father died. We'd kept in touch with the occasional letter and phone call since I first informed him of my new career in Singapore. Liza had rung me and suggested that if I wanted to say goodbye, I should get to Rockhampton Hospital in Queensland. Fast.

I found him slipping away. 'Hello, Dad,' I whispered, 'it's me, Shane. I came, Dad. I'm here now.' We'd hardly spoken over the last 47 years and nothing was about to change. It didn't matter that we wouldn't have a conversation. After all, I was the only one who'd have to live with whatever was said.

Only his hair had resisted the onslaught. He had a full head of wavy, black hair. As I combed it back from his clammy forehead with my hand, it was as though I was able to exorcise his demons with every stroke. Dad's breathing became less tortured, ebbing towards the final frontiers of sleep. I told him how much I'd missed him.

How I'd missed the footy games and the laughter and the talks about the birds and the bees and the picnics and the piss-takes and the politics between a father and a son. I told him how I'd ached for him to be there the night I won the Australian title. I told him I loved him. I told him I forgave him and I begged his forgiveness, too.

And I think he heard me, because a veil of peace fell across his face, softening his features, and his breathing hushed and slowed and stilled, and suddenly he was empty of the world at last. I hugged him and I cried four decades worth of tears.

Looking at my dead father, I realised how unimportant and petty our differences were, seeing only the similarities in our faces and in our foibles. The irony, of course, is that so often it's the things we share that repulse us; we don't see the other person so much as we see a reflection of what we resent in ourselves. Accepting and loving them is momentous, because it means that first we have accepted and loved ourselves. Dad's death awakened me to this truth, and I am indebted to him not so much for what he gave me in the living years, as for this, his final legacy.

I was asked to say a few words at the funeral.

*The measure of a man's immortality, in this world at least, is how he is remembered. My final memory of Dad is one I will always thank God for. I flew in from Singapore on Tuesday morning, arriving at the hospital at 8.30.*

*Dad was hanging in. He knew no other way. All his life, from working as a cook in deplorable conditions in the most inhospitable and isolated parts of Australia, to fighting disease, bad luck and ill health, my dad's been a battler.*

*But while they could take away half his bowel and both his kidneys, they couldn't remove his will to live. And so that's how I found him, struggling desperately for every breath. I was stroking his hair and telling him softly how much I loved him when his breathing slowed and stopped. It was 9.50. And do you know what? It occurred to me that even then Dad had not quit. He could not. It simply was not in his nature. Instead, it was God who had thrown in the towel. It was God who had exercised his authority as the Ultimate Referee. I'll always remember the 2000 Sydney Olympics as the time God said, 'Enough is enough', and called my dad home.*

I know that Talullah loves her mother because she protests too much. And I know too that part of her will drown in the depth of that love if she is unable to hug her mother before it's too late and she's cold and distant and meaningless as yesterday.

As for David, he's come to terms with his old man. He once felt like a victim, and although he was right, of course, I wondered how much his sense of self-pity would detract from his ability to work through and emerge from this crisis. Healing and hate are diametrically opposed. David wants to be just like me. What scares me, however, is that David doesn't actually know who I am – he only knows who I was. David and I were talking on the phone the other day. I told him about this book. He said he was proud of me and that he'd already been telling people my story for years.

Anna is 18 years old and living with her 30-year-old boyfriend, a well-meaning kid who obviously cares for her very much. She's no longer a Weaver any more, having changed her surname to match her mother's. Very occasionally, because her pride is stronger than her poverty, Anna writes and asks for money. Kate and I always send it. It's easier to send money than to give your child back her sense of hope.

Anna was always good and she was gentle. Underneath the swagger and the frown she still is. She deserved so much more than I gave her. And yet she bears no grudges. She doesn't blame anyone for her life. I asked her if she had any memories of growing up with me.

'Yes, I do, Dad,' she said. I braced myself.

'Do you remember the ducky-poohs? You used to take us to this park in Gosnells where there was a secret path that led to a place where the ducks swam. You couldn't see it from the road. You held my hand and we walked quietly, not talking, so we didn't frighten them. You had names for all of them and it felt like we were part of a secret world.

'And I'll never forget the time we were living at Federal Close and it hadn't rained for so long the ground was cracked. Then one day it thundered and poured down and you yelled for us to come outside and we all danced with you in the rain, laughing and splashing in the puddles. I have lots of happy memories. Dad. That's why I love you.'

I hung up the phone and I cried for Anna and I cried for me and I cried till Kate came in and asked me what the matter was.

How did Bradley turn out to be such an uncomplicated and genuine young man? Maybe it's because he had little to do with me in his formative years. He never bore the full brunt of the screaming and shouting like the older kids. (Not that I ever thumped Talullah or David. In fact, because of my strength and frightening temper, I had a self-imposed rule that when they misbehaved, they would get three spanks only with an open hand on the bottom; nevertheless, watching your father rant and rave and threaten your mother while smashing the house up can be a fearful experience for a child.) Terror and uncertainty weren't programmed into his psyche.

Bradley was never academically inclined, and left school at 15 to get a job at Burger King. They love his work ethic and sense of humour. He'll do well there, if he chooses to stay. If not, he'll do well wherever he goes because he'll be taking with him a good heart and a good attitude.

Last I heard he was in love and wanted to get married. Kate and I flew over to West Aussie for the engagement party. His fiancee is a bright and attractive young woman. Bradley was baptised last year and he lives with his fiancee's family. They've accepted Bradley as one of their own. He's still a Weaver, though, and will need my written permission to marry. Bradley turned 16 yesterday. There's no way in the world I'll be giving consent yet – he's way too young.

My youngest daughter from the dark ages is Kimberley. She was three when Charlene and I split for the last time. My oldest memory of Kimberley is driving past the house where Charlene and her rat-faced Romeo were living, and seeing a toddler looking back at me from the verandah as I slowed down to an intimidating crawl.

It was a hot day, and the two star-crossed lovers were sitting on the front verandah, sipping beers. They glowered at me in unison and I punched the horn in vicious combinations before speeding off in a screech of burning rubber. I didn't even think about the feelings of the wide-eyed child. As usual, I was only thinking about numero uno.

Time, sobriety and sanity combined to make me see that I needed to reacquaint myself with Kimberley. She came to spend Christmas 2000 with us in Singapore. The plan was that she would stay three-and-a-half weeks. Three days after she arrived she announced she was homesick and wanted to go home. I read an email she'd sent to David in the short time she was here. Obviously, she didn't know she was leaving a digital trail. And obviously, she was disappointed in me. I hadn't lived up to her expectations. We put her on a plane, gave her some money and said 'Merry Christmas'.

Although her mother and her stepfather were separated (again), I heard all the kids and Charlene re-grouped at her husband's house to share a traditional festive dinner except for Talullah, who wasn't talking to her mother, David, who made alternative arrangements, and Bradley, who opted for his girlfriend's house. So yes, maybe there is a Santa Claus, but the fat bastard wasn't delivering to Charlene that year. And what about the Reynard-Weavers? How were they faring in the 'good will among all men' stakes?

John Lennon is not dead. He's living in a government flat in Fremantle, Western Australia. With Tom Waits, the Rolling Stones and Lou Reed. Tony Weaver, however, died some time ago.

He died incrementally. Some of him froze in the blizzard of Dad's indifference. Some more was incinerated in the inferno of Dad's hate. The final essence of Tony atrophied and dropped off when he embraced the broad spectrum of drugs from pot to pills to IV therapy. Street drugs, chemist shit, home made, takeaway, eat it here, snort it there, smoke it, shoot it, lick it, stick it, it didn't matter, so long as it got you where you needed to go. Which, in Tony's case, is anywhere but here, wherever 'here' happens to be.

Sometimes, however, like a flashback to another time, the clouds part and splashes of the old Tony come crashing through like bright bolts of sunshine. The effect is all the more shocking because of the contrast with the monochrome of his everyday life.

His one true love is his music. The only time Tony sparks is when he turns on his beloved CD player. It's as though the surge of electricity energises him, reactivating his brain and stimulating the speech centre. Suddenly, he's wired and awake. Alive to every nuance of the music, he knows more about the meaning embedded in the lyrics and the arcane messages in the melody than any New York DJ. 'Listen to this, man. Check it out. Do you know what this means? Did you hear that?' He gets more than pumped up, he gets downright Krakatoa.

'Shut it, man,' he'll fume, if you try to get a word in edgeways. 'Just fucking listen, will ya!'

He insists that everyone pay homage to his acoustic and electric heroes. But the song doesn't last forever, and when the music dies, so does Tony. Pause. Everything goes back. Everything goes black. Black into the void. Black into the wall-eyed silence. Tony is locked into his own dance. It's called the Luckless Limbo and he's breaking all records for 'How low can you go?'

I pray he doesn't close his eyes and fall asleep like James, too deeply, too peacefully, too profoundly to ever be called back. Or that he doesn't follow Sarah, hurtling down the same highway to oblivion.

I don't think about Kelly much. But I have wondered how differently everything might have been for all of us, had Mum and Ryan stayed together. I doubt that he's ever given to such moments of introspection. I think about the time he sent Tony to do business with a smackhead whose evil temper was legendary, armed with a sachet of crushed aspirin.

Suffice to say that Kelly is now living under an assumed name in Queensland with his third wife and second daughter. I haven't spoken with him in over a decade. I don't hate Kelly any more; I don't hate crocodiles either, but that doesn't mean I'm going swimming next time I'm at the zoo.

Richard still finds it difficult to relate to people. He doesn't make friends, and he's still unequivocally and irrevocably unmarried. He's great with our kids, though, and Beth's kids, and all the kids in the family for that matter, snatching the fulfilment of family life vicariously wherever he can. It's a pity he left school so young; he's clearly the most intellectually endowed of all the Reynard-Weavers. He's also a gifted artist, having taught himself how to design and fire his own stained-glass work. Some of the most striking glasswork in the old churches and stately homes around Fremantle is my brother's handiwork.

Beth has found a new man. A good man who respects her and protects her. They have plans to marry. She is living in Gosnells with her kids, Sarah's daughter, Billie, and has even adopted Sarah's dog, 'BD' (Bloody Dog).

She's successfully completed her Higher School Certificate as a mature-age student, and is currently working as a caregiver in an aged people's hostel. That's appropriate, because a caregiver is precisely what my sister Beth is. In my absence, Beth has also taken on the demanding job of keeping an eye on Mum.

I try to call Mum every Sunday. We send her money each month and whenever there's an emergency, like when she needs to replace her glasses or her dog, Sherna, needs to go to the vet. I send postcards from the places I travel to for work or holidays. When I made my first trip to Hong Kong, I was working at Tequila. I was so excited, I found a post office in the airport and gushed a quick note off to Mum. I told her how this extraordinary journey to Hong Kong had started in our tiny, tawdry kitchen in Edward Street 35 years ago. I thanked her for putting me on the plane. And I meant it more than my words could ever hope to convey.

The Sunday phone ritual is always the same. I call her around 11 in the morning. There's no time difference between Perth and Singapore, and she's usually just come back from walking Sherna over the road to the shops to get the paper. I can tell by the first 'Oh, hello love' exactly what tone the rest of the call will take. But whether it's an almost childlike eagerness to embrace me in the minutiae of her life, or a desperate attempt to drown me in her twilight regrets, my reaction is the same. I read my emails while we talk. I hover between what I fear sounds like indifference and what I hope sounds like uninterrupted concentration.

She tells me about her trips to the St Vincent de Paul's and the Salvos, and her excursions to the $2 Shop, conjuring up an Aladdin's cave of plastic Gucci wannabelookalike sunglasses, cutesy picture frames and brightly coloured crap. She tells me how Perth Sundays are miserable because the world stops and there's not even anything on TV. She tells me about the road excavations outside her flat and somehow sees an analogy with the building of the Great Pyramids. She tells me how her best friend, both in this world and outside it, is Jesus. She tells me about the relentless heat and her annoying neighbours. More alarmingly, she tells me about encounters with elderly men who she's certain have designs on her body.

'I was walking Sherna, dear, and we were minding our own business like we always do, when his dog's lead, and it was *very* obviously a male dog, dear, got tangled up with my little Sherna's and really, it was just a little too close for comfort for Sherna and I, dear. He didn't seem to mind, I might add, and his dog was *very* obviously happy. But really, the last thing Sherna and I need in our life is a man, for goodness sake.'

I grunt in all the right places. I wince into the receiver. I yeah and nope and uh uh and tut tut and of course. I listen to the chronicle of her life with my ears stuffed with the cotton wool of denial. When Simon and Garfunkel sang about 'people listening without hearing', they were singing about my Sunday chats with Mum.

You see, I can't afford to open myself up. I can't afford to let her in. I can't afford to love her with the same senseless, unbridled, unqualified passion of my youth. Because if I do, her death will kill me. And even as I make this admission, I can see the selfishness of a man who is still looking for ways to stop the brunt of reality denting his carefully fabricated world. It's a knee-jerk reaction,

I suppose, from a time when a small boy's feelings were subject to the vagaries and vicissitudes of living with a sadist.

I can say I have no regrets, and it's true. But there is pain. Can you have one without the other? I think so. Regret implies a desire to go back and undo or change something. I have no such wish. I accept that the good and the bad are all part of the same thread, and that changing any of it would alter the fabric of my entire life. I am more comfortable with who I am today than I have ever been.

My pain comes from knowing that many of the choices I've made have hurt others. I have to live with that. You can't wound people and walk away scot-free. Like so many cliches it's true that what goes around comes around. If this sounds like my hands are tied, well yes, they are. But they're tied in prayer, one hand in gratitude for God's forgiveness, and the other hand in supplication for the comfort and healing of those I have harmed. And my life is a testimony to the fact that prayers are heard and answered. Especially those of the unlovely and the unworthy.

I'll probably never be able to sever all the tendons that tie me to the past. To a large extent, I still measure my value as a human being by the opinion of others. I still ache for Daddy to take me in his arms and say, 'My boy, you've done a man's job.' With one father who'd died long before he was buried, and another with all the compassion of a cactus, it's never going to happen.

I don't see so much of the confused and angry man I used to be any more. Except sometimes in the mirror, in a flash of fear in my eyes. But it passes quickly, and I've learned how to hide his face from others, most of the time, at least. Yet he's always with me, and I guess he always will be.

I accept the angry young man for who he is. I understand how he came to be so frightened, and why it's easier for him to scream in anger than in fear. But here's the most beautiful revelation: the angry young man can now accept me, too. He can accept the super boy who, disguised as a fat, middle-aged advertising executive, fights a never-ending battle for 'Truth, justice and sobriety'.

He doesn't resent the distance I try to put between us. He understands why I try to keep him bound and gagged and hidden in a room in the darkest part of me. I even think he's proud, albeit somewhat grudgingly, of what I've achieved. After all, he knows I did it for both of us.

As for my being less than perfect, like my friends in AA used to say, 'The road to recovery is still under construction.' This book is finished. I am not.

# EPILOGUE

I'M 48 AND FOUR-AND-A-HALF YEARS sober, and in the morning we'll be on a plane bound for Sydney. Looking in the mirror, I'm reminded of the severed heads of those executed men who had 'donated' their bodies to science. The ones I saw suspended in giant pickle jars on my trip to the cadavers' room at Sydney Uni. Close-cropped hair and features bludgeoned by time and fists and gravity, staring back dispassionately from their fishbowls, unblinking, seeing everything and seeing absolutely nothing at all. The glass had a magnifying effect, not unlike the special hand-mirrors you find in posh hotels, dramatising every blackhead and blemish, and turning wrinkles into deep-set fissures in the ravaged landscape of their faces. I have more hair sprouting from my ears than I do on top of my head. Recently, I read the results of a quiz where women were asked to vote on what they found more ugly, nasal hair or ear hair. I would've bet my furry balls on nose hair. And I would've ended up a eunuch! What's worse, a eunuch with ears like toilet brushes.

Blokes who are going bald invariably react in one of two ways. They either grow whatever hair they have as long as possible, arranging it artfully over the shiny bit, in a sort of sad, silly camouflage. Or they 'go with the flow', pun intended, and crop whatever's left super short. I got a number one yesterday. In so far as a 'number one' is a euphemism for urinating and a 'number two' refers to doing the full business, it sounds like someone has pissed on my head. Nothing so romantic really. It just refers to the closest setting on the barber's clip. It was also the cut I favoured in my fight days. The battle cut. Now I think of it, it's not far off the tonsorial style favoured by Saul. Kate says it makes me look like 'Stormin' Norman'. Appropriate for the journey back to Blacktown.

Mum still tells everyone who'll listen (as well as those who couldn't give a flying fig) that I was born with perfectly proportioned limbs.

'Yes, the doctors would come round in groups of six or eight at a time, dear, gawking and taking his measurements. My Shane was a model baby.'

I can't recall any of this myself, of course, but I do know that if it's true, my body has been in revolt since that auspicious start. Those arms and legs may have been perfect on a baby, but somewhere along the line they stopped short of perfection. Indeed, it's as though, when I reached my mid-teens, they just stopped altogether. My stunted stature didn't stop me winning an Australian boxing title, but, to my interminable irritation, it has always prevented me from crossing my legs and adopting the posture of careless abandon or studied indifference to which I so desperately aspire.

How the fuck can you be cool if you can't cross your legs? Can you imagine, I've spent my entire adult life secretly despising anyone with the ability to casually place one leg over the other without resembling a fat clown trying to get into the lotus position?

As well, since arriving in Singapore, I am the victim of a corporeal civil war in which my face and head are the targets. I am at the mercy of a florid rash that engulfs my forehead and the perimeters of my lower eyes. It attacks without warning, but is a fairly predictable assailant when I'm due to give a speech or do an important presentation. 'Roseate acne' apparently caused by stress, the doctor said, handing me a prescription for tetracycline.

Finally, a cruel and unrelenting case of mid-life psoriasis has turned my scalp into a salt mine. The only consolation is that my hair is so grey the fallout is not always immediately apparent. Dressed in my black kurta, however, I resemble a rotund, mobile lamington. I don't merely have 'bad hair days', with my face flaring like a beacon and my scalp snowing like an alpine resort, I have 'bad head days'.

Cyclops' eye has been ripped out, and hangs throbbing like an angry orb in the blood-streaked sky as we fly into Sydney's Mascot Airport. Kate, the kids, Mary, our maid, and me. 28 December 2001, and bushfires have ravaged the Blue Mountains and are tonguing the suburbs. Some mornings you can't see the Harbour Bridge from our hotel in Oxford Street.

'Why are those men holding hands, Daddy?' asks Olivia.

'Because they're good friends, Ollie.'

'But why are those ones kissing?' A guy aged around 30, dressed in bottom-hugging black velvet hot pants and a silver spangled singlet has his tongue buried down the throat of a bloke with close-cropped, orange hair.

'Because they're *really* good friends, Ollie.'

I'd forgotten that Oxford Street was home to Sydney's gay community. This was where the Blacktown boys went to wreak 'ultra violence' on 'those poo pokin' poofters'.

But that was a lifetime ago. Our current agenda has more in common with *The Partridge Family* than with *A Clockwork Orange*. The kids and Mary do all the touristy things, going to Taronga Park Zoo and Manly Beach, catching a ferry and trying to avoid the vigilant beggars who maintain a well-fed presence on what seems like every street corner. One guy carries a sign that reads 'I need a beer bad'. The world's most honest bum. I give him ten bucks.

Kate's brother lives at Mosman on Sydney's North Shore, and she gives him a call. Non-smoking, moderate drinking, devoted husband, doting dad, William has a degree in Theology and works in corporate finance. (For obvious reasons, I call him 'One in a William'.) His wife, Jane, is from Tasmania, and if there's any inbreeding in her family, it's paid handsome dividends. Tall, nice body, good teeth and adept at small talk and smiling radiantly on cue. With two perfect little boys, 'Fin' and 'Gus Bus', they comprise the copybook nuclear family.

Jane picks us up in their perfect Land Rover and drives us out to their perfect split-level home. While not exactly harbourside, it overlooks the water and you could just about spit on the Sydney Harbour Bridge except selfish neighbours have extended their lounge room. 'The kookaburras wake us in the mornings. It's splendid,' Jane says, beaming.

William cooks a barbecue on the raised verandah overlooking the water and we eat king prawns while waiting for our perfectly formed T-bones to turn medium-rare. I notice that Jane painstakingly de-veins her crustaceans before popping them into her mouth. Personally, I reckon the gritty colon of a prawn is the best bit, and besides, by forgoing the niceties, I'm able to scoff four of the buggers to her one. Anyway, I haven't come for the culture. I'm here to rattle skeletons and fill my lungs with the stale, dead breath of the old days. The bedwetter, the Weaver bastard and the boy who dreamed he was Superman. He's come home. Kate insists on making the trip back to Blacktown with me. She's heard so much about the place from me and Mum and the rest of us.

We hire a car in the city and turn the beast westward. For some reason, probably neuronal damage due to decades of piss, pot and punches to the head, I can't read a map to save my life. So Kate keeps a street directory on her lap and shouts a succession of lefts, rights and shit we've missed its, till we're finally out of the big smoke and cruising along the Great Western Highway.

We tune into Triple J and don't talk much, each of us locked into our own space. Paul Kelly sings 'Everything's Turning to White', based on the true story of three mates who go fishing in a river in Adelaide. They see the body of a young woman floating by, and choose to wedge her between some rocks rather than spoil their fishing trip by reporting it to the cops. After all, 'We'd come so far and she was going nowhere.'

Suddenly, maybe it was the reference to the water and the rocks, I remember the only time I ever saw Saul cry. I'm 12 years old. It's dark, about nine at night. I've walked out of the house and into the backyard to check for the silhouette lurching across the paddock. He's already at the fence and he's holding something in his arms, pressing it to his chest. 'Shane,' he whispers, 'come here, mate.' When I get closer, I see he's holding our sausage dog, Sweetie, and she's limp and lifeless. 'She got hit by a car,' he whimpers, pushing the dog's body towards me like a terrible gift. 'I don't know what to do. Help me, help me.'

So I snatch the dog from him like it's a sack of flour and say, 'Yeah, no worries,' marching off towards the creek. I know Sweetie's death will upset Mum and the kids, and it's better if they think she's just run away, or maybe been stolen by some dog lover. I have to put her where no one would ever find her. And so I wade into the creek and, weighting her with rocks, gently pin her dead dog's body to the creek bed. When I return to the house, Dad's tucking into heated-up rissoles and tomato gravy and his eyes catch mine. While my heart's torn, I look directly at him. And I smile.

Now, on the outskirts of Blacktown, the old landmarks strike like poison darts, scoring hits of recognition as we drive past: The East Blacktown Hotel, affectionately known as the EB, where I spewed up my false teeth on the night of my 21st birthday. When I peeled my eyes open the next morning, I couldn't be sure who I was, let alone where I'd lost them. But they were worth a few quid and wouldn't be easily replaced. I jumped in a taxi and retraced my steps of the previous night, knocking on the doors of friends and strangers, 'Have you seen me teeth?'

I got the driver to stop intermittently at the puddles of spew that marked my journey along the footpath. I never found my teeth, but I did discover that I must have eaten some pretty weird shit that night.

Next on the hit list was Blacktown Hospital, where I'd been stitched up after street brawls, pumped out after piss-ups and tested for liver dysfunction on several occasions. It was also Mum's first stop for having babies, or after overdosing or slashing her wrists. This is where Sarah ended up when the rabbit chomped her finger off. And where they operated on Kelly after the broken bottle split his thigh like a cleaver through a melon. It was the place they resurrected my mate the night he overdosed. My first three children had the dubious distinction of having entered the world via Blacktown Hospital.

It was around lunchtime, so we parked in town and scouted round for somewhere to eat. I spotted Bow's Chinese Restaurant in the main street. Twenty-five years on and it was still open for lunch and dinner, seven days a week, including public holidays. There was a time when Bow's was the most exotic place to dine in town. And the food was authentic, cooked by a real Chinese chef. In the old days, Jacko delighted in getting the waiter's attention with cries of, 'Hey, China!' Of course, the waiter never got the joke, but Jacko laughed like a drain. (Another of his party tricks was to get the lady at reception in clubs to page 'Mike Hunt'.)

Engagements, weddings, wooings, a win on the dogs, funerals, and all occasions special, sad and celebratory, Bow's was the logical, the only, venue. Kate and I popped in for lunch.

I turned back the clock and tucked into fried rice and crispy noodles with seafood. Kate went for beef in oyster sauce. Nothing had changed. Huge helpings and it was scrumptious. The only difference was, 25 years ago I brought my own cans of Tooheys because Bow's was unlicensed. Or a bottle of Liebfraumilch, if I was trying to get into a sheila's pants. 'Yeah, it means mother's milk, darlin',' I'd say, leering at her tits and doing my best man-of-the-world.

'Geez,' I said to the Chinese waitress, 'you must have been here 25 years.'

'Not me personally, mate,' she said, in her best, third-generation, true-blue, Ocker accent. 'But the restaurant's been going for 40, eh.'

After lunch we did a walking tour of the town. I showed Kate where the infamous Hood once sat, over the road from the railway station. It had been reduced to an anonymous office block. It didn't seem right. You're not allowed to build on a graveyard for a hundred years after planting the last corpse, and the same council ordinance should've applied to the ground the Hood had occupied. So many people were buried there. Today, I'm sure, many of them are ghosts who have wives in Ugg boots and grown-up kids who hate their guts. I can see them shuffling in their twilight years to treadmill jobs where the expectations and prospects are even more basic than the pay and their low-ceiling lives.

They are the walking dead, and whenever they raise a beer to their lips, they do so in remembrance of the Hood and its squalid congregation. In their cups, they are changed in the twinkling of an eye, returning to the drunken dogma of the old bar, where they must tarry until it's 'Time gentlemen, please'.

We walk around the corner and stop for a minute at the site of the old West End Milk Bar. This was where the drunken, stoned, belligerent hordes went to pig out on burgers and chips or whole chickens when our guts became rumbling caves and the demon munchies roared to be appeased. I saw more blues at the West End than anywhere except the Hood itself. The West End went out, literally, in a blaze of glory one cracker night. Legend has it that some legless yobbo threw a lighted cigarette into the fireworks display. I'm inclined to go with the 'insurance job' theory myself.

From there, we moved on to Westpoint, Blacktown's mega shopping centre. We headed for Kmart to stock up on 'fat' clothes that were impossible to get in Singapore where the majority of the population is noodle-thin. Mum worked here once. She loved it when I popped in to visit her on the job. I was so proud. She may have only been a 'floor lady', but in my eyes, Mum had the most critical position in the shop. Dressed in her black skirt and white blouse with her Anne Deacon nametag, she was the 'face' of Kmart.

Next stop, Blacktown Boys' High, where I entered the sausage machine as a frightened and thin mince patty, and emerged in 1972 as a terrified, fully fledged hamburger. Think McDonald's with a side serving of malice. 'Do you want any hate with that, sir?' I was hoping that we'd arrive at recess so I could walk across the quadrangle as one of the tallest kids for the first time in my life. But it's New Year's Eve and a school holiday, so Kate and I do the rounds alone. The old buildings look shabby and in dire need of a lick of paint and a good spit and polish. We walk down to the sports oval where I once stood as a cadet on parade, holding a 303 and wishing to Christ I had live ammo so I could open fire and shoot the fuck out of the bastards (the bastards being anyone in my sights).

Before we drive away, Kate takes some photos of me standing outside the front gate. The school motto, set within a shield framed by a spear on one side and a boomerang on the other, stands in the background: 'Learn to live'. A few of us did. But a lot of us failed with distinction.

Then it was time. This was why we'd come. Driving down the main road, I wonder what I'll find waiting for me at Edward Street. Will Saul be in the front yard? Should I confront him? Would he even know who I was? I turn into Edward Street and drive slowly to number 63. There, I turn the car around and park opposite the house, in getaway mode. Thirty years and they still haven't put a bridge over the storm-water channel that used to be our beloved creek. The front door of 63 Edward Street still opens onto a dead end. A barricade blocks the road to stop drunk or distracted drivers plummeting into the brackish water or pissy trickle, depending on the season. Today it's a pissy trickle.

Me and Jimmy called it 'The Talking Pole', and we'd spend hours leaning against it and yakking about football and girls and music and how our lives would be transformed when we had our degrees. We never arranged a time to meet there. We simply found ourselves drawn to the same place at the same time whenever one of us had something on our mind. Today, the street is silent. There's no sign of life. The windows in the houses are empty as eyes. The doors closed as minds. No barking dogs or shouting children. No laughter or screaming. No comment. It's a street with Alzheimer's.

But I remember. I look at the old house and it looks back at me. We've both changed. The bleak fibro walls are gone, updated with a trendy white permalum veneer. The venetian blinds are gone, replaced with bright, colourful curtains. 'That's my bedroom,' I whisper to Kate, pointing at the room on the far right, half-expecting the curtains to part, revealing a sad-eyed little boy. The wood and wire front fence has gone. Sixty-three Edward Street is a pretty little cottage with an immaculately kept garden out front and an awful secret inside.

We walk around to the side of the house where parkland ensures no neighbour's house will ever encroach. I look over the fence and see the manicured lawn that's the legacy of a boy's donkeywork one heartless, oven-baked night more than three decades ago. A few raucous Hawaiian shirts flutter on the clothesline, and I know Saul would never be seen dead in anything like them. Maybe he's rented the place out, or even sold it. The tomato garden has fallen back on itself and has been subsumed by the emerald green grass. There is no evidence it ever existed. Like everything that happened in that house, the evidence is all in my mind, and in the fitful memories and haunted sleep of the survivors.

Kate takes a few photos of me standing by the letterbox that proclaims 63 Edward Street. I don't smile.

'Come on, Kate,' I say, 'let's see if the McKinnons are still there.'

We drive round to 93 Block Street and the former home of my good friend and confidant, Jimmy, whose backyard abutted ours. Along with Mrs Roberts' place next door, this was one of the 'safe houses' I'd run to with Kelly and Tony when fear split the night and spilled over into our dreams and I was lucky enough to be able to shepherd them out. I walk up the path and back into the 1960s. The front door is open, and I tap respectfully on the screen door.

Mrs McKinnon shuffles to the door. She has a walking frame for support and her face is scrunched up in concentration as she peers through the dusty screen. 'Yes?' she says.

'It's been a long time, Mrs McKinnon, but it's me, Shane Weaver. Shane Reynard.'

'Saul's brother?' she replies. 'You're Saul's brother?'

'No, I'm his son, his stepson, Shane.'

'Oh,' she says, opening the door. 'Yes, I remember you. Come in.'

The lounge room is spotlessly clean. The curtains are drawn. Having never been in one, it's like I imagine a parlour to be, ill lit and stuffy with yesterday's air, the musty smell of wet dogs and the mildew bouquet of a lifetime of memories. Real people have been replaced by framed photographs that will never change or disagree or forget to be there when it matters. The hungry light introduces an old woman who reminded me of Olive Oil when I was a kid and indeed still does. Except now there's one feature that removes her from the safety and sanctity of a comic book. Her mouth and nose are ravaged by cancer.

'I remember you,' she says, 'you used to knock on my door late at night. When the fighting got too much.' And she closes her eyes for just a second to see me way back then.

I introduce her to Kate. She offers us a drink, although she says she doesn't have much, just some cold water. We say no thanks, we've just had lunch.

'I wondered what happened to you,' said Mrs McKinnon.

I compress my life into 45 seconds, saying that I've remarried, have three more kids, bringing the tally to eight, and that we live in Singapore. I say I've changed my name back to Weaver.

She tells me that her husband, Ken, passed away some ten years earlier and now, except for her dogs, she lives alone. One of her three sons, Fred, lives around the corner in Edward Street. His second marriage is going down the toilet. Another son works for the post office and lives in the Blue Mountains. She's worried about Don because of the fires. James (she never called him Jimmy) is living in Hunters Hill with his wife, Lucinda, and their eight-year-old daughter. She describes Lucinda as 'a lovely girl', and she's happy to give us her eldest son's phone number.

We talk about old Mr and Mrs Smith who used to live next door. She explains how they've passed on, but I know about that and we don't go into details. We speak, too, about the man who lived over the road. I'd forgotten about Mr Rose. He came home drunk one night and fetched his baby from its cot, placing the child gently next to his sleeping wife. Then he chopped them up with an axe. The next morning, it was Mrs McKinnon who saw him naked out in the front garden. He was hosing blood from his face and body. She went to the house next door and called the police. Eventually, when new people moved into the house, we wondered if they had any idea why they got the place at such a bargain.

It seems all the old neighbours have passed on or moved on, except for Mrs McClean down the road, the wife of a local policeman who died in a car accident many years ago. Mrs McKinnon says she felt sorry for Phil when he was alive, as he had the job of identifying the bodies of the axe-man's family and was usually allotted the task of cleaning up when anyone in this neck of the woods fucked up – which happened with alarming regularity.

'You know, someone should write a book about Block Street,' she nodded, smiling with half a lip.

It's time to go and I ask her if she minds having a photograph taken with me. She says she'd rather not, pointing to her face. 'Well, I'll have a big hug then,' I say, and I hold her and feel a surge of gratitude and grief for this bone-thin old lady whose kindness had meant so much when a young boy in wet pyjamas needed a hot Milo, some toast and somewhere safe to hide.

It's New Year's Eve and we plan to stop at the Sydney Fish Market and buy lobsters and oysters so we can feast in our hotel room and maybe catch whatever we can of the fireworks through the window. As we drive away, Kate says, 'What a nice old lady. And sharp as a tack.' I barely hear her. I'm listening to a faraway sound from a long, long time ago when I was someone else, someone I hardly know.

## SPIDERS TALKING,  Shane Reynard aged 15

*Tired to death*
*I crawl under the house.*

*We three brothers*
*Have our rooms here*
*In the chambers*
*Of the underbelly*
*Of the beast.*

*Sometimes*
*I am so lonely*
*I talk to spiders*
*Like me*
*Shrinking in corners*
*Gulping the darkness with multiple eyes.*

*The floorboards creak*
*Overhead*
*The dead-leg shuffle*
*Daddy's going to sleep*
*To drown*
*In drunken*
*Unremembering.*

*The world falls silent*
*Save the invisible roar*
*Of a million spiders*
*Screaming.*

# TO MY FAMILY

MANY SELF-DOUBTS LOOM AND HOVER when you're alone in your head in a place called Blacktown. Writing my memoir took me back to places and people I've been hiding from for nearly half a century. And now it's done, I realise it's just the beginning.

To those who are hurt by how I have drawn them, I'm sorry. This was not my intention. Where my words are scathing, it is a reflection of what I felt and thought at that time; it's no indication of my feelings now. Indeed, maybe it's more a representation of who I was, rather than of who you were. I can live with that, and I hope you can, too.

Mum, I love you to the point of bursting. If my gratitude for the sheer totality of your sacrifice is not evident, it's because I lack the words, and perhaps even the courage, to admit it to myself. But there would be no story to tell without you. Without you, Mum, there would be nothing.

To my 'first born', as one of my daughters once distinguished herself and her siblings from my kids with Kate, I see you every time I look in a mirror. (Hope that's not too disturbing a thought!) You are as much a part of me as my cornucopian nose. I love you, and I am proud of you all. You have forgiven me my selfishness, my stupidity and my savagery. I can never repay you for that.

To Georgie-fish, Ollie-bean and Pippo, one day you may read this book and say of me, 'We never knew this man. We never knew him at all.' And I will be the happiest dad in the world.

My rock of Gibraltar, Kate, what can I say? You saw the alcoholic transformed into the workaholic. You put up with the mood swings and puff your way resolutely through the anti-smoking crusades. And you still see someone loveable where others might see naught but a cranky old man. I love you, my darling, and count my blessings that you love me too. My second tattoo, a blood red rose with the date inked on a scroll around the stem, marks the occasion of my second marriage. I still haven't remembered a single anniversary. Like I always say, it's not that I don't care, it's just that I forget to look at my tattoo on the right day.

My sisters and brothers, I am comfortable with the bridges and the chasms that bring us together or keep us apart. We built the bridges against all odds with our own hands, and the chasms, they only exist where it would be dangerous or useless to try to breach the gap.

Someone once said 'History is written by the victors'. Were it necessarily so, I would have edited my own part to become someone much more agreeable. The truth is not always pretty, but it is never as ugly as a lie.

# THANK YOU

My agent, Fiona Inglis, for your unswerving faith. My publisher, Fiona Henderson, for your grand vision. My editor, Kim Swivel, for your insight, uncommon sense and sensitivity. Sophie Ambrose and Vanessa Mickan for never taking their eye off the ball.

Gordon Dawson, for giving a 32-year-old piss pot and ex pug a break.

Wayne Saxton, Yvonne Renshaw, Terry Morris, Roger McMillan and Anne Humphries, for your friendship and support in tough times.

Lou Myers and 'Sugar Ray' Wheatley, for teaching me how to face my fears and rearrange them with my fists.

Matthew Atkinson, for hiring what he called a 'giant' when I'm only five foot seven.

Jerry Smith, for reading the first draft and fanning the fire.

Graham Kelly and Shayne Pooley, for letting me piggyback on your genius at work (and hey, Shayne, thanks for the terrific cover, mate).

Lyn and Bill, for giving me the greatest gift of all. Your daughter.

Justine Lee for reading bits of the second draft and presenting me with a copy of the *Superman* video.

Thanks to you all, I can fly!